Back to Basics:

Chess Openings

by

Carsten Hansen

2021
CarstenChess

Back to Basics: Openings
by
Carsten Hansen

ISBN: 978-87-93812-75-8

© Copyright 2010, 2021

Carsten Hansen

All Rights Reserved

First published as "Back to Basics: Openings" by: Russell Enterprises, Inc., P.O. Box 3131, Milford, CT 06460 (ISBN: 978-1-888690-44-6). Original Cover design by Janel Lowrance and Zygmunt Nasiolkowski

For more material and updates to this and other books by Carsten Hansen, please visit:

www.winningquicklyatchess.com

If you enjoyed the book, please make sure to write a short review on Amazon or where you purchased the book; Carsten will very much appreciate that.

Table of Contents

Author's Dedication

*To my mother, who taught me to play chess,
and my father, who motivated me to improve.*

Bibliography

Collins, Sam, *Understanding the Chess Openings* (Gambit Publications, London, 2005)

Donaldson, John and Hansen, Carsten, *A Strategic Opening Repertoire* (2nd edition, Russell Enterprises, Milford, 2008)

Emms, John, *Play the Open Games as Black* (Gambit Publications, London. 2000)

Giddins, Steve, *How to Build Your Chess Opening Repertoire* (Gambit Publications, London, 2003)

Hansen, Carsten, *Improve Your Positional Chess* (Gambit Publications, London, 2004)

Larsen, Bent, *Åbningsspillet i skak* (Samleren, Copenhagen, 1965)

Matanovic, Aleksandar, ed., *Encyclopaedia of Chess Openings*, Vols. A-E, (Sahovski Informator, Belgrade)

Nielsen, Peter Heine and Hansen, Carsten, *The Sicilian Accelerated Dragon* (Batsford, London, 1998)

Nimzowitsch, Aron, *Mit System* (Hernovs Forlag 1977)

Seirawan, Yasser, *Winning Chess Openings* (Everyman Chess, London, 2003)

Watson, John, *Mastering the Chess Openings*, Vol. 1 (Gambit Publications, London, 2006)

Introduction

Thanks for getting this book. You have probably started playing chess quite recently and you are looking for a quick climb up the ladder to chess excellence. So, openings may be the place to start because openings come first in the game, and therefore should be your first topic of study, right?!

Well, perhaps not. In fact I would recommend you first take a look at some of the other books in this series on tactics and endings, as these will help you better realize the advantages from the positions this book will hopefully help you obtain. Having noted that, this book will certainly assist you gain a solid understanding of chess openings.

Openings in chess are quite the temptress, and many players spend year after year studying, yet never mastering them. In fact, when it comes to chess, there are on average 1-3 new opening books, CDs or DVDs released in any given *week*, 52 weeks a year. Therefore keeping up with the development of all openings is extremely difficult.

However, this book is not out to teach everything there is to know about openings, but it will help you understand and play openings much better. It will also help instill a sense of balance in your study of openings,

give you some direction about how to obtain better results from your openings and how to approach a variety of situations relevant to our topic of openings.

The book is divided into the following chapters:

Chapter 1
My Own Experiences with Openings

This first chapter will give you a more general introduction to the opening, including how I have approached the study of openings, which types of books I have worked with and most importantly, the mistakes I have made over the years, and how you can best make use of my experience, including, of course, how to avoid repeating my mistakes.

Chapter 2
Opening Principles

In this chapter, we will examine the basic principles pertaining to development, which squares are important, and how to get yourself ready for the next phase of the game after the opening – the middlegame .

Chapter 3
How do I decide which opening to choose?

This chapter will cover topics such as why some openings are played more frequently, why some are played less frequently, which openings are good and which are not, what you should consider when putting your opening repertoire together, how to work with repertoire books, and much more. The answers are not always as simple as we would like.

Chapter 4:
An Introduction to Opening Theory

Chapter 4 will give you a good handle on how to deal with the succeeding chapters, which all concern themselves with opening theory. It covers terms such "slight advantage," "with compensation," and many other similar terms of art, which you encounter time and again when studying opening theory, but which you may find difficult to get a feel for when working on your own.

Chapter 5
The Open Games

This will cover all openings that start with 1 e4 e5.

Chapter 6
The Semi-Open Games

This chapter will cover openings starting with 1 e4, but where Black replies with something other than 1...e5.

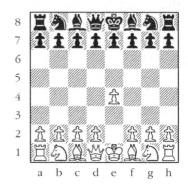

Chapter 7
The Closed Games

Games that start with 1 d4 d5 are covered in Chapter 7.

Chapter 8
The Semi-Closed Games

Like its counterpart, Chapter 6, this chapter will cover openings starting with 1 d4, but where Black replies with something other than 1...d5.

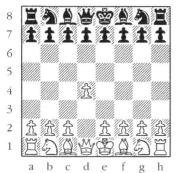

Chapter 9
Flank Openings

A wonderful mixture of what remains, such as more mundane openings like 1 c4 , 1 Nf3, 1 f4, and 1 b3 as well as more bizarre choices like 1 b4, 1 g4, 1 Nc3 and several others.

Chapter 10
Where do I go from here?

In this chapter, I will give you pointers about how to continue your studies and how to apply your new-found knowledge.

Remember, chess is supposed to be fun, and while studying openings at length will pay some rewards – a few quick wins and some good positions – studying chess openings constantly may become boring unless you are already one of the world's best players. Therefore, take a measured approach, spread out your studies over a period of time, and follow the advice offered in this book. You will certainly be on your way to better results for a long time to come.

> *In many openings where the lines are finely balanced, the player with the better understanding has an excellent chance for winning the game.*

Chapter 1

My Own Experiences with Openings

Early Lessons

My first experiences with chess openings came back in 1978. I was six years old and participating in one of my first scholastic tournaments. I knew little more than how the pieces were moving. My opponent, whose name I can't recall, must have sensed my insecurities. The game went like this: 1 e4 e5 2 Bc4 Nc6 3 Qh5 Nf6 4 Qxf7+ mate.

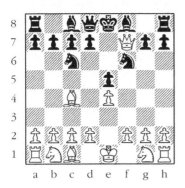

My dad, who was an experienced player rated just under 1900, and who had taken me and some other children to the tournament, saw this. Acknowledging my terrible defeat, he suggested to my opponent that we play another game for practice before the next round. My opponent reluctantly obliged, and mated me in a similar fashion in the second game as well! This is the first tournament experience I remember.

The next incident regarding chess openings came several years later. I remember playing a lot of games in the interim, often with decent results, but not showing much actual talent. In the spring of 1982, I participated in another scholastic tournament in my home town of Søndersø on the Danish island of Funen. My results were unremarkable; I think I scored something like 3 points of a possible 7, so I didn't win a prize in my age group. However, my younger brother, Bent, did. What an unmitigated disaster!

Being a young man of action, I decided that this would be the last time he would win a prize a tournament when I didn't. In an earlier tournament, I had won a book on the 1978 World Championship match between Karpov and Kortschnoi. The story line had grabbed my attention, and moreover my sympathies lay with the defeated challenger, Kortschnoi. Now, having to study chess for the first time in my life, I had to decide on what to study, and having noticed that Kortschnoi favored the English Opening, 1 c4, it became a natural choice for me.

That summer, I went through all my father's copies of the Danish chess magazine, *Skakbladet*, to locate games with 1 c4, and whenever I came across one, I played through it. In the beginning I couldn't understand a great deal, but as the weeks passed, I began to pick up more than just the basic moves. The games were played by many of the greatest players of that era: Botvinnik, Smyslov, Petrosian, Kortschnoi, Uhlmann, Geller, Polugaevsky, Ivkov, and of course my compatriot Larsen, just to mention some of the more prominent names guiding the white pieces.

Towards the end of the summer, I played my first tournament after gaining all this new knowledge. The result was an unqualified success. I won the scholastic group, which had a number of children several years older than I with the score of 7 out of 7. That certainly inspired me to do more. While studying, for some reason one particular setup attracted me more than any other: 1 c4, 2 Nc3, 3 g3, 4 Bg2, 5 e3, 6 Nge2, 7 0-0 and then 8 d4. I even won a miniature with it: 1 c4 e5 2 Nc3 Nf6 3 g3 Nc6 4 Bg2 Bc5 5 e3 d6 6 Nge2 Be6 7 d4:

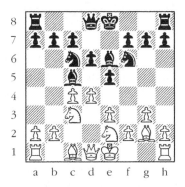

Black resigned, because after 7...exd4 8 exd4 Bb4, White wins a piece with the pawn fork 9 d5.

My next project was a book by Bent Larsen, *Åbningsspillet i skak*, which means "The Opening Play in Chess." In some ways, the book resembles the volume you are reading right now, while in other ways it is very different. For example, we will spend a lot of time examining the different opening variations; in Larsen's book, written in 1965, the section covering all the openings was reduced to a single chapter. The philosophy was that some knowledge is good, but don't overwhelm the reader. After studying Larsen's book, I decided to try a few other openings, e.g., the Caro-Kann (1 e4 c6)

against 1 e4; the Nimzo-Indian (1 d4 Nf6 2 c4 e6 3 Nc3 Bb4);

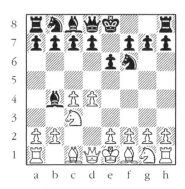

and the Queen's Indian (1 d4 Nf6 2 c4 e6 3 Nf3 b6)

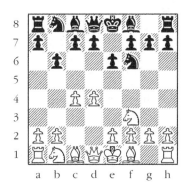

against 1 d4. Other openings were not considered at that time.

While these openings remained an integral part of my repertoire for the next few years, I also added a number of other openings to my arsenal. With White, I started playing 1 Nf3, and on occasion, I even dared 1 e4, particularly if I had played a particular opponent before and had trouble as White in my English Opening. As Black I started playing the Sicilian Accelerated Dragon (1 e4 c5 2 Nf3 Nc6 3 d4 cxd4 4 Nxd4 g6)

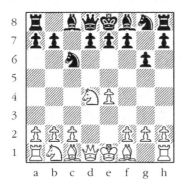

as well as the Scandinavian (1 e4 d5 2 exd5 Qxd5 3 Nc3 Qa5)

the last being very popular after Larsen used it to beat Karpov; I was also assisted by an excellent book in Danish

on the Scandinavian by the Danish master (and later correspondence grandmaster), Niels Jørgen Fries-Nielsen. I also took up the Queen's Gambit as Black in reply to 1 d4 Nf6 2 c4 e6 3 Nf3,

only then playing 3...d5. Not all of this was inspired by actual studying and playing, but playing the same thing all the time bored me, even if the results were reasonably good.

I have found that playing and studying a number of different openings also expands your overall knowledge and understanding of the game much quicker than if you concentrate on a few openings all the time.

After a couple of bad experiences with 1 c4, I began to use 1 e4 as my main opening. While it meant that I had to learn a massive amount of new opening theory and was punished severely several times when I did not have a clue about certain variations, it had the benefit of giving me a broader understanding of many types of positions and pawn structures that I had not previous been familiar with.

As my overall game improved, I began to vary my openings more. For example, as Black I played every variation of the Sicilian with some frequency. My results in the Sicilian, quite predictably, were horrendous. I lost several games in spectacular fashion, simply because I couldn't remember the theory and therefore often mixed up the variations quite badly. After a few rapid-play tournaments with several quick losses, I decided to settle on two lines in the Sicilian: the Dragon (1 e4 c5 2 Nf3 d6 3 d4 cxd4 4 Nxd4 Nf6 5 Nc3 g6)

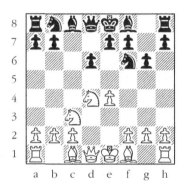

and the Sveshnikov (1 e4 c5 2 Nf3 Nc6 3 d4 cxd4 4 Nxd4 Nf6 5 Nc3 e5).

Of course, nowadays, the enormous amount of theory in these lines might prohibit most students from taking them both up at the same time, but back then, theory developed somewhat more slowly and the access to information

wasn't as easy or quick; you relied on chess magazines – in my case *Chess Informant* – as well as opening monographs, (released quite infrequently compared to today's pace of publishing) and finally, *Batsford Chess Openings* by Keene and Kasparov. I still have my old, nicely maintained copy autographed by both authors. It served me well in those early years.

Mistakes and Experiences

Looking back at how I studied and allocated my time on openings over the years, I can now see a pattern of erroneous decisions, wasted time, inconsistent and irrational work, with the occasional smart moves.

From the previous section, you may recall that I indiscriminately studied a large volume of games with one particular starting move, 1 c4. Based on my immediate better results, you may have come to the conclusion that this was a smart move. Well, it wasn't! What was worse, I repeated the mistakes many times over, because when I found a theoretical article, such as the "Game of the Month," which in those days was often were written by the famous Yugoslav grandmaster Svetozar Gligoric and which contained a number of theoretical references, I would look all the games up in *Chess Informant* and then play through the entire game, again without understanding very much of what was going on.

Almost any time spent on actual chess will help you improve your game. Some approaches, however, are better than others. For example playing over games by the best players in the world without having much understanding of why

11

certain moves are being played or knowing why certain moves are mistakes and other are not, is not really a productive use of your time. Of course, I did not have an overabundance of material at that time as there were very few books that were aimed at players at my level, and those that were did not appeal to me in the beginning.

What I should have done was to start out with the book by Larsen (the one I eventually picked up later), and read it from cover to cover. When it came to the theoretical section, I should have played over all the examples. This would have enabled me to learn first the basics of understanding the openings, and then, when playing through the opening variations, it could have given me ideas which openings to choose for my repertoire. Ideally, if you have a coach or acquaintance – rated at least 1600 – you might seek some additional help in this process. They can help you stay clear of some of the pitfalls, so that, for example, you do not decide to select openings that require deep strategic understanding. A case in point would be, for example, the Ruy Lopez, also known as the Spanish Game, which arises after 1 e4 e5 2 Nf3 Nc6 3 Bb5 and is an integral part of almost any grandmaster's repertoire in which 1 e4 is played regularly.

Another example is the Grünfeld Indian Defense (1 d4 Nf6 2 c4 g6 3 Nc3 d5) *(D)*, which players like Kasparov, Fischer and Botvinnik all played regularly, but knowing how to combat the white center and understanding the large volumes of theory are subjects you should not work on when you first start out.

When studying openings, I have made

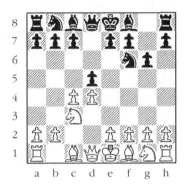

nearly every mistake known, and I would encourage you to learn from my mistakes. While I am reasonably happy with the results I ultimately attained, I am certain I could have made better progress if I had spent my time on openings more productively. The lessons I want you to remember are:

(1) Don't study material that is far too advanced for you without the assistance of a stronger player.

(2) Don't spread your opening repertoire too thin, but focus on a few openings and understand the typical plans well.

(3) Don't buy every book that is available on a particular opening. If the opening is an important part of your repertoire, buy one that is aimed at your level and that has received good reviews.

(4) Don't spend more time on the opening than you do on the middlegame and endgame, because without a good understanding of all aspects of the game, you will rarely be able to take advantage of the good positions you reach from the opening.

Chapter 2

Opening Principles

Before discussing opening repertoires and theory, it is important to understand some of the basic principles of opening play, because without a solid understanding of these principles, the material presented in the following chapters may be appear incomprehensible, and the real reasons behind many of the moves may elude you.

If you have played for some time, but made no real progress, the reason could well be that you don't fully understand some of the basic principles. Therefore, take your time going through this chapter, even if you think you have seen it all before. Also, in the coming chapters on opening theory, when you encounter a move that doesn't seem obvious, try to look at the basic principles discussed in this chapter.

Occasionally, however, you will encounter moves that appear to follow no principles at all. In addition, there are countless exceptions to established principles, which perhaps would be better considered as rules of thumb. However, just because you see the best players in the world break basic opening principles, don't think you can do the same and get away with it. They have a well-defined sense of danger that allows them to determine when they can push the envelope and when they cannot, and even then, they sometimes lose quickly. Studying this chapter carefully should help you avoid many of these kinds of disasters.

Main Objectives of Opening Play

I am confident that you already have a clear idea of what you should aim for in the opening, but matters are not always cut and dry. We often stray from what we know is right, chasing an illusion or an ill-conceived idea. So let us remind ourselves of the basic priniciples behind opening variations and moves:

(1) Getting pieces developed onto good, relevant squares.

(2) Finding a safe place for the king.

(3) Controlling the center of the board.

(4) Reaching a playable position that you understand how to play.

These are all very broad definitions and can mean different things when applied to different openings, but they are all important. We will discuss these objectives, both individually and in relationship with each other in the sections below. The fourth objective, however, should be regarded as most important: reaching a playable position that you understand how to play. By this I don't mean that you must have an advantage or winning position as White, nor do you have to equalize in all openings as Black, but you should not be clearly worse. Furthermore, you should understand the openings you play, which means that you have a clear idea what both the objectives and main plans of the opening are.

I emphasize this because many experienced players dive into opening books with the avowed purpose of learning a massive amount of theory as quickly as possible. Unfortunately, as often turns out to be the case, sometimes even when faced with a position with which he should be familiar, a player doesn't remember what to do with the good position that was reached. This lesson is one that I will repeat several times in this book, because reaching a playable position that you understand how to play is a cardinal rule that you must never forget or break, no matter how tempted you are to do so.

The Center

In the opening, the center is the most important part of the board. The center proper consists of the following four squares: e4, d4, e5, d5

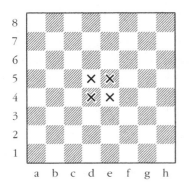

and to that we can add the extended center which includes the c4, c5, f4, f5, d3, e3, d6 and e6 squares.

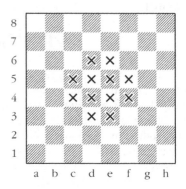

Your pawn play and piece development should focus on and around these squares. This of course can be interpreted in countless ways, so let me give some examples.

In the Open Games, play starts with **1 e4 e5**.

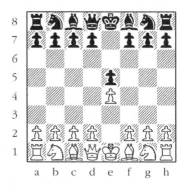

Each player has not only occupied a square in the center (e4 and e5 respectively), but also controls another square (d5 for White, and d4 for Black) as well as a square in the extended center (f5 and f4). Furthermore, the moves have the added benefit of

Don't study material that is far too advanced for you without the assistance of a stronger player.

opening lines for the bishops on f1 and f8. The game could continue with **2 Nf3** (attacking the pawn on e5, and also aiming in the direction of the d4-square) **2...Nc6** (protecting the e5-pawn, and also looking at d4) **3 Bc4** (developing a piece and controlling the c4- and d5-squares) **3...Bc5** (this is similar to White's 3rd move) **4 Nc3** (taking control over the d5-square and guarding the e4-pawn) **4...Nf6** (attacking the e4-pawn and fighting for the d5-square) **5 d3** (guarding the e4-pawn and opening the diagonal for the dark-squared bishop on c1) **5...d6** (with similar motives) **6 0-0** (getting the king to safety) **6...0-0** (ditto), and so on.

This is quite elementary, so let us return to the position after Black's 3rd move.

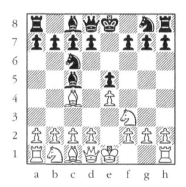

As you will discover in the theoretical section, chapters 5-9, White has more options to choose from in this position. A common choice is **4 c3**, which perhaps at first glance does not look like much, as it only guards the d4-square, but White has other ideas in mind. For instance, if Black now plays **4...d6** to guard the e5-pawn one more time and prepare the development of the bishop on c8, White will then play **5 d4**,

placing a second pawn in the center. If play now continues **5...exd4 6 cxd4 Bb6 7 Nc3**, White has gained control over the center, has more space and freer development, as his position is less restrained compared to Black's somewhat passive set-up. This doesn't mean that Black is lost in this position, but only that White has an easier game plan to follow.

In the classical Closed Game, there is a similar interaction: **1 d4 d5 2 c4 e6 3 Nc3 Nf6 4 Bg5 Be7 5 Nf3 h6 6 Bh4 0-0 7 e3 Nbd7**

and so forth. As you can see, every move, with the exception of Black's kingside castling which brings the king to safety, fought for the center. Note that the bishop move Bg5 also was part of the plan by pinning the knight and thereby restricting its ability to compete for the d5- and e4-squares. Black's attempts to first release the pin by ...Be7 and later threaten the bishop are designed to eliminate the white bishop's sphere of influence.

With that in mind, how are moves such as 1 b3 and 1 g3 evaluated, since they don't seem to fight for the center? Well, in some ways they do compete for central control because the bishops will go to b2 or g2, from where they will support pawn advances and further development that aims to fight for the center; the battle is not abandoned, just postponed to a later time when more pieces are developed. For instance, in the Queen's Indian, Black does not always start the fight for the center right away: **1 d4 Nf6 2 c4 e6 3 Nf3 b6 4 Nc3 Bb7 5 a3** (preventing the pin by ...Bb4 that immobilizes the knight and fights for the center) **5...g6**

6 d5 Bg7 7 e4. This theme also occurs in the King's Indian Defense, where Black lets White take over the center completely: **1 d4 Nf6 2 c4 g6 3 Nc3 Bg7 4 e4 d6 5 f4 0-0 6 Nf3**

and one might think that white is clearly better, but moving all those pawns in the opening also constitutes potential weaknesses Black can eventually target; guarding against Black's counterplay is not as easy as it seems. In the Alekhine Defense, Black provokes White to take control of the center: **1 e4 Nf6 2 e5 Nd5 3 d4 d6**, and now **4 c4 Nb6 5 f4**

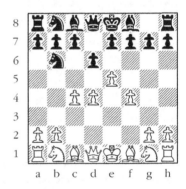

looks more tempting than it actually is. In fact the top players in the world normally restrict themselves to playing **4 Nf3**, happily holding on to the space advantage gained, but not initially striving for more.

I will finish the discussion of the center off with a quote by Tarrasch: "If you have no center, your opponent has a freer position. If you do have a center, then you really have something to worry about!" Keep that in mind.

Pawn Play in the Opening

At this point, let's discuss pawn play, which seems to be relatively easy to understand, but in fact can be very difficult to master. While it is very tempting to conquer the center with pawns, looks can be deceiving. I have played many lines with both Black and White where I attempted absolute control of the center, but after apparently having reached my goal, my opponent started attacking my "impregnable" center from the wings and the front, playing around it, and all of a sudden I found myself with an inferior position. I could not maintain the apparently strong center and the weaknesses that formed when it was created. This taught me an important lesson, one that the German grandmaster Siegbert Tarrasch had put forth more than a century ago: each pawn move constitutes a weakness. While you most certainly have to move your pawns to develop your pieces, you should limit yourself to what is necessary, and save the rest for later, as has already been note in the example with the Alekhine Defense.

Determining where the balance lies is another thing altogether, difficult to assess unless you already have some experience with the opening you are playing. Therefore, before you venture out in an attempt to conquer the world, do not start shoving all your pawns forward willy-nilly. It is, in my opinion, better to err on the side of caution, limiting yourself to a potentially smaller

advantage, rather than to weaken your position unnecessarily aiming for a large advantage, only to face the unfortunate consequences of having rushed your pawns forward too soon. This was underscored by Tarrasch (again!) when he said: "Nothing so easily ruins a position as pawn moves." It makes more sense, particularly in the opening, to keep pawn moves to a bare necessity, but by studying the openings you intend to play, you will quickly learn which pawn moves are normal and which are seen less frequently. Until you feel very confident in your handling of the pawns in a given opening, stick to the tried-and-true pawn moves.

Pawn Structures

While the moving of pawns is routinely handled when openings are studied, more often than not the related topic of pawn structures is overlooked. There has been a recent trend, however, to give this important subject more attention, and there are now opening books that deal with this – and these are the books that you should be using in your study of openings (see chapter 10 for some guidance on opening books). If you come across an opening book you are considering purchasing, make sure to look for the treatment of pawn structures somewhere; if you don't find it, you may well wish to pass on the book!

In order to understand an opening well, it is essential to comprehend the significance of the key pawn structures of the opening and its main variations. If you glibly pass this off with "Sure, no problem," then you are really in for a surprise. For instance, the following pawn structure

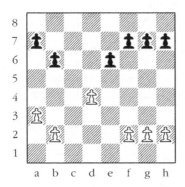

can occur in openings as different as the Caro-Kann Defense (1 e4 c6), the Nimzo-Indian (1 d4 Nf6 2 c4 e6 3 Nc3 Bb4) and the Queen's Gambit Accepted (1 d4 d5 2 c4 dxc4), just to mention some of the more popular openings. The pawn structure with an isolated d-pawn is both fascinating and difficult to understand; indeed, several books have been dedicated to this topic and its related structures. When I started out in chess, I was absolutely terrified of ending up with an isolated pawn and even more so a doubled pawn, because I was never shown what the benefit of these structures could be and therefore if I ended up with such a position I thought I was essentially on the verge of already losing. In contrast, if I played against them, I played with a sense of destiny, thinking I was already on the path to a full point on the board, even if my opponent actually had the better position.

The reason that understanding pawn structures is so critical is that they usually dictate a lot of the play on both sides and therefore if you are unable to "read" your pawn structure correctly, you could well be setting the wrong

course for your game plan and will be punished accordingly. Let's us look at some actual examples.

From the French Defense: **1 e4 e6 2 d4 d5**, and now White will obtain similar pawn structures after a variety of moves: **3 e5, 3 Nd2 Nf6 4 e5** or **3 Nc3 Nf6** (or 3...Bb4 4 e5) **4 e5**. In all cases, the pawn center is closed with the following central structure:

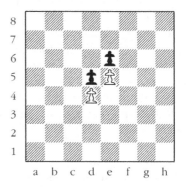

The pawn structure gives White a space advantage in the center, but furthermore it "points" in the direction of Black's kingside, thus indicating that White should most likely target his play on that side of the board. Black, on the other hand, will likely focus his attention on the queenside, because his pawns "point" in that direction. However, if Black exclusively focuses his attention on the queenside, he may well find himself getting mated on the kingside before anything ever happens on the queenside. Therefore, Black often makes a pawn break with ...f7-f6, attacking the e5-pawn, changing the direction of the game. This can be seen in the following line: **1 e4 e6 2 d4 d5 3 Nd2 Nf6 4 e5 Nfd7 5 Bd3 c5 6 c3 Nc6 7 Ne2 Qb6 8 Nf3 cxd4 9 cxd4 f6**

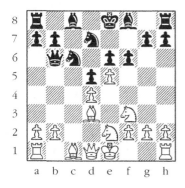

10 exf6 Nxf6, and all of a sudden the overall game plan for both sides has changed.

In the main line of the Classical King's Indian, the plans for both players are also defined early on: **1 d4 Nf6 2 c4 g6 3 Nc3 Bg7 4 e4 d6 5 Nf3 0-0 6 Be2 e5 7 0-0 Nc6 8 d5 Ne7 9 Ne1 Ne8 10 Be3 f5 11 f3 f4 12 Bf2 g5**

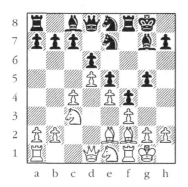

Here it is even more apparent that Black will attack on the kingside and White on the queenside.

In other openings, it can be more difficult to determine, for example, when both central pawns have been exchanged or if the position is symmetrical, because it may then appear that both players have the same plan.

That may be the case, but in those instances where the pawn structure is completely symmetrical, the final decision often depends on the placement of the pieces and where they are pointing, as well as where it possibly would be relevant to make a pawn break.

It is easy to generalize, less easy to setup concrete rules, and impossible to tell exactly how you should treat pawn structures without knowing the opening from which it arose and where the pieces, in particular the minor pieces, are placed on the board. I repeat: do not start playing an opening unless you have at least a rudimentary understanding of the most frequently occurring pawn structures in that opening.

Minor Pieces

When discussing development of the pieces, the main consideration really concerns the minor pieces. The German theoretician Siegbert Tarrasch wrote that, as a rule of thumb, knights should be developed before bishops. This is nearly always the case and worth keeping in mind, though there are of course many exceptions. For example, both **1 e4 e5 2 Bc4**, the Bishop's Opening, and the Trompowsky, **1 d4 Nf6 2 Bg5**, are mainstream openings yet both break the rule of knights before bishops.

A common pattern of development is knight, bishop (from the same wing), then knight again before bishop on the other side. The minor pieces should be developed to squares where they are as influential as possible considering the opponent's position and pawn

19

structure, and they should not be liable to be attacked right away. Does it matter if you play a bishop to g5 and it is then attacked with ...h6? Not really, unless neither Bxf6 nor Bh4 is a good move.

Major Pieces

While getting the so-called "major" pieces – the queen and rooks – involved in the action right from the beginning has some appeal to beginners, it is usually a very good idea to wait a bit and only get these pieces into play once the minor pieces have been developed and the king has been tucked away. While there are numerous examples of openings (e.g., the Center Game, the Scandinavian Defense) in which the queen in particular is developed early, the major pieces, because of their value, easily become targets of simple threats from the opponent's developing pieces. As a result, an early development of a queen or rook can lead to loss of important tempi and put you behind in development. For instance, if White attempts the Fool's Mate, **1 e4 e5 2 Qh5 Nc6 3 Bc4**, Black can parry the threat with **3...g6** and gain additional time after **4 Qf3 Nf6 5 Ne2 d6**, and Black is obviously doing fine.

As a rule, the queen should be developed after the minor pieces, but is often developed before the rooks in an attempt to clear the back rank, allowing the rooks to connect. However, it should only be developed to a square where it is not likely to be attacked immediately, and where it may actually play a role in the future game plan.

The development of the rooks is a more difficult issue, because it is not always

apparent where they belong. A good rule of thumb is to place them on files that are either open or likely to be open shortly. For example, the Petroff Defense (a/k/a the Russian Game): **1 e4 e5 2 Nf3 Nf6 3 Nxe5 d6 4 Nf3 Nxe4 5 d4 d5 6 Bd3 Be7 7 0-0 Nc6 8 Re1**

is an example of the former, and the King's Indian, Fianchetto Variation, of the latter: **1 d4 Nf6 2 c4 g6 3 Nf3 Bg7 4 g3 d6 5 Bg2 0-0 6 0-0 Nbd7 7 Nc3 e5 8 e4 c6 9 Qc2 Re8 10 Rd1**.

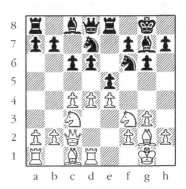

Both sides have prepared for the eventual opening of the center by Black with **...exd4**. However, you should not automatically play the rooks the d- and e-files because the pawn structure may dictate something entirely different. For example, in another line of the King's

Indian, Black places a rook on e8, only to see White close the center: **1 d4 Nf6 2 c4 g6 3 Nc3 Bg7 4 e4 d6 5 Nf3 0-0 6 Be2 e5 7 0-0 Nbd7 8 Qc2 Re8**, and now White can play **9 d5**, after which one of Black's best options is to move the rook back to f8.

Another good place for a rook is behind an advancing pawn, where it will not only support the pawn, but will also be ready in case the file opens up, e.g., **1 c4 e5 2 Nc3 Nc6 3 g3 g6 4 Bg2 Bg7 5 Nf3 d6 6 0-0 Nf6 7 d3 0-0 8 Rb1**

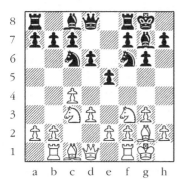

supporting the advance of the b-pawn.

In some openings, it is not immediately obvious where the rooks belong and indeed they could be placed logically on several different squares. In such cases it is helpful to study games of strong players to see how they may have handled the proper placement of the rooks. An example of an opening where it is not entirely clear what is best is the Exchange Variation of the Queen's Gambit Declined: **1 d4 d5 2 c4 e6 3 Nc3 Nf6 4 cxd5 exd5 5 Bg5 Be7 6 e3 0-0 7 Bd3 c6 8 Nf3 Nbd7 9 0-0 Re8 10 Qc2 Nf8**.

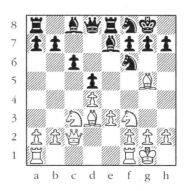

There are many good plans in this position. One such is to play **11 Rab1**, preparing the advance of the b-pawn, a common plan in positions with this pawn structure, but **11 Rae1** is also played here. This looks rather strange, placing the rook behind the e3-pawn, leaving no squares available for the f1-rook. The plan is to open the center, which can be accomplished, for example, with **11...Ne4 12 Bxe7 Qxe7 13 Bxe4 dxe4 14 Nd2 f5 15 f3 exf3 16 Nxf3 Be6 17 e4**, while if Black plays something more modest like **11...Be6**, then White will reply **12 Ne5** followed by **13 f4**, and all of a sudden both rooks are ideally placed.

The issue of rook development is even more complicated when considered in the context of their relationship with the placement of the minor pieces. Players of all strengths struggle with these sophisticated issues; they are not easy to master.

King Safety and Castling

Checkmate ends the game and as the king is a vulnerable piece that can only move one square at a time, it is not likely to be able to defend itself very well from checks. Therefore, it is a good policy to get the king into safety as soon as possible. This is usually done by castling. Castling kingside is seen in nearly all openings, but in sharp, risky lines, it is not uncommon for the players to castle queenside. For instance in the Sicilian Defense, White very often castles queenside in order to launch an attack against Black's king which will normally be found on the kingside: **1 e4 c5 2 Nf3 d6 3 d4 cxd4 4 Nxd4 Nf6 5 Nc3 e6 6 Be3 Be7 7 Bc4 0-0 8 Qe2 a6 9 0-0-0 Nc6**

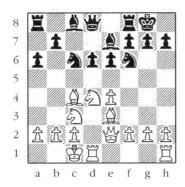

with a position in which White will advance the pawns on the kingside against the black king and Black in return will attack with the pawns and pieces on the queenside.

In some openings, one side will leave the king in the center because it is ultimately the safest place for the time being: **1 e4 c5 2 Nf3 d6 3 d4 cxd4 4 Nxd4 Nf6 5 Nc3 a6 6 Bg5 e6 7 f4 Be7 8 Qf3 Qc7 9 0-0-0 Nbd7 10 g4** *(D)*

and it is now too dangerous for Black to castle kingside and therefore he will instead focus on finishing his

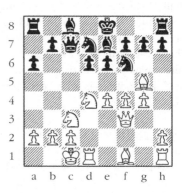

development and prepare an attack against White's king on the queenside with **10...b5** followed by **...Bb7** and **...Nc5**.

As mentioned in the section on pawn play, you should limit pawn moves in front of the castled king to a bare minimum and only then to what the position dictates. It is quite common to play either h3 or ...h6, giving the king some "room to breathe," but if the opponent has yet to castle or has castled queenside, this innocent move can constitute an immediate weakness that the opponent can target by launching a kingside attack: **1.e4 c5 2.Nf3 Nc6 3.Bb5 g6 4.Bxc6 dxc6 5.h3 e5 6.d3 f6 7.0-0 Nh6 8.Be3 Nf7 9.Nc3 g5** (Black starts the attack on the kingside, even before his own king is castled) **10.Nh2 h5 11.g4 Be6 12.b3 Qd7 13.f3 Rh7 14.Ne2 hxg4 15.hxg4 Nh8 16.Ng3 Ng6 17.Nf5 0-0-0 18.Rf2 Nf4**, and Black is clearly better (Psomiadis-Kotronias, Ikaria 1997). Therefore, unless strictly necessary, do not commit to any pawn moves in front of the king until you feel confident that it will not become a target right away and you know where your opponent is castling.

22

Flank Play

Some openings lend themselves to flank action more than others. "Flank Openings" are those that refer to play on the a-, b-, c-, f-, g-, and h-files. Early advances of the b- and c-pawns are particularly characteristic, with kingside pawn advances in the opening being less common. The English Opening, 1 c4, is an example of this. For instance in the following line: **1 c4 e5 2 Nc3 Nc6 3 g3 g6 4 Bg2 Bg7 5 d3 d6 6 Nf3 f5 7 0-0 Nf6**

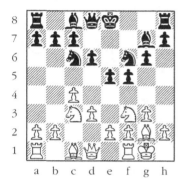

White already at this stage readies himself for queenside action with **8 Rb1**, intending b2-b4-b5. There are numerous openings where this is a feature, but as in this example, it is important to remember that any flank play should only be taking place in conjunction with healthy development, with a particular goal in mind and with a reasonably stable center. The reason for queenside flank play being more common than kingside flank play is that in most openings, both sides will castle kingside and thus pushing the kingside pawns forward weakens the king's safety. Please keep in mind that, as previously mentioned, you should not invest too much time on one project before you have more or less completed your development and gotten your king into safety.

As with any rule, there are exceptions that need to be considered. When one is deciding whether or not to pursue flank play in the opening, such considerations are: will it facilitate or accelerate your development; slow down your opponent's; or gain control over crucial squares? A combination of these ideas may be found in the Benko Gambit, which otherwise appears to contradict normal opening principles: **1 d4 Nf6 2 c4 c5 3 d5 b5**.

Both sides are just starting to develop their pieces. White has more space in the center and easier access to piece development, yet Black offers up a pawn out of the blue. How can that possibly work for Black? The idea behind this opening is that Black, after **4 cxb5 a6 5 bxa6 Bxa6 6 Nc3 g6**, followed by ...Bg7, ...d6, ...0-0, obtains quick development in return for the pawn, opening files on the queenside. This puts White under pressure, with White having to be particularly careful how exactly to bring out his pieces.

There is a well-known maxim which states that improperly prepared flank action should be countered by activity in the center. This is the reason that the center has to be reasonably stable. If you have good control over the center, either with pieces or pawns, and the opponent doesn't have any pawn breaks (or other active play) available in the center, you may be ready for play on the flanks.

Gambit Play

One of the more attractive, if not amusing elements of opening play, is that of gambit play, that is, when one side sacrifices material, usually one or more pawns, in an attempt to achieve a lead in development, force the opponent into a passive position or create weaknesses in the opponent's position in an attempt to hang on to the sacrificed material.

In the 19th and early 20th centuries, gambit play was much more common at top levels than it is today. For instance, it was not unusual to see the top players essay the King's Gambit, **1 e4 e5 2 f4**, or the Evans Gambit in the Italian Game, **1 e4 e5 2 Nf3 Nc6 3 Bc4 Bc5 4 b4**.

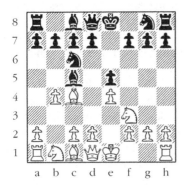

The Evans was even played several times in matches for the world championship.

Although the Queen's Gambit, **1 d4 d5 2 c4**, strictly speaking is not a gambit – because Black cannot successfully hang on to the pawn after **2...dxc4 3 e4** or **3 Nf3** followed by **4 e3** – it can lead to gambits, such as the Anti-Meran, that are currently popular at the top levels of today's chess, e.g., **1 d4 d5 2 c4 c6 3 Nf3 Nf6 4 Nc3 e6 5 Bg5 dxc4 6 e4 b5 7 e5 h6 8 Bh4 g5 9 Nxg5 hxg5 10 Bxg5 Nbd7 11 exf6**

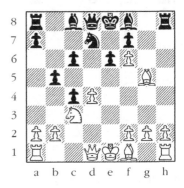

or the Anti-Moscow Gambit **1 d4 d5 2 c4 c6 3 Nf3 Nf6 4 Nc3 e6 5 Bg5 h6 6 Bh4 dxc4 7 e4 g5 8 Bg3**

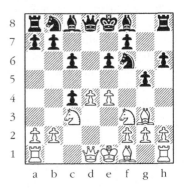

Both openings lead to massive complications that require very detailed knowledge.

At club level, gambit play is seen much more frequently and playing gambits is a good way to learn about the value of material as well as how to seek compensation for sacrificed material.

A good rule of thumb when playing gambits is that you at least should obtain two tempi of development in return for a pawn, but this is a rather inexact calculation, because many other factors play into the determination of whether there is sufficient compensation for the sacrificed material. For example, if the opponent simultaneously is forced into a passive position or to accept a structural weakness, then one tempo may be more than enough.

Pawn Grabbing

Personally, I have never enjoyed being material behind at any stage of the game and have therefore not liked playing gambits, but rather felt more comfortable accepting sacrificed material and then hanging on to it, although that can be a rather dangerous undertaking in the opening. The key to successfully accepting gambit pawns in the opening is to know how much is too much and to be ready to return material in exchange for other advantages. You should usually not allow yourself to get too far behind in development or weaken your position too much in an attempt to hang on to a pawn.

"Poisoned" Pawns

A further sub-topic to gambit play and pawn grabbing is that of poisoned pawns. The label "poisoned pawn" derives from the idea that neglecting development, casting caution to the wind, may be dangerous – poison – to one's position. Traditionally, in the opening, the pawns on b2 and b7 are considered to be "poisoned" because grabbing them with the queen can only be done so at expense of a great deal of time as well as considerable danger, as the queen runs the risk of not returning safely.

An unfortunate example of my own is the following:

H. Nielsen-Ca. Hansen
Søndersø 1984

1.e4 c5 2.Nf3 Nc6 3.d4 cxd4 4.Nxd4 g6 5.Nc3 Bg7 6.Be3 Nf6 7.Be2 Qa5?

I had played the line 7 Bc4 Qa5 (see "Opening Traps" below) with success, but in my youthful ignorance, I failed to see the problem with the opening strategy in this game until it was too late.

8.0-0 Qb4? 9.a3 Qxb2??

I recall that alarm bells were going off in my head, but I could not see what my 400-point higher-rated opponent had in mind against this pawn grab.

10.Na4

Don't buy every book that is available on a particular opening.

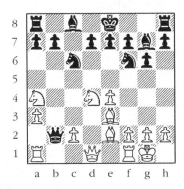

Oops! The queen is trapped, and I dutifully resigned, learning a memorable lesson about both pawn grabbing and poisoned pawns. **1-0**

There are several theoretical lines in which one of the players can take the poisoned pawn and get away with it. For example, in the Sicilian Najdorf, the Poisoned Pawn Variation has been employed successfully by the likes of Fischer, Kasparov and Anand: **1 e4 c5 2 Nf3 d6 3 d4 cxd4 4 Nxd4 Nf6 5 Nc3 a6 6 Bg5 e6 7 f4 Qb6 8 Qd2** (Note that after 8 a3, as in my game above, Black cannot play 8...Qxb2 on account of 9 Na4, winning the queen, but Black does not have to take the pawn) **8...Qxb2**.

Although the pawn-grab in the Najdorf is the most well-known, other openings that have poisoned pawn variations involving the b2-pawn, include the Torre Attack (**1 d4 Nf6 2 Nf3 e6 3 Bg5 c5 4 e3 Qb6 5 Nbd2**), and the Trompowsky (**1 d4 Nf6 2 Bg5 c5 3 d5 Qb6 4 Nc3**).

But there are also other poisoned pawn variations, for instance, in the French Winawer. **1 e4 e6 2 d4 d5 3 Nc3 Bb4 4 e5 c5 5 a3 Bxc3+ 6 bxc3 Ne7 7 Qg4**, in

which Black often allows White to take on g7 after **7...Qc7**, e.g., **8 Qxg7 Rg8 9 Qxh7 cxd4 10 Ne2**, with a sharp game. See the theoretical section in chapter 6.

While grandmasters and other strong players regularly get away with taking these poisoned pawns, there is absolutely no reason for you to follow in their footsteps; it simply involves taking too many risks and usually requires a level of calculation and theoretical knowledge that may far exceed your current level.

Moving Pieces More Than Once

This should be a rather obvious principle to follow, but because there are some blatant exceptions to the rule, some players have a hard time determining when it applies and when it does not. For instance in the Main Line Ruy Lopez, we see White repeatedly move his light-squared bishop: 1 e4 e5 2 Nf3 Nc6 3 Bb5 a6 4 Ba4 Nf6 5 0-0 Be7 6 Re1 b5 7 Bb3 d6 8 c3 0-0 9 h3 Na5 10 Bc2 c5. Despite the bishop ending up staring at its own e4-pawn, White normally tries to preserve this bishop which acts as a thematically cohesive part of White's position. In general, you should not move a piece unless the piece is threatened, will be threatened, or if there is otherwise a very specific reason

Opening Traps

Many players are attracted to opening traps because they present the possibility of winning a game quickly, or at least obtaining a very good position right from the outset. While I certainly understand this and have always had a couple of opening traps included in my repertoire, they must have sound underpinnings to be truly effective, because an unsound approach will more often than not leave you with the worse position if your opponent doesn't fall into the trap. To illustrate the difference between a sound and an unsound trap, let us have a look at a couple of examples. The first is from the Sicilian Accelerated Dragon:

1 e4 c5 2 Nf3 Nc6 3 d4 cxd4 4 Nxd4 g6 5 Nc3 Bg7 6 Be3 Nf6 7 Bc4 Qa5

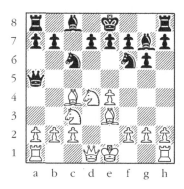

In this position Black has the obvious threat of 8...Nxe4, because the knight on c3 is pinned. White can remove the king from the pin by playing 8 0-0, after which the game will normally continue with 8...0-0 9 h3 d6 10 Bb3 Bd7 with chances for both sides. This is standard theory and has been played many times. But some players with White wants to enter the so-called Yugoslav Attack lines of the Sicilian, in which White castles queenside and will therefore opt for either 8 Qd2 or 8 f3, both moves being part of the Yugoslav Attack setup for White and both apparently eliminating the pin on the c3-knight. However, both moves are clear mistakes:

(a) 8 Qd2? Nxe4! 9 Nxc6 (or 9 Nxe4 Qxd2+ 10 Nxd2 Nxd4 and Black has won a pawn) **9...Qxc3! 10 bxc3 Nxd2 11 Kxd2 bxc6**, and Black is a pawn up with the clearly better position.

(b) 8 f3? Qb4 9 Bb3 Nxe4! (again the loose knight on d4 is a problem) **10 Nxc6 Bxc3+! 11 bxc3 Qxc3+ 12 Ke2 dxc6**, and White cannot capture the knight on e4 by 13 fxe4 because of 13...Bg4+, winning the queen.

I have had the opportunity to have six players fall into this trap against me over the years, mostly as a junior, but even grandmasters have played 8 f3 and been punished for it. As noted, there is no harm done if White avoids the trap. Another trap I have had success with, but no longer play, is the following one from the Smith-Morra Gambit:

1 e4 c5 2 d4 cxd4 3 c3 dxc3 (accepting White's gambit can be quite dangerous because White obtains a large lead in development as compensation, and defending Black's position is not to everybody's taste. A solid alternative is 3...Nf6, leading to a line in the so-called Alapin Sicilian – 2 c3.) **4 Nxc3 Nc6 5 Nf3 e6 6 Bc4 Nf6 7 0-0 Qc7 8 Qe2 Ng4!?**

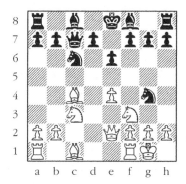

Black's play thus far looks fairly harmless, but the last move contains a lot of poison as one of my opponents (and he is not alone, many have fallen for this trap) found out after the normal-looking move...

9 h3?? Nd4!

and White can resign because 10 Nxd4 allows 10...Qh2 mate, whereas 10 Qd3 Nxf3+ 11 Qxf3 Qh2 mate is only a move better, and other moves lead to the loss of White's queen. Obviously, neither 9 h3 nor 8 Qe2 are forced, and White has many reasonable alternatives that give excellent play for the gambit pawn, another reason why I have given up this trap in addition to it now being fairly well-known.

An example of a less sound trap is the following:

1 e4 e5 2 Nf3 Nc6 3 Bc4 Nd4?

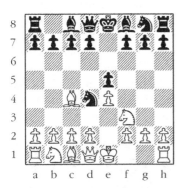

This is a rather crude trap, but I have seen some scholastic players fall into it because the temptation of the loose pawn on e5 with the threat to f7 was simply too much to pass up: 4 Nxe5?? Qg5! 5 Nxf7 (5 Bxf7+ Ke7 is not much of an improvement for White who will lose

a piece in this variation) 5...Qxg2 6 Rf1 Qxe4+ 7 Be2 Nf3 mate. This looks simple and neat, but White will likely smell the rat and simply obtain the clearly better chances with...

4 Nxd4 exd4 5 0-0 and White is ahead in development with the better pawn structure.

Many books are devoted to the subject of opening traps and miniatures; some are worth a read, but many are not. My suggestion is to avoid traps unless they are a natural part of the openings you play, in which case they are also much more likely to be effective.

The Differences between Openings

As noted in the previous sections, each opening has its own characteristics, pawn structures, piece development and plans. It is very important to keep that in mind when you are playing. Do not automatically assume that because a move is good in one opening that it is just as good in another one; you have to look at the each position individually and determine which move makes the most sense. When your opponent has made a move, write it down and look at the position carefully and use the model described in the last segment in this chapter, it will help you make better choices.

Before You Make a Move

By now, I'm sure you feel ready for the next chapters, to tackle bigger topics as well as opponents, but before moving ahead I will ask you to memorize a little tool that I use myself. I have recommended it to my students over the years as well as to the readers of my book *Improve Your Positional Chess* (Gambit Publications, 2004). It will help you to avoid most serious errors as well as make better, sounder decisions, both short-term and long-term. Before making a move you need to consider:

- King safety
- Pawn structure and placement
- Piece coordination and placement
- Unprotected pawns and pieces
- Weak squares
- What would your opponent do on move?

This seems like a rather long list, and but once you get in the habit of using it, it doesn't take that long go through it, and often it can be done by asking how each player's last move has affected the position.

Let's quickly run through it the list:

King safety – In the opening, one of your main goals is to get your king placed safely, out of harm's way, though of course "safety" is a relative term.

Pawn structure and placement – Most long-term plans are determined by pawn structure and how the pawns are configured on each wing. Entire books have been written on individual types of pawn structures and while knowing and understanding all of them is a huge task, you should initially focus on the most common ones that arise in the openings you play.

Piece coordination and placement – Normally when using the list to decide on moves, your pieces are already developed, but in the opening you are making decisions that will affect both the coordination and the distribution of the pieces for some time to come, because you may not have time to correct an incorrectly placed piece until some time later when you have completed your development. Therefore, you must make developing moves with care. This is of course closely connected with knowing some of theory of the openings you are playing, but it is equally related to the pawn structure. In the event that you have never encountered an opening variation and the accompanying pawn structure, make sure that your take sufficient time to find the optimal squares for your pieces.

Unprotected pawns and pieces – While developing your pieces will inevitably leave some pawns and pieces unprotected, what really matters is the extent of their vulnerability. Miniatures (games of 20 moves or less) are often won as a result of one side's leaving pieces unguarded or poorly coordinated – Forewarned is forearmed!

Weak squares – Pawn moves create weaknesses, often permanently, so be wary of making unnecessary pawn moves. In particular, be especially careful of moving pawns which are in front of your king, as the resulting weaknesses may be difficult to correct.

What would your opponent do on move? – This is a simple yet effective way to avoid obvious mistakes. By trying to determine what your opponent's plans and threats may be, you can often prevent their realization.

Note that this formula holds for the entire game, although there are some exceptions of a technical and practical nature in the endgame, but books dedicated to these specialized topics may be consulted for more information.

Chapter 3

How do I decide which openings to choose?

In this chapter, we will look at the process of selecting openings and putting an opening repertoire together, as well as how to deal with set-backs in your chosen openings. We will also look briefly about preparation for a specific opponent.

Choose Some Openings You Like

Studying opening theory can give you misconceptions about your own abilities as well as your capacity to memorize and play certain lines well. This is a very common mistake and one I have made several times, but having learned from my past errors, I have now selected some openings that suit me well and in which it is unlikely that I will fall victim to some novelty in a sharp line or where I may not be completely familiar with latest developments.

Many players make serious mistakes in this phase and end up choosing openings that don't match their skill level and pay for it with lost games and lost confidence.

Keep the following guideline in mind: As Black, you need one main opening against 1 d4, one against 1 e4, and consistent and considered responses to 1 c4 and 1 Nf3. As White pick one opening move, for example 1 e4, and make sure you have a considered response to Black's main replies. For example against the Sicilian, 1...c5, you decide to play 2 Nf3, and when Black answers 2...Nc6 or 2...d6, you play 3

Bb5(+) and against 2...e6, perhaps you choose 3 d3. Against all other moves, initially work it out over the board. The same procedure goes for Black's other main replies, such as 1...e5, 1...e6, 1...c6, and 1...d6. Write down your choices instead of just making a mental check list, that way you avoid gross oversights. Here is an example of how to do this:

Black - against 1 e4
1...e6
- 2 d4 d5
a) 3 Nc3 Nf6
a1) 4 Bg5 dxe4 5 Nxe4 Be7 6 Bxf6 gxf6
a2) 4 e5 Nfd7 5 f4 c5 6 Nf3 Nc6 7 Be3 a6
b) 3 Nd2 Nc6
c) 3 e5 c5 4 c3 Qb6 5 Nf3 Bd7
d) 3 exd5 exd5
d1) 4 Nf3 Nc6
d2) 4 Nc3 Nf6
d3) 4 Bd3 Nc6
- 2 d3 d5 3 Nd2 c5 4 Ngf3 Nc6 5 g3 Bd6 6 Bg2 Nge7

When you are done with your repertoire against White's main openings, you can make a quick outline of what to do against other openings such as 1 Nc3, 1 b3, 1 b4, 1 g3 and 1 f4, and then move on to the white repertoire. The level of detail is up to you, but I would advise against making it too detailed, because then it will take too much time.

However, I cannot recommend that you include any dubious gambits or sidelines as part of your main repertoire.

At some point you will encounter an opponent who is prepared and you may pay dearly. Similarly, do not think you can match the repertoires of top grandmasters; their repertoires are far to detailed and will contain several very theory-laden lines that you will have no capacity to learn properly and even less chance of understanding.

This phase may seem cumbersome and unnecessary, but take my word for it: There is nothing easier than to start studying material that has nothing to do with the openings you had initially selected, resulting in wasted time and effort. Therefore take your time, and don't be afraid to change your opinion a couple of times before settling on an opening and its main lines. It is better to retain flexibility at this stage rather change your mind later, when you have invested hours in studying the theory.

Familiarize Yourself with Your Opening Choices

At this stage, I recommend you revisit the relevant chapters and sections in this book that concern themselves with the particular lines you have chosen. Once you have accomplished that task, play over games with the openings you have chosen. These games can be found in a number of places. I prefer the games to contain some annotations, for example, like many found in chess magazines. Lacking that, there are many (perhaps too many) games available online, both with and without annotations, and they also serve you well. Annotated games can be found on a number of websites such as ChessCafe, ChessBase, The Week in Chess or in the web archives of numerous on-line newspapers.

When studying games from online sources, you will often find that they are available in several commonly used formats: PGN, ChessBase or Chess Assistant. In order to access these games you will need a "game viewer." There are PGN-viewers available multiple places on line, and a product like ChessBase light, which is available for free on the www.chessbase.com website and is quite excellent for these purposes as it reads multiple formats.

In this phase, it is also worthwhile to get a book on the opening in question, but pick carefully; it has to be a book that is suited to your level of understanding, so an encyclopedia or very advanced monograph is out of the question.

Having located relevant material, you should spend fair amount of time to acquaint yourself with both the theory, and more importantly the typical ideas and strategies in the opening, as well as the transition from opening to middlegame, as well as the middlegame itself arising from you chosen openings.

Play the Openings in Games with Shorter Time Limits

After having worked over the theory and gained some understanding of the opening, test the opening in games with shorter time limits, ideally rapid-play games with at least 20 minutes per player for the entire game, but 5-minute blitz games played on-line can also be useful. The reason for this exercise is that you get some experience playing the opening and that you keep score of the moves played. Yes, you record the moves in the rapid games too, at least until you have 5-7 minutes left. Keeping score of the game will help you in the next stage.

Learn from Your Mistakes

This seems so obvious, but the vast majority of players do not take the necessary time to go over the games afterwards and pinpoint what went well and what went badly. The latter is particularly important, because you need to look critically at every game to gain an understanding of where your strengths and weaknesses are, both when playing a particular variation, but also in general. When going over the games, preferably do so with the assistance of a coach, a stronger player or alternatively a chess engine. Another person is the most ideal, because he is more likely to ask why you played one move and rather than another. If working with a chess engine, you have to ask yourself the questions, while still being honest to yourself when answering.

A good tool in this phase is to print out a diagram of each position where you made a mistake. You may set the criteria yourself for creating the diagrams, but in any event, they should serve as a healthy reminder of the mistakes you made, also helping you to avoid making similar mistakes in the future. Once you have tested the opening to the extent that you feel reasonably confident about your understanding of it, you can move on and include the opening in your repertoire.

How to deal with setbacks, refutations and bad games

If you have played chess for a while, you will inevitably have games where you apparently never had a chance and were beaten badly. What do you do in

those situations? Many players use such games as an excuse to start playing another opening. But if you do this every time you have a bad game, then you will soon run out of openings in addition to spending a disproportionately large amount of time on the opening phase of the game, compared to the middlegame and endgame. Furthermore, the reason for the bad game is normally not the opening, but rather your failure to remember the theory or understand the opening well enough.

As you will notice in the theoretical section of this book (chapters 5-9), most openings lead to either equal play or a slight advantage for one side. That means that if you were clearly worse or even losing out of the opening, you made a mistake and before you play that opening again, you need to find out where and why you went astray. Note that the margin of error in the opening is somewhat bigger compared to both the middlegame and endgame, where, particularly in the endgame, a lost tempo can lead to an instant loss, while an inaccuracy in the opening will usually only lead to a slight disadvantage. Therefore you can often get away with a few minor mistakes at that stage.

If you feel an opening variation has been refuted, then you will either have played a very dubious opening from the outset, with the logical consequences, or simply have played an otherwise sound opening badly. The fact of the matter is that the odds for your opponent refuting an established opening are rather small.

Should you feel that you are constantly being punished in some part of your repertoire, you have to take extra time to work over the games to see where you went wrong, and work over the lines in question with the help of the opening monograph that you used when studying the opening originally. Until you have gone through this process, my advice is to not even think about switching openings.

Opponent-specific preparation

If you participate in tournaments regularly, you will frequently run into an opponent whom you know reasonably well and with whose openings you wil be familiar, just like he probably knows what you are likely to play. So what should you do in those situations? Play something outside your repertoire to surprise him or play your usual opening? In my opinion, it very much depends on the individual situation, such as the situation in the tournament, and the psyche of both you and your opponent. In my games, I have many times side-stepped my standard repertoire both to make my opponent uneasy and to avoid possible "home" preparation by my opponent. In some cases it has paid off handsomely, but in other cases I have been punished in similar fashion. Therefore I will advocate the following approach; stay within your repertoire unless:

(a) Your opponent consistently plays a dubious line, you know a refutation, and what to do if he plays another variation of that particular opening; (b) You have just lost a bad game in key part of your repertoire and you know that your opponent will likely follow that path too. This notwithstanding, it still pays off more frequently than not to play a line within your current repertoire, even if it means that you need to play a less

critical line; or (c) Your opponent reacts badly to surprises and spends too much time in such situations, but you also understand the opening in question well enough to play it with some confidence.

What is best, 1 e4 or 1 d4?

As a long-time 1 c4 player, I could be cheeky and say neither. Despite claims to the contrary, such as Fischer's "Best by test" comment about 1 e4, there is literally no way to tell if one move is better than another. In my opinion, it entirely depends on the playing style and temperament of the individual player. Often 1 e4 is considered to lead to sharper, open positions, whereas 1 d4 leads to somewhat more closed strategic positions, but these are broad generalizations which may be highly inaccurate, because individual variations can make 1 d4 openings as sharp as the sharpest 1 e4 openings, which in return can lead to dull, maneuvering positions that are more common after 1 d4.

Several authorities claim that it is best for a chess player's development to play 1 e4 in the formative years, but personally I don't think it is terribly important. However, what I have seen much too often is a talented player restricting him or herself to a very limited opening repertoire incorporating a few different types of pawn structures and thereby limiting the player's exposure to a wider variety of positions, holding back the player's development as an all-round player. The Swiss grandmaster Viktor Kortschnoi has said that implementing new openings into your repertoire keeps your game fresh and broadens your understanding of chess overall. You should heed his advice, but not do it too frequently.

Chapter 4

An Introduction to Opening Theory

Before we move to the chapters that discuss the individual openings, we need to examine some elements required to study and understand opening theory. If the signs and expressions below seem confusing, do not worry, eventually you will know them by heart.

Symbols

In most opening books, there will be a list of symbols with some brief explanations about what these symbols mean, but for the inexperienced student or reader, these explanations may not be sufficient, and we look a little closer at them in this segment.

! A good move or a strong move. This obviously is a very general explanation. For example, if 1 e4 is a good move, why doesn't it deserve a "!"? The exclamation point is given to a move that is better than the average move, and not a forced or "only" move or a move that is in some positive way surprising or unusual. But even all of these "rules" don't explain the full picture, because moves that deserve an exclamation point are often a difficult to find, surprising or gutsy, or maybe they just stop the opponent in his tracks. Whenever you see an exclamation point, pause to take stock and see if you can understand why the move was awarded it.

!! This should only be given to exceptional, truly surprising and very strong moves, basically an extra degree of everything described above for "!".

? A weak or bad move. This symbol is awarded to moves that significantly worsen a position or unnecessarily reduce the potential in one. For example, if you are winning and play a move that decreases the advantage significantly, it merits a question mark. Similarly, if an equal position worsens and becomes a clearly inferior position, it also deserves a question mark. It can also be given if a move makes a difficult position clearly worse or extends the possibility of a win considerably. If you don't understand why a question mark is given, then stop and analyze the position a bit until you feel you have a clear idea why the move is bad.

?? A blunder or a losing move. This symbol is normally used if a truly terrible move is played, such as moves that lose immediately, throw away a win or transform an equal position to a lost one.

!? An interesting and possibly good move. This symbol is given to a wide variety of moves, both good and better-than-average moves, but which also have the quality of creating an interesting position or an interesting line of thought, underscoring the unique thinking behind the move. Moves that are awarded an "!?" may be – but are not necessary always – the best move in the position.

?! A dubious move. This symbol is awarded to moves that are not completely bad, but that are clearly inferior to other possible moves.

34

+= **or** =+ A slight advantage for White or for Black. This evaluation is given for those small advantages that are often of a fleeting nature or are of a size that will be insufficient to secure a win without further weak or inferior moves from the other side. A slight advantage can consist of many things: a strong center, a space advantage, better placed pieces, control over an important file or diagonal, a misplaced piece, or a weakened pawn structure such as a doubled or isolated pawn. For a strong player, such an advantage may be sufficient to put an opponent under pressure for a long time, and maybe even lay the foundation for eventually winning the game, but for most players a slight advantage will rarely amount to much and should definitely not deter you from playing an opening if you like the positions that arise from it, even if the theory gives a slight preference for this position to the other side. In many cases it can be worthwhile taking on positions that are considered slightly inferior if you know, understand and play them well, because your opponent will more often than not be in the same "comfort zone."

+/- **or** -/+ A clear advantage for White or for Black. If a slight advantage develops into a more obvious one, perhaps of a more constant nature, or remains a more permanent factor in spite of other features of the position changing. A clear advantage can also be a material one, such as a pawn or an exchange.

+- **or** -+ A decisive advantage for White or for Black. If the advantage for one side or the other is sufficient to win the game, this symbol should be used.

Again it can apply to any number of advantages, such a material advantage, a winning attack, a passed pawn that cannot be stopped and the like. It can also be a positional advantage where the weaker side cannot prevent penetration or is completely tied up.

= An equal position. You would think that this is the simplest one to describe, but an equal position can be so many different things, such as a dull symmetrical position where neither side is able to improve the position, but it can also be dynamically balanced, where one weakness compensates for another. So if you don't understand why a position is equal, even or balanced, look and dig a little deeper until you feel you have gained some understanding why a position has been designated "=".

Phraseology

There are also a number of phrases that are commonly found in chess books.

Unclear This expression is used too frequently by annotators and authors who can't be bothered to get to the bottom of a position, and therefore it should be regarded with some suspicion when encountered. On the other hand, there are plenty of positions that are genuinely unclear, for example, where the players have castled on opposite sides and it is difficult, if not impossible, even with exhaustive analysis, to determine who will strike first and obtain an advantage if one is even to be had. It can also be applied to positions that have so many imbalances (see below) that it is difficult to determine how to weigh them individually and against each other.

Double-edged A double-edged position may be an unclear position, but it can also be a sharp position in which both sides have chances. There can be double-edged positions that favor one side, but where the other side has sharp counterplay.

Initiative The initiative is the ability to create threats, and therefore is not necessarily a lasting advantage. By its very nature, it is a fleeting advantage, which may disappear if the other side successfully parries the threats. However, if the defending side has troubles defending against the threats, the initiative can develop into a real advantage. Also note, that if you don't use the initiative, it will likely disappear and the opportunity for a real advantage with it.

Imbalance An imbalance is a number of different elements in the white and black position. Some examples are material imbalances, such as a bishop pair against knight + bishop; pawn structures such as one side having three pawns on both wings, whereas the other side has two pawns on the queenside and four pawns on the kingside; or one side has a doubled or an isolated pawn, while the other side doesn't. An imbalance is not necessarily a disadvantage, but it could be. Positions without imbalances may often be quite boring, but again, this may not necessarily follow.

Compensation In terms of opening theory, compensation will usually be for one or two pawns, a piece for a couple of pawns or knight/bishop for a rook. If you don't have full compensation for sacrificed material, we may be talking about dealing with an actual advantage. As you will see in the coverage of the opening theory in the following chapters, this is a very frequently used term and it covers a wide variety of situations. However, while "with compensation" may be the objective evaluation by stronger players and theoreticians, you have to make a subjective evaluation yourself, deciding whether you think that the positional compensation is sufficient for you if you intend to sacrifice the material in your own games or if it isn't. This is an important process and is one you must do for yourself when studying opening theory.

Transposition In many openings there are several transpositions available within individual lines, but occasionally transpositions happen from one opening to another, such as in the following example: 1 c4 c5 2 Nc3 Nc6 3 Nf3 g6 4 d4 cxd4 5 Nxd4 Bg7 6 Nc2 Nf6 7 e4, and now we have moved from a line in the Symmetrical English to the Maroczy Bind in the Sicilian Accelerated Dragon (1 e4 c5 2 Nf3 Nc6 3 d4 cxd4 4 Nxd4 g6 5 c4 Nf6 6 Nc3 Bg7 7 Nc2). Transpositions are worth looking out for because if you are unaware of their existence you can end up in an opening or variation you don't know particularly well or didn't intend.

Plus / minus This is another way of describing an advantage or disadvantage for one side or the other.

Counterplay In itself counterplay is hard to define or measure, because it is used very broadly. Counterplay can be something akin to "equal chances" or a "balanced position," but it is also frequently used when one side has a small advantage, but when used with a limiting phrase such as "and Black has counterplay" it indicates that whatever advantage the other side may have, it certainly is not one-sided.

Lead in Development Unlike the previous term, a lead in development is both obvious and tangible. Some of the older masters such as Tarrasch counted tempo advantages as compensation for pawns won or sacrificed, but that is a very inaccurate science, and I don't encourage you to try to determine any lead in development by exactly how many pieces you have developed compared to your opponent. For instance, if a game starts with 1 b3 d5 2 Bb2 c5 3 Nf3 f6 4 e3 e5 5 Be2, it is clear that White has developed more pieces, while Black so far has only moved pawns. Yet, in this position, White does not have an advantage, because Black is able to develop his pieces freely and to good squares without any major interruption from White. Therefore what you should be paying attention to is the quality of development, i.e., developing the pieces to active squares and moves that allow for keeping the king safe, such as clearing the path for the king to castle.

Also note that the development of the queen and rooks are in most opening lines something best left for later, when the pawn structure has been defined and you therefore more easily can determine which squares are optimal for the plan you wish to follow. All too frequently, I see games with inexperienced players, in which the queens get developed much too soon, or where the rooks, after castling, are blindly placed on the e- and d-files, irrespective of what otherwise is happening on the board.

With the Idea of Or "intending," is something worth paying attention to when studying openings, because it defines a plan or intention from one side. This can also be described as a variation containing moves from both players, or a probable line or a sequence of moves.

"Only" Move This term is most frequently used when considering middlegames and endgames, but occasionally it is also used when discussing openings, where either one or more moves must be played by one side in order to avoid a quick loss. However it is just as frequently used to describe the unique move that gains an advantage or allows a player to equalize.

Different Styles of Presentation

Opening theory is usually presented in one of three ways, though occasionally, they are combined.

(1) Encyclopedic
This type of presentation uses tables of variations, with individual numbered variations, and alternatives given in footnotes. For new players, I cannot recommend books that use type of presentation, because the explanatory prose that elaborates typical plans and ideas is usually absent, thus leaving the student without any clear idea why certain moves are played or even preferred over other apparently equivalent moves. Another problem is that encyclopedic works are often rather

costly and do not get updated as regularly as monographs that concentrate on individual openings. The benefit is of course that the reader gets a wider presentation of openings and variations than monographs provide.

(2) Tree

In older opening monographs, the tree-style presentation was used almost exclusively, and while it is still seen nowadays, it is usually in works aimed at players with advanced skills. The tree-style can be recognized by the variation being split up in A, B, C, etc. and then numbered as the variations break up further, so that you may be able to see something like "A1542." A presentation of this kind can be both confusing and overwhelming to the less experienced player, but for the more advanced player, variation trees allow more clarity and assurance that all relevant lines are being covered in a particular work. Unless the variations are supported by sufficient narrative, I don't recommend books of this type to beginners and less experienced players, because the phrase "can't find the forest for the trees" explains it well – there is simply too much information to obtain a good picture of what is truly happening in a particular opening or variation.

(3) Main Game

For inexperienced players, I think the model that bases opening discussions on more or less complete games that are fully annotated, though with a main focus on the opening and early middlegame, is the ideal. Opening books such as the *Chess Explained* and *Starting Out* series are ideal for players who are not yet that advanced but who at the same time would like to learn how to play a particular opening well, and both of these series have based their presentation on mostly complete games.

Final thoughts before studying the next chapters

From the outset, you should understand that you will not be able to remember all the theory you will come across in the next five chapters, nor should you try to do so; it is a waste of time.

"Theory" is mostly a collection of main and other important lines, which can help steer you generally in the right direction. However, you should also use these lines to see which ones you prefer as you begin to put together your repertoire.

Finally, don't try to go through too many chapters and variations in one day, because you will get confused. As described in chapter 1, I once did this myself, and the consequences of my half-baked approach meant that I took up too many different lines, didn't understand them, mixed them up and lost a lot of games.

When you are done with the chapters on theory, go back to chapter 3 before again moving forward and reading chapter 10.

> *Do not start playing an opening unless you have at least a rudimentary understanding of the most frequently occurring pawn structures in that opening.*

Chapter 5

The Open Games

For a very long time, the world's best chess players focused almost exclusively on 1 e4 e5 openings, the so-called "open" games. Therefore most of the openings in this chapter have a long history and complicated variation trees, some of which make little or no sense. Many chess coaches have either written or spoken about the benefits of starting out in chess by playing these openings because they give an excellent balance for your understanding of the game. The openings presented below vary from the mundane and boring to the intrinsically complicated and confusing, and in many cases backed by volumes of theory that can be difficult to understand. But fear not, in all of the openings presented here, there are ways to avoid the most difficult and theory-heavy lines.

Scotch Game and Scotch Gambit

Some years ago world champion Garry Kasparov took up the Scotch Game as White, making the statement that it is the only serious alternative to the Ruy Lopez (3 Bb5) for White after 1 e4 e5 2 Nf3 Nc6. It is still seen quite frequently at top level, but nowhere near as often as the Ruy Lopez, which is strategically far more complex. On the plus side for the Scotch Game fans, black players don't invest nearly as much time in the Scotch as they do on the Ruy Lopez, so there are plenty of opportunities to surprise opponents.

1 e4 e5 2 Nf3 Nc6 3 d4 exd4 4 Nxd4

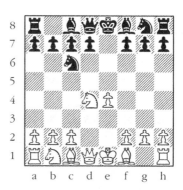

While the official starting position of the Scotch is 3 d4, the vast majority of the games continue with 4 Nxd4. The alternatives are 4 Bc4, the Scotch Gambit, which will be covered below, and 4 c3, which is the Göring Gambit and can be found in the gambit section.

Now Black's main moves are 4...Bc5 and 4...Nf6, and each has its own section, but occasionally Black tests other moves such as 4...Bb4+, 4...Qh4 and, to a lesser extent, 4...Nge7 and 4...Qf6. The first option, 4...Bb4+, is considered a solid move and has been played by a number of grandmasters who have not been afraid to deviate from the most well-trodden paths, whereas 4...Qh4 is very risky, intending to pick up White's e4-pawn at a cost of lagging development and often sacrificing the right to castle. Therefore I cannot recommend this move to anyone except those that love living life on the edge and can stand defending a scary position for some time, hoping to eventually emerge relatively unscathed.

Scotch Gambit

The main problem for White in the Scotch Gambit is that the opening usually transposes into something else rather quickly; some of these lines are quite interesting, whereas others offer less chances for an interesting game.

1 e4 e5 2 Nf3 Nc6 3 d4 exd4 4 Bc4

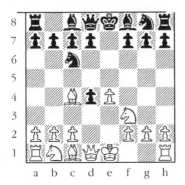

The starting position of this gambit; Black now has the option of playing 4...Nf6, taking the game into the lines that will be discussed in the section on the Two Knights Defense.

4...Bc5!

This is the simplest option for Black.

5 c3

White invites Black to take the pawn on c3, but if Black accepts the challenge with 5...dxc3, White recovers the pawn with 6 Bxf7+ Kxf7 7 Qd5+ Kf8 8 Qxc5+ d6 9 Qxc3, with a better game for White. Also 5...d3 6 b4 Bb6 7 0-0 and 5...d6 6 cxd4 are better for White. Thus far, everything looks quite promising for White. Black however has another simple solution...

5...Nf6!

And when White now plays 6 cxd4, Black plays 6...Bb4+, and we have reached the Møller Variation of the Italian Game, which is covered below. If it had been White intention to play the Italian Game, he would probably have played 3 Bc4 straightaway, though with this move order, White has avoided some possible lines in the Two Knights Defense.

4...Bc5 Variation

At the highest levels, this particular variation has been Black's preferred choice for quite some time, and as a result, the theory of this line has expanded at a very rapid pace, and even fairly obscure sidelines are now seen regularly in grandmaster games.

1 e4 e5 2 Nf3 Nc6 3 d4 exd4 4 Nxd4 Bc5

Black attacks the white knight, forcing White to commit to one plan. In addition to the main lines which will be covered below, White has also tried 5 Nf5, but this can be met adequately a couple of ways: 5...g6 6 Ne3 Nf6 7 Nc3 0-0 8 Bd3 Re8 and the sharper 5...d6!? (or even

5...d5), and here White should play 6 Ne3, with equal play, as 6 Nxg7+ Kf8 7 Nh5 Qh4 8 Ng3 Nf6 9 Be2 Ne5 gives Black ample compensation for the pawn.

5 Be3

The old main line is 5 Nb3, but Black is considered to be fine after 5...Bb6 6 a4 a6 7 Nc3, and here Black has the choice between 7...Nge7, 7...d6 and 7...Nf6, in each case with approximately even chances.

Originally it was thought that 5 Nxc6 was inadequate for an edge because of 5...Qf6!?, threatening mate on f2 as well as the knight on c6 and therefore avoiding the doubled c-pawns. However, it has since been determined that after 6 Qd2!?, Black should accept the doubled pawn with 6...dxc6 anyway in order to avoid lagging behind in development. Now the theoretical main line runs 7 Nc3 Be6 (7...Ne7 is also fully playable) 8 Na4 Rd8 9 Bd3 Bd4 with chances for both sides.

Quite recently, White has preferred a somewhat curious looking move, 6 Qf3!?, offering Black the opportunity to give White doubled f-pawns. The theoretical verdict isn't quite in yet, but Black appears to be in good shape after both 6...Qxf3 7 gxf3 bxc6 8 Be3 Bxe3 9 fxe3, but at the higher levels, Black usually prefers the immediate 6...bxc6, waiting to exchange on f3 when it suits Black better.

5...Qf6 6 c3

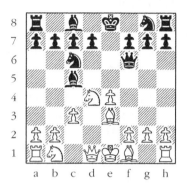

White can also consider the sharp and unclear 6 Nb5!? to avoid the mountain of theory in the main line, but Black should be fine after 6...Bxe3 7 fxe3 Qe5 8 Nd2 Kd8.

6...Nge7 7 Bc4

Another option is 7 g3, but 7...h5 is fine for Black.

7...Ne5

Also 7...0-0 and even 7...b6 are fully playable for Black.

8 Be2 Qg6 9 0-0 d6

Black cannot afford to take the pawn on e4: 9...Qxe4 10 Nb5, and Black is essentially lost.

10 f3 0-0 11 Kh1

And Black can choose between the solid 11...Bb6 and the sharper 11...d5, in both cases with adequate counterplay.

> ***Don't spend more time on the opening than you do on the middlegame and endgame.***

4...Nf6 Variation

This line is often called the Mikenas Variation. Black's idea is to provoke White to advance his pawns to squares where protecting them will leave structural weaknesses and further force White to develop pieces to awkward squares. Black in return concedes a fair share of space, and unless he is careful, he can end up with a passive position without counterplay. A delicate balance.

1 e4 e5 2 Nf3 Nc6 3 d4 exd4 4 Nd4 Nf6 5 Nxc6

5 Nc3 leads to the Scotch Four Knights, covered below.

5...bxc6 6 e5 Qe7

It is not immediately obvious why this move is a good idea, but after a few moves, things start getting clearer. The alternative, 6...Nd5 7 c4 Nb6 8 Bd3, is pleasant for White.

7 Qe2

An awkward square for the queen, where it blocks the development of the light-squared bishop.

7...Nd5 8 c4

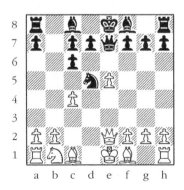

This is the starting position of the Mikenas Variation. Black now has two equally viable lines to choose from.

8...Ba6

Taking advantage of White's queen being on e2 by pinning the c4-pawn. The alternative is the immediate 8...Nb6, and then after 9 Nc3 (if 9 Nd2, then 9...d6 or 9...Bb7 10 b3 0-0-0 promises Black a decent game.) 9...Qe6 (or 9...a5!?) 10 Qe4 Ba6 11 b3 with a complicated position where both sides have their share of the chances.

9 b3 g6

The alternatives include 9...g5!? (to develop the f8-bishop, but also to prevent f2-f4), 9...Qh4 and 9...0-0-0; they all are considered more or less adequate for equal chances.

10 f4 f6 11 exf6 Nxf6 12 Bb2 0-0-0

And once again we have a sharp position with more or less equal chances.

Four Knights Game

For years the Four Knights Game had a reputation of being exceedingly dull because of the symmetrical nature of the Spanish Four Knights line. But in the 1980s the opening had a revival, particularly in the hands of several of the strongest English grandmasters such as Short and Nunn. Since then the opening's popularity has declined again, though it still appears even at grandmaster level.

1 e4 e5 2 Nf3 Nc6 3 Nc3 Nf6

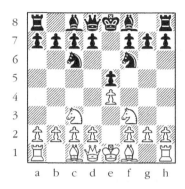

Here the paths diverge. In addition, 4 Bc4 will take the game to the Italian Four Knights and then finally White has the overly solid 4 Be2 and the somewhat bizarre 4 a3 that intends 5 d2-d4 without allowing Black to play ...Bb4.

Spanish Four Knights

Of the different versions of the Four Knights, this main line of the Spanish Four Knights is probably the least interesting to most people, but strategically it is rather intriguing and this is undoubtedly why it became more popular in the early 1990s.

4 Bb5

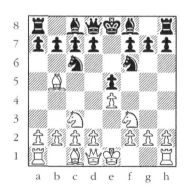

4...Bb4

While this is seen most often, Black has a major alternative in the Rubinstein Variation, which immediately takes the game in a sharper direction, often at the cost of a pawn, the price for taking a "boring" opening in a more exciting direction: 4...Nd4!?

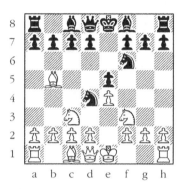

and now White has a number of options available, but the critical lines are the ones in which White play 5 Ba4. After 5...Bc5 (5...Nxf3+ 6 Qxf3 is more solid, but also slightly better for White, whereas 5...c6 also leads to sharp play) 6 Nxe5 0-0 7 Nd3 Bb6 8 e5 (also 8 Nf4 is seen quite frequently, but Black is doing fine in that line after both 8...c6 and 8...d5) 8...Ne8 9 Nd5 d6 (9...c6 usually transposes to the main line after 10 Ne3 d6) 10 Ne3 c6 (10...Qg5!? 11 exd6 Nxd6 with compensation for the pawn or 10...dxe5 11 Nxe5 Qg5 12 Nc4 f5 with a sharp position) 11 c3 Nf5 12 0-0 Bc7, and once again Black has compensation for the pawn. More recently, White has also taken a liking to the more solid 5 Bc4, which gives a balanced game, but where the stronger player has a good chance of playing for a win without taking unnecessary risks.

5 0-0 0-0 6 d3 d6 7 Bg5

White sometimes sidesteps the main lines by playing the slightly odd-looking, but perfectly logical 7 Ne2, intending c2-c3, Ng3 and d3-d4.

7...Bxc3

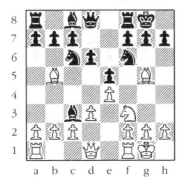

With the pin on the f6-knight, Black cannot afford to allow White to play Nc3-d5. Therefore Black cedes White the bishop pair.

8 bxc3 Qe7

This is considered best, intending to deal with the pinning bishop on g5 by re-routing the knight on c6 via d8 to e6; 8...h6 9 Bh4 Bd7 is also fully playable.

9 Re1 Nd8 10 d4 Ne6 11 Bc1!?

It has been determined that this is the best square for the bishop, but White has played both 11 Bd2 and 11 Bh4 with decent success, so these moves cannot be entirely dismissed either.

Now Black can choose between 11...Rd8, 11...c5 and 11...c6, all of which have been used by top grandmasters, though the last two are the more popular options. The chances are approximately

equal, with a prolonged strategic battle ahead in each case.

Scotch Four Knights

When studying the theory of the Scotch Four Knights you will find an interesting mix of players, well-known and virtually unknown, along with material that spans a period from the 1880s through today. It is not currently particularly popular at grandmaster level, and it is doubtful whether it truly ever will become a topical opening at that level again, simply because it doesn't offer the degree of strategic complexity that is required for grandmasters to give it their full attention.

4 d4

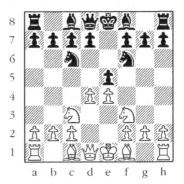

4...exd4

A sharper alternative is 4...Bb4, which leads to considerable complications.

5 Nxd4

White can also essay the Belgrade Gambit which arises after 5 Nd5.

While it presents Black with some problems, especially if not prepared, Black can get a decent game in several ways: 5...Be7 (5...Nxe4 is what White is hoping for, and while playable, both 5...Nxd5 and 5...Nb4 lead to complications with which White likely will be more familiar than Black. The text move, 5...Be7, is a simple solution that lead to equal play) 6 Bf4 (6 Bc4 is answered by 6...0-0 7 0-0 d6, and 6 Nxd4 by 6...Nxd5 7 exd5 Nxd4 8 Qxd4 0-0, and in both cases Black has equalized rather effortlessly) 6...d6 7 Nxd4 0-0 8 Nb5 Nxd5 9 exd5 Ne5 with a pleasant position for Black.

5...Bb4 6 Nxc6 bxc6 7 Bd3 d5 8 exd5 cxd5 9 0-0 0-0 10 Bg5 c6

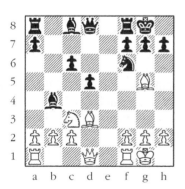

This is pretty much the starting position of the Scotch Four Knights. Now White has a number of options available including 11 Qf3 and 11 Ne2, but the next move is the most popular continuation and also the most critical for both players.

11 Na4 h6 12 Bh4 Re8 13 c4 Bd6 14 cxd5 cxd5 with mutual chances.

Four Knights Fianchetto

This variation is often called the Glek System after grandmaster Igor Glek who has played this system repeatedly with very good results despite theory condemning it as fairly innocuous.

4 g3

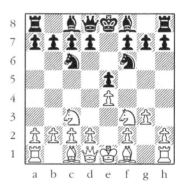

You may notice some similarities in the theory and that of 3 g3 in the Vienna Game, and in some cases the variations transpose. If you are going to play this line, you should have a rudimentary knowledge of both lines.

4...Bc5

In my opinion, this is the better move for Black in this position, but according to standard theory, Black is also doing fine after 4...d5, e.g., 5 exd5 Nxd5 6 Bg2 Nxc3 7 bxc3, and now both 7...Bc5 8 0-0 0-0 9 Re1 Qf6 and 7...Be7 8 0-0 0-0 9 Re1 Bf6 are supposed to lead to equal play, but White, usually being more familiar with the resulting positions, tends to score well in both lines.

5 Bg2 d6 6 d3 a6 7 0-0

White can also play 7 h3, though after 7...h6, play tends to continue down similar paths as our main line, e.g., 8 0-0 Be6.

7...Be6 8 Be3 Bxe3 9 fxe3 Ne7! 10 Nh4 c6 and a sharp position with chances to both sides has arisen.

The Italian Game

There are a couple of openings in this chapter where the lines vary from fairly unexciting to high adrenaline, throw-in-the-kitchen-sink type of openings. The Italian Game is one of those and once you become more familiar with the lines, I'm certain you will agree.

1 e4 e5 2 Nf3 Nc6 3 Bc4 Bc5

We will cover 3...Nf6, Three Knights Game, in the next section. Now White can take the game in very different directions based on his choice of move in this particular position.

Italian Four Knights

4 d3 Nf6 5 Nc3 d6

This line is without a doubt one of the dullest lines of the entire Italian complex, but also one that I have played or faced numerous times as a scholastic player. It is a fairly simple setup, where the players have more or less identical plans, and usually the better player wins because of a better ability to create and take advantage of favorable imbalances.

6 Bg5

After 6 Be3, Black should not exchange on e3, allowing White to open the f-file, but rather play 6...Bb6, followed by 7...Be6 and a similar retreat by White. The text move aims to create a little more action.

6...h6 7 Bxf6

Keeping the pin with 7 Bh4 does not accomplish anything; it rather invites Black at a later stage to try ...g7-g5, taking the bishop entirely out of the game and initiating a kingside attack for Black.

7...Qxf6 8 Nd5 Qd8 9 c3 Ne7 10 d4 Ba7 with chances for both sides.

Evans Gambit

One of White's sharpest approaches in the Italian Game is the so-called Evans Gambit invented by Capt. William Evans in the 19th century. It was all the rage towards the end of that century and was debated intensely in the matches between Steinitz and Chigorin for the world championship. Nevertheless, this variation has never been refuted and is somewhat regularly employed by the English grandmaster Nigel Short and was even used a couple of times by Kasparov against other top grandmasters.

4 b4!?

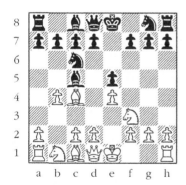

White sacrifices a pawn and hopes in return to gain time to expand in the center and develop his pieces more easily.

4...Bxb4

Black can also decline the gambit with 4...Bb6.

5 c3 Ba5

If Black plays 5...Bc5 or 5...Be7, White can play the desired 6 d4 with less risk. With the text move, Black pins the c3-pawn, thus not allowing White to take back with the c-pawn after 6 d4 exd4.

6 0-0

6 d4 is nevertheless possible, e.g., 6...exd4 (or 6...d6!?) 7 0-0 Nge7 8 cxd4 d5 9 exd5 Nxd5 with sharp play and chances for both sides.

6...d6 7 d4 Bb6 8 dxe5 dxe5 9 Qb3 Qf6 10 Bg5 Qg6 11 Bd5 with a sharp position and approximately even chances.

Max Lange Gambit

This line should not be confused with the Max Lange Attack, which is discussed in the section on the Two Knights Defense.

4 0-0 Nf6 5 d4!?

Although advocated in several repertoire books as a weapon for White, this line was never subject to much scrutiny, but when Movsesian convincingly beat Adams with the opening in Wijk aan Zee 2009, even casual observers started paying attention. However, Black should be fine provided he knows what he doing.

5...Bxd4

This seems like Black's safest continuation.

6 Nxd4 Nxd4 7 f4 d6 8 fxe5 dxe5 9 Bg5 Be6

While this is the main line, a recent recommendation of American grandmaster Roman Dzindzichashvili is 9...Qe7, and then after 10 Na3, Black plays the deep 10...Rg8, preparing to open the g-file when White exchanges on f6.

10 Na3 Qe7 11 c3 Nc6

And White has good compensation for the sacrificed pawn; the pin of the f6-knight virtually guarantees that White will win the pawn back when he so desires.

Møller Attack

While still plenty of fun for the initiated, the Møller Attack has entirely disappeared from top level play since an idea for Black was introduced by the Hungarian grandmaster Lajos Portisch in 1969. It did not refute White's play, but it left him with no hope of an advantage. Nevertheless, this line is still seen in correspondence chess games

between strong players, leaving the impression that this opening may still be played with some hope of success.

4 c3 Nf6

The only real alternative to this move is the solid and somewhat passive 4...Qe7, e.g., 5 d4 Bb6 6 0-0 d6 7 h3 Nf6 8 Re1, which leaves White with more space and an easier game, although Black's position is perfectly playable and theoretically equal.

5 d4!?

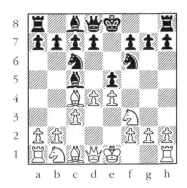

White continues as if Black's moves don't matter. The more reserved 5 d3 is covered below in the Pianissimo segment.

5...exd4 6 cxd4

6 e5 d5 7 Bb5 Ne4! 8 cxd4 Bb6 9 Nc3 0-0 is fine for Black, and 6 0-0 dxc3 can take the game to Scotch Gambit, whereas 6...Nxe4 is a line in the Two Knights Defense.

6...Bb4+ 7 Nc3

This is the classical main line, named after the Dane Jørgen Møller who was one of the strongest Scandinavian players around the end of the 19th century. As mentioned in the introduction to this segment, this line is not seen very often any more. White usually deviates at this juncture with the more solid 7 Bd2, and after 7...Bxd2+ 8 Nbxd2 d5 9 exd5 Nxd5, a draw is often agreed when 10 Qb3 Na5 11 Qa4+ Nc6 11 Qb3 (11 Bb5 Bd7 at least lets the game continue, but isn't seen very often) 11...Na5 follows. If Black wants more, he can try either 10...Nce7 or 8...Nxe4!?, the latter leading to very sharp play that supposedly is fine for Black, but he really needs to be prepared for this line.

7...Nxe4! 8 0-0! Bxc3! 9 d5!

The previous few moves have been established as the only way for White to play for an advantage and the only way for Black to keep the balance, but at this juncture Black has a couple of moves to choose from.

9...Bf6

The main line, but 9...Ne5 10 bxc3 Nxc4 11 Qd4 0-0 12 Qxe4 Nd6 13 Qd3 is also possible, with equal chances.

10 Re1 Ne7 11 Rxe4 d6 12 Bg5 Bxg5 13 Nxg5 h6

Another option is 13...0-0, though the answer 14 Nxh7!? will likely terrify some players, but Black should be okay after 14...Kxh7 15 Qh5+ Kg8 16 Rh4 f6 17 Bd3 f5!, and Black can defend.

14 Qe2! hxg5 15 Re1 Be6 16 dxe6 f6! 17 Re3

White has compensation for the pawn, but not much more.

Giuoco Pianissimo

A lot less committal than the Møller is the Pianissimo. Rather than pressing forward, White takes the necessary time to develop pieces before making a move in the center. At the same time, Black is allowed to do the same. This line is seen quite often at grandmaster level, even in games between the very highest rated players in the world.

4 c3 Nf6 5 d3

Note that this variation often arises via the Two Knights Defense: 3...Nf6 4 d3 Bc5 5 c3.

Reach a playable position that you understand how to play.

5...d6

Black often plays ...a7-a6 either here or on one of the next moves in order to be able to retreat the dark-squared bishop to a7 rather than to b6. However, often the lines will transpose.

6 0-0

White has several alternatives at this juncture, and while many of them allow transposition to the main line, of independent significance is 6 b4!?, aiming to gain space on the queenside, e.g., 6...Bb6 7 a4 a6 (or 7...a5!?) 8 0-0 0-0 9 a5 Ba7 10 Bb3 Ne7 11 Bb3 Ng6 with chances for both sides.

6...0-0 7 Bb3 a6 8 Nbd2 Ba7 9 h3 h6 10 Re1 Be6

This position is considered the main line and can be reached a number of ways, and is assessed as about equal.

Two Knights Defence

Black's sharpest response to the 3 Bc4 is undoubtedly the Two Knights Defense which immediately provokes a reaction from White:

1 e4 e5 2 Nf3 Nc6 3 Bc4 Nf6

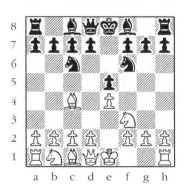

Now White has a choice to make: take it slow and continue development with 4 d3, or try to punish Black with either the very direct 4 Ng5 or the sharp 4 d4.

The Quiet System

If White is not easily provoked, then it is likely that White will opt for this continuation, building up the position slowly and developing pieces rather than getting involved in chaotic hand-to-hand combat.

4 d3 Be7 5 0-0 0-0 6 Bb3 d6 7 c3

This very much resembles some of the lines in the Ruy Lopez discussed below.

With Black inviting sharp play with his 3rd move, it is quite possible that this type of play is not what he is looking for.

7...h6 8 Nbd2 Re8 9 Re1 Bf8 10 h3 Be6

And the chances are more or less even.

White plays 4 Ng5!?

While world championship candidate Siegbert Tarrasch scoffed at this move, it has many followers. White makes a clear threat against the weakest spot in Black's position; now Black has to come up with a decent response.

4 Ng5 d5

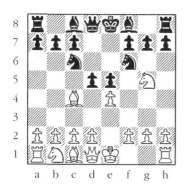

This is an obvious choice, blocking the bishop and apparently leaving White's knight hanging in mid-air on g5; if only matters were that simple.

Black's only alternative is the Traxler Counter-Attack, also called the Wilkes-Barre, 4...Bc5, which apparently ignores White's threat against f7. Claims of having refuted this line have appeared periodically, but is as far as I know it is still viable, if only theoretically, because the analysis of this line is massively complicated and nearly impossible to reproduce at the board unless you have a book or a computer to remind you of all the moves, e.g., 5 Nxf7 (at the moment, this is considered the critical continuation, but previously 5 Bxf7+ Ke7 6 Bd5 was considered best) 5...Bxf2+! 6 Kf1 Qe7 7 Nxh8 d5 8 exd5 Nd4 9 d6! Qxd6 10 Nf7 Qc5, and Black may be fine. If none of this makes sense to you, don't worry – it doesn't to most people, which is a good reason to stay away from this line.

5 exd5 Na5

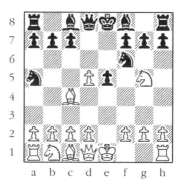

When I was younger, I thought White was winning after 5...Nxd5 6 Nxf7, (the so-called Fegatello or Fried Liver Attack), but what none of my opponents managed to find was that Black is actually doing fine after 6...Kxf7 7 Qf3+ Ke6 8 Nc3 Ncb4, even if the defense of Black's position is by no means is easy. Therefore, White should play the Lolli Attack, 6 d4!, which is far more problematic for Black.

But in addition to the text move, Black actually has two other moves at his disposal, neither of which are particularly easy to understand: (a) 5...b5 (the Ulvestad Variation) 6 Bf1 (6

Bxb5 Qxd5 is fine for Black) 6...Nxd5 (6...Nd4 transposes to line (b) below) 7 Bxb5 (now that Black does not have ...Qxd5 available any longer, this makes good sense) 7...Bb7 8 d4 exd4 9 0-0 Qf6 with an unclear position; and (b) 5...Nd4 (Fritz Variation) 6 c3 b5 7 Bf1 Nxd5 8 cxd4 Qg5 9 Bb5 Kd8 10 Qf3 Bb7 11 0-0 Rb8 with another crazy position that appears to be devoid of any kind of chess logic.

6 Bb5+ c6 7 dxc6 bxc6

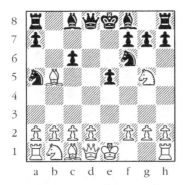

Black has sacrificed a pawn and hopes that his easier access to developing the minor pieces will provide an initiative that will counterbalance the material investment.

8 Be2

It begs explanation why White does not just play 8 Qf3. This move has actually been played by several strong players, but although White after 8...Rb8 can win a second pawn with 9 Bxc6+, he should prefer 9 Bd3 to avoid getting too far behind in development.

8...h6 9 Nf3

Both Steinitz and Fischer gave preference to the odd-looking 9 Nh3,

but Black is should be doing fine in this line.

9...e4 10 Ne5 Bd6 11 d4!? exd3 12 Nxd3 Qc7

And now after 13 b3 0-0 14 Bb2, White has an extra pawn, but Black's active pieces more or less compensate for the material imbalance.

Max Lange Attack

The Two Knights Defense is replete with complicated and convoluted lines that can be difficult to navigate without serious and thorough study, and the Max Lange Attack certainly belongs in this group.

4 d4 exd4 5 0-0

White has a couple of alternatives at this juncture: 5 Ng5 which is fine for Black after 5...d5!? 6 exd5 Qe7+ 7 Kf1 Ne5 provided Black knows the theory, and 5 e5, which is the so-called Modern Attack. After 5...d5 (both 5...Ne4 and even 5...Ng4 can be played, even if they are a bit more provocative than the main line) 6 Bb5 Ne4 7 Nxd4 Bd7 (an alternative is 7...Bc5!?) 8 Bxc6 bxc6 9 0-0 Bc5 10 f3 Ng5 11 f4 Ne4 12 Be3 Bb6, with chances for both sides.

5...Bc5

This leads to lines which boggle the mind. A simpler, more solid approach is 5...Nxe4 and now after 6 Re1 d5, White should play 7 Bxd5! Qxd5 8 Nc3 Qa5 9 Nxe4 Be6 10 Bd2 (or 10 Neg5 0-0-0 11 Nxe6 fxe6 12 Rxe6 Bd6 with a satisfactory position for Black) 10...Bb4 11 Nxd4 Nxd4 12 c3, and here Black should be fine after both 12...Be7 and 12...0-0-0.

6 e5 d5 7 exf6!?

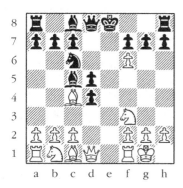

If White prefers a calmer alternative, then the option of 7 Bb5 Ne4 is still available, transposing into the Modern Attack above.

7...dxc4 8 Re1+

In spite of appearances, 8 fxg7 Rg8 9 Bg5 Be7 10 Bxe7 Kxe7 is fine for Black.

8...Be6 9 Ng5 Qd5!

Note that 9...Qxf6 loses a piece to 10 Nxe6 fxe6 11 Qh5+.
10 Nc3 Qf5 11 Nce4 0-0-0 12 g4 Qe5 13 Nxe6 fxe6 14 fxg7 Rhg8 15 Bh6 d3 16 c3 d2 17 Re2 Rd3

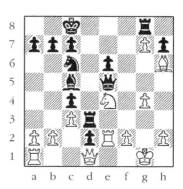

And we have reached the critical position of the Max Lange Attack; the theory continues on for some time, but needless to say, you shouldn't even think about entering this line with either color unless you have studied it very carefully.

Third Move Deviations

The openings covered in this segment are seen only infrequently and are not of any particular consequence, but it is worth knowing the basics.

The Hungarian Defense

The pure version of this variation is seen very rarely these days because it is quite passive.

1 e4 e5 2 Nf3 Nc6 3 Bc4 Be7

If White now plays 4 d3, and Black then follows up with 4...Nf6, we have a line that normally originates in the Two Knights: 3...Nf6 4 d3 Be7, but with the present move order White should play more actively.

4 d4

4...d6

On 4...exd4, White may be tempted to play 5 c3 because of 5...dxc3? 6 Qd5, which looks like it wins straight away, 6...Nh6 being answered by 7 Bxh6, but 7...0-0! wins the piece as a result of the threat against the b2-pawn and the bishop on h6, and the fact that 8 Bc1 is answered by 8...Nb4 9 Qd1 c2. However, 8 Bxg7 Kxg7 9 Nxc3 gives White an edge, and so does 5...d3 6 Qb3 Na5 7 Bxf7+ Kf8 8 Qa4. But White's best is the simple 5 Nxd4 d6 6 0-0 Nf6 7 Nc3 with an obvious space advantage. Black has played a Philidor with the knight on c6, not a good combination.

5 d5 Nb8 6 Bd3 Nf6 7 c4 and White has the better chances.

Three Knights Game

The Three Knights Game only arise if Black declines to go in for the Four Knights, but generally speaking, White should be able to gain a small advantage, and therefore Black would be better advised to enter the Four Knights.

1 e4 e5 2 Nf3 Nc6 3 Nc3

3...g6

Other moves include 3...Bb4 and 3...Bc5.

4 d4 exd4 5 Nxd4

A sharper alternative is 5 Nd5, e.g., 5...Bg7 6 Bg5 Nce7 (6...Nge7? loses to 7 Nxd4 Bxd4 8 Qxd4! Nxd4 9 Nf6+) 7 Nxd4 c6 8 Nc3 h6 with approximately equal chances.

5...Bg7 6 Be3 Nf6 7 Qd2 0-0 8 0-0-0 d6 9 f3 and White has the better chances.

Ponziani Opening

As with many of the other openings in this chapter, the Ponziani has a long history, but in the case of the Ponziani, it isn't particularly distinguished, though a few strong players have given it some attention, in particular the Yugoslav grandmaster Dragoljub Velimirovic and the Swedish grandmaster Jonny Hector. Objectively speaking, it should not cause Black many headaches because equality can be obtained in several ways, but if White is well prepared, Black must be careful.

1 e4 e5 2 Nf3 Nc6 3 c3

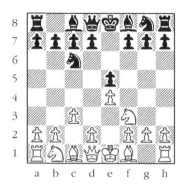

White intends to follow up with d2-d4 on one of the next moves, but unfortunately for White, Black has to move first.

3...Nf6

Black attacks the pawn on e4, forcing White's hand. The main alternative is the sharper 3...d5, which leads to double-edged play after both 4 Qa4 and 4 Bb5, e.g., 4...dxe4 5 Nxe5 Qg5 6 Qa4 Qxg2 7 Rf1 Bh3 with chances for both sides.

4 d4

Anyway, but 4 d3 is obviously rather passive and leads, after 4...d5, to a Reversed Philidor.

4...Nxe4 5 d5 Ne7

The alternative is 5...Nb8 6 Nxe5 Qe7 7 Qd4 Nd6 8 Qe3 Nf5 9 Qe2 d6, and both sides have chances.

6 Nxe5 Ng6 7 Qd4 Qe7 8 Qxe4 Qxe5 9 Qxe5 Nxe5 10 Bf4 Bd6 and Black has equalized.

The Ruy Lopez

Of all chess openings, the Ruy Lopez is one of the oldest, best and most analyzed. I suppose you can call it the granddaddy of chess openings. It is in the repertoire of all serious players who open with 1 e4 and has been featured in the repertoire of every world champion.

1 e4 e5 2 Nf3 Nc6 3 Bb5

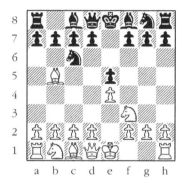

With this move we reach the Ruy Lopez, also known as the Spanish Game, both giving credit to the Spanish priest, Ruy Lopez, who in the 15th century supposedly was the first to discover and play this move. The bishop attacks the knight on c6, which is guarding the pawn on e5, but as we shall see shortly, it isn't a question of an immediate threat, but rather long-term pressure against Black's center.

The main move now is 3...a6, but first, let's have a look at some of the lesser alternatives, several of which have had their time in the spotlight, even quite recently.

The Bird Variation

The least logical of the above continuations is Bird's move, where the knight leaps for the second time as Black agrees to a doubled pawn.

3...Nd4?!

Nowadays this move is rarely seen at the top level, and only then as a surprise weapon. The idea is to eliminate White's pressure against the e5-pawn by exchanging White's knight on f3. With accurate play by White, this move is insufficient for equality, but against an unprepared player with the white pieces, Black has decent chances, e.g., when Khalifman played it against Kasparov and got away with a draw in their first encounter with this line.

4 Nxd4 exd4 5 0-0 c6

You would think that with Black already significantly behind in development, getting pieces into the game would have been Black's first priority. The problem for Black is White's rapid control of the center and the kingside.

6 Bc4 d5 7 exd5 cxd5 8 Bb5+ Bd7 9 Re1+ Ne7 10 Bxd7+ Qxd7 11 Qh5

This is by no means the only continuation for either side, but it illustrates well some of the problems Black encounters. In our final position, Black is behind in development, has central doubled pawns with the king stuck in the center.

The Cozio Defence

It seems logical that if the knight on c6 is threatened, then the other knight should protect it.

3...Nge7

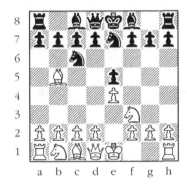

However logical it may appear, this move is also quite passive and blocks the development of the dark-squared bishop. Black will deal with this problem by either playing ...g7-g6 to fianchetto the bishop or ...Ne7-g6, guarding the e5-pawn and clearing the path for the bishop on f8.

4 0-0

White has other options, including 4 Nc3 and 4 d4, both of which should lead to a slighter better game for White, but Black is solid in any event. In the main line, White wants to grab the center and hopes to capitalize on his easier development.

4...g6 5 c3 Bg7 6 d4 exd4 7 cxd4 d5 8 exd5 Nxd5 9 Re1+ Be6 10 Bg5 Qd6 11 Nc3 and White has the better chances.

The Fianchetto Variation

This line was a favorite of world

56

champion Vassily Smyslov, leaving Black with a solid if somewhat passive position, although given the right circumstances, Black will be able to develop satisfactory counterplay.

1 e4 e5 2 Nf3 Nc6 3 Bb5 g6

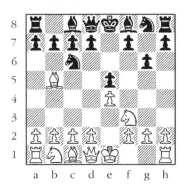

It looks a little strange to spend another pawn move to develop the bishop to g7 from where it will be staring at the e5-pawn. The point is that White sooner or later will have to open the center, after which the bishop will be excellently placed on g7.

4 d4

The main alternative is 4 c3, and then 4...d6 5 d4 Bd7 6 0-0 Bg7 leaves Black with another solid position. The text move is more aggressive.

4...exd4 5 Bg5 Be7

Black can also play 5...f6, but that isn't particularly aesthetically pleasing either.

6 Bxe7 Ngxe7 7 Nxd4 d5 8 Nc3!? dxe4 9 Bxc6+ Nxc6 10 Nxc6 Qxd1 11 Rxd1 bxc6

And after this series of exchanges, White has a slightly better game thanks to his superior pawn structure, but Black is certainly still in the game.

The Steinitz Variation

Those players who fancy Black's setup in this variation usually play 3...a6 4 Ba4 and only then 4...d6, allowing Black some more flexibility compared to the line given below.

3...d6

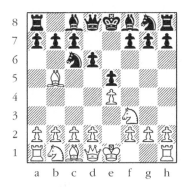

This is another fairly passive setup for Black and one which is only seen rarely in modern praxis.

4 d4 Bd7 5 Nc3 exd4

Or 5...Nf6 6 Bxc6 Bxc6 7 Qd3 Nd7, and White has more space and the slightly better chances.

6 Nxd4 g6 7 0-0 Bg7 8 Bxc6 bxc6 9 Re1

and White has the somewhat easier game.

The Cordel Variation

One of the oldest lines to counter the Ruy Lopez is the Cordel. Black's response is quite logical, developing a bishop to an active square and preparing to castle.

3...Bc5

4 c3

After 4 0-0, Black will often play 4...Nf6, transposing the game to the Berlin Defense.

4...f5

Black can also play 4...Nf6, after 5 d4 Bb6 6 0-0 Nf6, we once again have a line from the Berlin. The text move is much sharper.

5 d4 fxe4 6 Bxc6 dxc6 7 Nxe5 Qd5 8 Bf4 Bd6 and White has a slightly better game, but Black's position is dynamic and if nothing else, he has the pair of bishops.

The Schliemann/Jaenisch Gambit

While seen occasionally at the higher levels, the Schliemann/Jaenisch has been very rare at the highest levels except for a rare appearance here and there. So it was for many years, until Azerbaijani phenom Teimur Radjabov

took it up recently and achieved good results with it against some of the very best players in world, including world champion Viswanathan Anand and former FIDE world champion Veselin Topalov.

White appears to have decent chances to obtain an edge, but Radjabov's argument is that Black's chances are no worse than in any other variation or opening. This is a lesson worth remembering.

3...f5

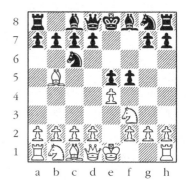

4 Nc3

This is White's most common choice, but for a while in Radjabov's games it seemed like White's best option was 4 d3, which should offer White a slightly better game. Other reasonably good choices include 4 d4 and 4 Bxc6.

4...fxe4

A sharper alternative is 4...Nd4, but it has been established that White is clearly better after 5 Ba4 Nf6 6 Nxe5 Bc5 7 Nd3 Bb6 8 e5 Ne4 9 Nd5 0-0 10 0-0.

5 Nxe4 Nf6

Black can also opt for 5...d5, but after the sharp exchange 6 Nxe5 dxe4 7 Nxc6 Qg5 8 Qe2 Nf6 9 f4 Qxf4 10 Ne5+ c6 11 d4 Qh4+ 12 g3 Qh3 13 Bc4, White has the upper hand, but needless to say, matters are still very complicated.

6 Nxf6+ Qxf6 7 Qe2 Be7 8 Bxc6 dxc6 9 Nxe5 0-0 10 0-0 Bd6 11 d4

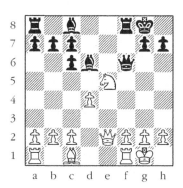

And White has an extra pawn, but Black has dynamic counterplay as compensation. Whether this counterplay is quite enough to fully compensate for the pawn is an entirely different question and likely a matter of taste and style.

The Berlin Defence

While never quite disappearing from the repertoires of the world's strongest players, this variation received a tremendous boost in popularity when Vladimir Kramnik used it as the cornerstone of his opening repertoire in his successful challenge in 2000 to Garry Kasparov for the world championship in London. This popularity has never waned and the Berlin Defense to the Ruy Lopez has taken its place in the opening

repertoires of some of the strongest players in the world.

1 e4 e5 2 Nf3 Nc6 3 Bb5 Nf6

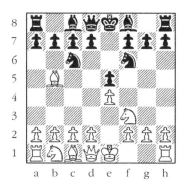

The starting position of the Berlin Defense, but there are several sub-variations that are popular in their own right.

4 0-0

This is the normal move for White, but if White wants to prevent the popular main line, 4...Nxe4, there is also either 4 d3 or 4 Qe2, though neither move represents any major problems for Black, who equalizes without too much effort.

4...Nxe4

Nowadays this move is played almost exclusively in this position, but there are a couple of alternatives that deserve attention: (a) 4...Bc5 5 c3 (White can also play 5 Nxe5 after which both 5...Nxe4 6 Qe2 and 5...Nxe5 6 d4 are supposed to deliver a slight edge for White, but also, unlike the main line, lead to simplifications) 5...0-0 6 d4 Bb6 7 Bg5 h6 8 Bh4 d6 9 Qd3 Bd7, and White has a slightly better game; and (b) 4...d6 5 d4

Bd7 6 Nc3 exd4 7 Nxd4 Be7 8 Re1 0-0 9 Bxc6 bxc6 10 Qd3, and again White has the upper hand.

5 d4 Nd6

Black aims for the so-called Berlin Wall Variation, the line that took center stage as a result of Kramnik's use of it particularly in the 2000 world championship match against Kasparov. The alternative is 5...Be7 6 Qe2 Nd6 7 Bxc6 bxc6 8 dxe5 Nb7, which looks bizarre, but is an accepted line for Black; one continuation for White now is 9 Nc3 0-0 10 Re1 Nc5 11 Be3 Ne6 12 Rad1, and White has the somewhat better chances, but Black's position is solid and not without counterplay.

6 Bxc6 dxc6 7 dxe5 Nf5 8 Qxd8+ Kxd8

We have reached the starting position of the Berlin Wall Variation, which has been the battleground for an almost endless stream of top encounters the last ten years.

9 Nc3

Another option for White is 9 Rd1+, but after 9...Ke8 10 Nc3, Black can safely choose between 10...Be7, 10...Ne7 and 10...a5, all with approximately equal chances. After the text move, White has

the flexibility to choose which rook to put on d1 or whether to do something else entirely.

9...Ke8

This is still the most popular move, but there are other interesting choices for Black such as 9...Bd7 (Kramnik's choice against Kasparov), 9...a5, 9...Ne7 and 9...h6.

10 h3 h5

It is a good indication of the fast development of the theory of this line, that this move now is considered the main line, closely followed in popularity by 10...b6. The three main lines in the respected *Encyclopedia of Chess Openings* published in 2000 are hardly being played anymore – 10...h6, 10...Ne7 and 10...a5. The main point behind the text move is to make g2-g4 less attractive for White.

11 Bf4 Be7 12 Rad1

And White has more space, is better developed and appears to have the initiative, but Black's position is very solid, full of latent resources and White has to be quite careful not to overstep his boundaries. White may have a slight advantage, but it is hardly more than that.

Ruy Lopez Main Lines

The main lines of the Ruy Lopez are the ones starting with the move attributed to the 19th-century American genius Paul Morphy: 3...a6. There is a tremendous volume of theory in these lines, but even so, there is plenty of room for original play, as there numerous lines that are less theoretically intensive. However, there are also plenty of lines that most players should stay away from, partly because of the mass of theory, but also because they are so strategically complex that most of us will simply not understand the play that ensues.

Exchange Variation

While the Exchange Variation undoubtedly has a reputation as a boring opening, it isn't entirely deserved. Lasker used it to beat Capablanca in one of the most famous games ever played, their encounter at St. Petersburg 1914. Fischer used the opening repeatedly with good results against top opposition. Former Dutch world championship candidate Jan Timman has played the opening throughout his career, and last but not least, FIDE world champion Rustam Kasimdzhanov used the opening repeatedly with good results in the knock-out tournament in which he gained the title.

1 e4 e5 2 Nf3 Nc6 3 Bb5 a6 4 Bxc6 dxc6

Black can also play 4...bxc6, but Black falls behind in development. So effectively, this is the starting position of the Exchange Variation. White can

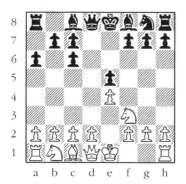

now go for the utterly boring 5 d4 exd4 6 Qxd4 Qxd4 7 Nxd4 that results in any hopes White may have had for an advantage to evaporate.

5 0-0

White cannot win a pawn with 5 Nxe5 because of 5...Qd4, but with the text move White threatens 6 Nxe5 and Black has to address this threat.

5...f6

There are numerous alternatives at this juncture such as 5...Ne7, 5...Qe7, 5...Be7, 5...Qf6, 5...Bd6, 5...Bg4 and last but not least 5...Qd6, which is probably Black main alternative to the text move. Now White can either play the slower 6 d3 followed by Be3 and Nbd2 or the more direct 6 Na3, intending Nc4, forcing Black to address this immediate threat, which can be done with either 6...b5 7 c3 c5 8 Nc2 or 6...Be6 7 Qe2 f6 8 Rd1 c5 9 c3 Bg4 in both cases with approximately equal chances.

6 d4 exd4

Black can also play 6...Bg4, after which the normal continuation 7 dxe5 Qxd1 8 Rxd1 fxe5 9 Rd3 Bd6 10 Nbd2 Nf6 with a fairly even position.

7 Nxd4 c5 8 Nb3 Qxd1 9 Rxd1 Bg4 10 f3 Be6 and the chances are about level.

4th Move Alternatives for Black

Before entering into the territory of the real main lines, there are a number of lesser, but not entirely insignificant lines we need to cover.

1 e4 e5 2 Nf3 Nc6 3 Bb5 a6 4 Ba4 d6

This is the Steinitz Variation Deferred we touched briefly upon when discussing the Steinitz Variation above. But in this more flexible form, there are truly amazing variety of lines, sharp, passive, solid, aggressive and something in between.

However, Black also has a couple of other lines at this juncture that deserve a brief mention: **(a) 4...f5** is a bad version of the Schliemann/Jaenisch Gambit and is best countered with 5 d4! exd4 6 e5 Bc5 7 0-0 Nge7 8 c3, and Black is behind in development with a worse position; **(b) 4...b5** 5 Ba4 Na5 is the so-called Norwegian Variation, which was pioneered by Norwegians and has occasionally attempted to be revived by some of their more recent grandmasters, but nevertheless, it is still a dubious line, e.g., 6 0-0 (even 6 Bxf7+ is playable, but quite unnecessary) 6...d6 7 d4 Nxb3 8 axb3 f6, and while Black's position is reasonably solid, he is behind in development with numerous structural weaknesses.

5 c3

The main move, but also here there are alternatives to consider: **(a) 5 c4** Bd7 6

Nc3 g6 7 d4 exd4 8 Nxd4 Bg7 9 Be3 Nge7 with approximately equal chances; **(b) 5 0-0** Bg4 (5...Bd7 is more solid, but after 6 c3 play will usually transpose to our main line after 5 c3) 6 h3 h5!? 7 d4! Qf6 8 Bxc6+ bxc6 9 Nbd2 Be6 and 7...b5 8 Bb3 Nxd4 9 hxg4 hxg4 10 Ng5 Nh6, in both cases with an advantage for White; and **(c) 5 Bxc6+** bxc6 6 d4 f6! 7 Be3 Ne7 8 Nc3 Ng6, and while Black's position looks quite passive, it is very solid and contains plenty of latent counterplay; the chances are fairly even.

5...Bd7

The normal Steinitz move, but Black also has the so-called Siesta Variation available: 5...f5, which spices up the game immediately, e.g., 6 exf5 Bxf5 7 0-0 (7 d4 e4 8 Ng5 Bf5 is fine for Black) 7...Bd3 8 Re1 Be7 9 Bc2!? (on 9 Re3, Black plays 9...e4) 9...Bxc2 10 Qxc2, and White is ready to break in the center with the d-pawn.

6 d4 g6

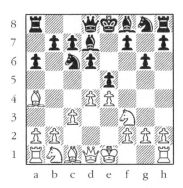

Another solid option for Black is 6...Nge7, e.g., 7 0-0 Ng6 8 d5 Nb8 9 c4 Be7 10 Nc3, and White has more space and the upper hand.

7 0-0 Bg7 8 Re1

White can also consider 8 dxe5, 8 d5 and 8 Be3. The last two in particular offer White good chances for a small plus.

8...Nge7 9 d5 Na5 10 Bxd7+ Qxd7 11 Nbd2

And White is marginally better thanks to more space and the initiative.

The Archangel, New Archangel and Møller Variations

In the 1980s three lines became immensely popular and these related lines are what we are going to discuss in this segment.

1 e4 e5 2 Nf3 Nc6 3 Bb5 a6 4 Ba4 Nf6 5 0-0 b5

The Møller deviates at this juncture, when Black plays the immediate 5...Bc5!?.

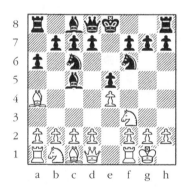

There is a lot of theory on this line, but not as much as its two cousins also covered in this section. One line runs 6 c3 b5 7 Bc2 (Black's move order allows White to play this directly instead of going first to b3, but some players prefer 7 Bb3, transposing into the New Archangel) 7...d6 (7...d5 has also been played quite a bit, but opening the center this soon isn't without risk, when White is ahead in development) 8 a4 Bg4 9 h3 Bh5 10 b4 Bb6 with chances for both sides.

6 Bb3 Bb7

In the New Archangel, Black plays 6...Bc5 instead, postponing the fianchetto of the light-squared bishop. After 7 c3 d6 8 a4 (White can also play 8 d4, but after 8...Bb6 9 a4, we are back in the same line) 8...Rb8 9 d4 Bb6 10 axb5 axb5 11 Na3 0-0 12 Nxb5 Bg4, and the pin on the knight on f3 along with Black's pressure on the white pawn center compensates for the sacrificed pawn.

7 Re1

One alternative to this is the very sharp 7 c3, inviting all sorts of madness, e.g., 7 c3, after which one line runs as follows: 7...Nxe4 8 d4 Na5 10 9 Bc2 exd4 10 b4 Nc4 11 Bxe4 Bxe4 12 Re1 d5 13 Nxd4 c5 14 bxc5 Bxc5, with a very complicated struggle ahead.

A safer, and nowadays a more popular, choice is 7 d3, after which 7...Be7 transposes to the Closed Variations, but 7...Bc5 8 a4 0-0 9 Nc3 b4 10 Nd5 Nxd5 11 Bxd5 d6 is about equal.

7...Bc5 8 c3 d6 9 d4 Bb6 10 a4 0-0 11 Bg5 h6 12 Bh4 and now Black can choose between 12...exd4 13 cxd4 Re8, 12...Re8 and 12...Qe7, in all cases with a complicated strategic middlegame battle ahead.

5 Qe2 and Other Early Deviations

White's last chance to deviate before entering variations with some of the most massive opening theory will now be discussed here. Objectively speaking, the lines should be fairly harmless, but because they are seen much less frequently, White has a decent chance for surprising his opponent at this juncture.

1 e4 e5 2 Nf3 Nc6 3 Bb5 a6 4 Ba4 Nf6 5 Qe2

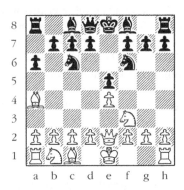

Now both 5 Bxc6 (If White wants to make the exchange on c6, he should either play it on the 4th move or on the 6th) and 5 Nc3 offer White no real chances of an edge, but 5 d4 is a different story, though Black can get a decent game after 5...exd4 6 e5 Ne4 7 0-0 Nc5.

Last, but not least, is the unassuming 5 d3 after which White intends to build up slowly with c3, Nbd2, 0-0, Re1, Nf1,

Ng3 and so on. It doesn't look like much and it really shouldn't be, but Black nevertheless has to be careful, because with a well-timed d3-d4 at some point, White may be able to seize the initiative.

5...b5 6 Bb3 Bc5 7 c3 d6 8 d3 h6 9 0-0 0-0 and the chances are about even.

Open Variation

The Open Variation has experienced a couple of revivals. First Bent Larsen brought it back to life in the 1960s, but it soon disappeared again, and then later in the 1970s Viktor Kortschnoi started playing it regularly with good results. Despite an occasional setback, for example an amazing game by Kasparov against Anand in their 1995 World Championship match, the opening is still seen with some frequency at grandmaster level.

1 e4 e5 2 Nf3 Nc6 3 Bb5 a6 4 Ba4 Nf6 5 0-0 Nxe4

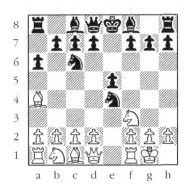

This is a very provocative reaction to White's opening play. Black makes the claim that despite the fact that White is well ahead in development, Black can snap off the white e-pawn and easily weather the storm.

6 d4

Neither 6 Qe2 nor 6 Re1 offer White any real chances of an advantage. With the text move, White wants to open the position to take advantage of Black's lack of development and vulnerable king that is still on the open e-file.

6...b5 7 Bb3 d5 8 dxe5 Be6

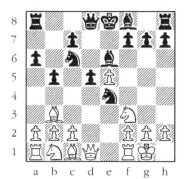

We have reached the starting position of the Open Variation, which is steeped in theory and generally should be avoided unless you either have a prepared sideline or really have spent a lot of time memorizing and understanding the theory of this line.

9 c3

Two alternatives for White are: **(a) 9 Qe2** Be7 10 Rd1 0-0 (10...Nc5 is also played) 11 c4 bxc4 12 Bxc4 Bc5 is about even, but quite complicated; and **(b) 9 Nbd2** Nc5 10 c3 d4 (with this move Black continues to provoke, but 10...Be7 and 10...Bg4 can also be played) 11 Bxe6 (both Karpov and Kasparov have preferred the ultra-sharp 11 Ng5!? in world championship matches. The idea is that 11..Qxg5 is answered by 12 Qf3, regaining the piece, though it is by no means clear that White is better in this

line) 11...Nxe6 12 cxd4 Ncxd4 13 Ne4 (here 13 a4!? is a worthwhile alternative) 13...Be7 14 Be3 Nf5 15 Qc2 0-0 16 Rad1 Nxe3 17 fxe3 Qc8, with a sharp position in which both sides have their share of the chances.

9...Bc5

Black can also play the more solid 9...Be7, for instance 10 Nbd2 Nc5 11 Bc2 Bg4 12 Re1 0-0 (or 12...Qd7) 13 Nf1 Bh5 14 Ng3 Bg6, and White is perhaps a little better after 15 Be3, but only time will tell by how much.

10 Nbd2 0-0 11 Bc2 Nxf2!?

Normally it is not considered a particularly good idea to give up two minor pieces for a rook and a pawn under similar circumstances, but in this

case it has been established as a main line option for Black – the so-called Dilworth Attack. The "saner" alternatives are 11...Bf5 12 Nb3 Bg6 13 Nfd4 Bxd4 14 cxd4 and 11...f5 12 Nb3 Bb6 13 Nfd4 Nxd4 14 Nxd4 Bxd4 15 Qxd4, both marginally better for White.

12 Rxf2 f6!

Opening the f-file is the only way to

claim compensation for Black for the uneven exchange on f2.

13 exf6 Bxf2+ 14 Kxf2 Qxf6 15 Nf1 Ne5 16 Be3 Rae8

While established opening theory claims White to be slightly better, it is easier to play Black than White.

Closed Variations

In my opinion, some of the most strategically complicated opening lines in all opening theory can be found in the following sections. The play can be rather convoluted and nearly impossible to understand for the uninitiated, yet I see many inexperienced players head into these lines, knowing a fair share of the theory, but not understanding why the moves are being played.

1 e4 e5 2 Nf3 Nc6 3 Bb5 a6 4 Ba4 Nf6 5 0-0 Be7

are the starting moves in all of the remaining lines in the coverage of the Ruy Lopez.

Delayed Exchange, Worrall Attack and Other 6th Move Alternatives

White can still avoid some of the heaviest theory, but even the lines in this section have been the topic of fairly intense research and are regularly played at grandmaster level, even by the very highest rated players in the world.

6 Qe2

This is the Worrall Attack, which not too long ago was the main subject of an absolutely massive tome on the Ruy Lopez.

The main alternatives are: **(a) 6 d4** exd4 7 Re1 (or 7 e5 Ne4 8 Nxd4 Nxd4 9 Qxd4 Nc5 10 Nc3 0-0 is about equal) 7...0-0 (7...b5 8 Bb3 d6 9 Bd5 Bb7 with a complicated game is also possible) 8 e5 Ne8 9 c3 dxc3 10 Nxc3 with compensation for the pawn; **(b) 6 Bxc6**, the so-called Delayed Exchange Variation, which makes more sense now when Black has committed to developing the bishop to e7 and therefore is less interested in spending another tempo guarding the e5-pawn with ...Bd6. This means that Black normally will have to retreat the remaining knight to d7 and often play ...f7-f6. After 6...bxc6, White has tried a handful different moves: 7 Re1, 7 Qe2, 7 Qe1, 7 Nc3 and 7 d3, of which the last is probably the best, e.g., 7...Nd7 8 Nbd2 0-0 9 Nc4 (9 b3!? is also worth a try) 9...f6 (preparing to move the knight to a more active square) 10 Nh4!? Nc5 11 Nf5 Bxf5 12 exf5 Qd7 with chances for both sides; and **(c) 6 d3**, often used whenever the Marshall Attack is in vogue, like the last several years. One of the main lines runs as follows: 6...b5 7 Bb3 Bb7 8 Nc3 (White can also play 8 c4, but this should not worry Black too much either) 8...0-0 (or 8...d6 9 a4 Na5 10 Ba2 b4 11 Ne2 c5 12 Ng3 0-0 with equal chances) 9 Bd2 d6 10 a4 Na5 11 Ba2 b4 12 Nd5 Nxd5 13 exd5 c5, and again Black has equalized.

6...b5 7 Bb3 0-0 8 c3 d6

Black can also play the more aggressive 8...d5, and after 9 d3 Re8 10 Re1 Bb7 11 Nbd2 Nf8, the chances are more or less balanced.

9 d4

There are several other interesting options for White, e.g., 9 a4 and 9 Rd1.

9...Bg4 10 Rd1 exd4 11 cxd4 d5 12 e5 Ne4 13 Nc3 Nxc3 14 bxc3 Qd7 and both sides have their share of the chances, but the play is quite complicated.

Anti-Marshall

With the emergence of the Marshall Attack as one of Black's primary answer to the Ruy Lopez at top levels over the last few years, the need for alternatives to the main lines has become apparent. Therefore White has resorted to two moves that prevent the Marshall.

6 Re1 b5 7 Bb3 0-0

Black's last move is usually an indication for White's alarm bells to sound, because the normal 8 c3 can now be met with the Marshall Attack, a sharp gambit that currently seems to be in the black repertoires of nearly every world class player. The Marshall will be covered in the next section.

If Black does not really intend to play the Marshall, 7...d6 may be played first and then after 8 c3, 8...0-0 will take the play to the Closed Main Lines. However, after 7...0-0, White has to make a decision whether to avoid the Marshall altogether or to allow it.

8 a4

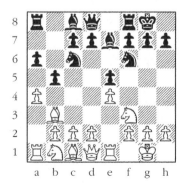

White also frequently plays 8 h3 at this point, and this can take the game to the Closed Main Lines after 8...d6 9 c3, but more often Black will attempt to take advantage of White's move order by playing 8...Bb7, and then after 9 d3, Black can choose between the Chigorin-like 9...d6 10 a3 Na5 (or 10...Nb8, intending 11...Nbd7) 11 Ba2 c5 with chances for both sides or Aronian's favorite move, the Marshall-like 9...d5!? 10 exd5 Nxd5 where 11 Nxe5 Nd4 gives Black decent compensation for the pawn and therefore 11 a4 has been given preference by players such as Anand.

Two other lines for White that prevent the Marshall are 8 d3 and 8 d4, both of which have also seen a lot of activity the last few years.

8...b4 9 d4

Or 9 d3 d6 10 Nbd2 Na5 11 Ba2 Be6 12 Bxe6 fxe6 with a complicated middlegame ahead, where the chances are approximately level.

9...d6 10 dxe5 dxe5

Black can also play 10...Nxe5. After the text move, White will normally continue with 11 Qxd8 Rxd8 12 Nbd2 Bd6 13 a5 h6 14 Bc4, after which he has an apparent advantage, but not much more than that.

The Marshall Attack

The American grandmaster Frank Marshall was one of the strongest players in the early part of the 20th century and even played a match for the world championship. Marshall loved sharp tactical games and several

of the opening variations that bear his name should appeal to players who enjoy sharp chess. The Marshall Attack first grabbed the attention of the chess world at an encounter between the future world champion, the great Cuban player José Raúl Capablanca, and Marshall, New York 1918.

6 Re1 b5 7 Bb3 0-0 8 c3 d5

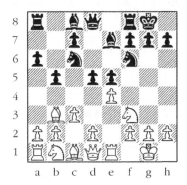

This fascinating gambit seems to go in and out of fashion at regular intervals. In the 1960s, it was Spassky and Tal, but as mentioned above, it now seems that all of the top players – even more positionally oriented players – have the Marshall in their repertoires.

9 exd5

This is only critical reply to the Marshall, although White has also tried 9 d4 to avoid the theory-laden main lines.

9...Nxd5 10 Nxe5 Nxe5 11 Rxe5 c6 (D)

In the stem game, Marshall played 11...Nf6, intending ...Bd6, ...Nf6-g4 and ...Qh4. Capablanca parried Marshall's attack and won a brilliant game. Nowadays, this line is seen very rarely; the same goes for 11...Bb7 which has also seen some attention over the years.

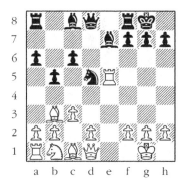

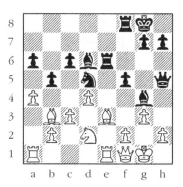

12 d4

White has several other adequate alternatives, for example 12 d3, 12 g3 and 12 Re1, all of which have been used frequently in recent years.

12...Bd6 13 Re1

13 Re2 has also been popular, but Black should be fine after 13...Qh4 14 g3 Qh3 15 Nd2 Bf5, with chances for both sides.

13...Qh4 14 g3 Qh3 15 Be3

Two interesting choices are 15 Bxd5 cxd5 16 Qf3 Bf5 or Petrosian's 15 Re4, which is best met by 15...g5 in order to prevent White from playing Rh4. Both lines lead to positions where Black is supposed to have full compensation for the sacrificed pawn.

15...Bg4 16 Qd3 Rae8 17 Nd2 Re6

Also 17...f5 is fully playable.

18 a4 f5 19 Qf1 Qh5 *(D)*

This and the alternative main lines have been played numerous times and the evaluation of which line is the most critical from either side seems to be in

constant flux, although really beyond the scope of this book. If you are interested in this opening, you should study separate literature devoted to this variation and the latest games and theory available online. Some general thoughts on openings of this nature can be found in the chapter "Which openings should I choose?"

Closed Main Lines

In this final section in the coverage of the Ruy Lopez, we will quickly look at the large amount of theory that exists in these lines. As previously mentioned, the lines are very difficult to understand, because the main lines are the result of over 100 years worth of trial and error by the best players in the world. Therefore, trying to work out why one move is better than another is nearly impossible and so are attempts to memorize the theory because its volume is so enormous.

6 Re1 b5 7 Bb3 0-0 8 c3 d6 9 h3 *(D)*

This prevents ...Bg4 and thus prepares the advance of the d-pawn, which nevertheless is played in two different widely different variations: **(a) 9 d3** is

69

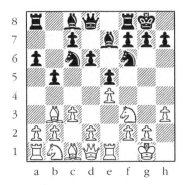

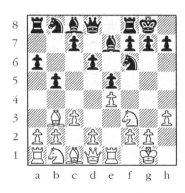

rather slow, but still of interest because it avoids the heaviest theory and allows the player with the better understanding to play for a win with less risk, but Black is still fine after 9...Na5 10 Bc2 c5 11 Nbd2 Nc6 12 Nf1 Re8; (b) 9 d4 is frequently seen at grandmaster level and is regularly played by American grandmaster Gata Kamsky. The main line continues 9...Bg4 10 Be3 (or 10 d5 Na5 11 Bc2 c6 12 h3 Bc8 13 dxc6 Qc7 with about even chances) 10...exd4 11 cxd4, and now Black can choose between 11...Na5 12 Bc2 c5 or 11...d5 12 e5 Ne4, in both cases with chances for both sides.

In the diagrammed position, Black has an amazing selection of interesting moves available, of which the most important are: **(a) 9...Be6**, named after the late Soviet grandmaster Ratmir Kholmov: 10 d4 Bxb3 11 axb3 (11 Qxb3 is also played, but it is not as critical as the text move) 11...exd4 12 cxd4 Nb4 13 Nc3 c5 (the point of the previous move) 14 Bg5, and White is perhaps slightly better; **(b) 9...h6**, the Smyslov Variation; it often leads to lines in the Zaitsev Variation if the players so desire, but there is also plenty of independent theory in this line too: 10 d4 Re8 11 Nbd2 Bf8 12 a3 (12 Nf1 is a good alternative) 12...Bb7 13 Bc2 Nb8 14 b4 Nbd7 15 Bb2 g6 with chances for both sides. **(c) 9...Nb8**,

the Breyer Variation, looks odd. Why make this knight retreat this early? Black thinks that the knight is more ideally placed on d7, where it does not block the advance of the c-pawn and the scope of a bishop on b7. This line has been a favorite of world champion Boris Spassky and grandmaster Alexander Beliavsky to mention but a few: 10 d4 Nbd7 11 Nbd2 Bb7 12 Bc2 Re8 13 Nf1 Bf8 14 Ng3 g6 15 a4 c5 16 d5 c4 with a strategically complex struggle ahead; **(d) 9...Nd7** bears the name of world champion Anatoly Karpov. After 10 d4 Bf6 (Black can also play 10...Nb6) 11 a4 Bb7, White can choose between 12 axb5, 12 Na3, 12 Be3 and 12 d5, of which the last perhaps is best, trying to take advantage of Black's somewhat artificial set-up, but it is entirely a matter of taste; **(e) 9...Bb7** 10 d4, Re8

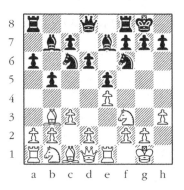

also closely associated with Karpov as it bears the name of his long-time second Zaitsev and was popularized by Karpov. This line has been heavily developed thanks to repeated use by many of the world's leading players over the last four decades. One main line runs: 11 Nbd2 (11 Ng5 Rf8 12 Nf3 Re8 with a draw by repetition, played numerous times, including several times by Karpov as Black) 11...Bf8 12 a4 (12 d5 and 12 Bc2 are two good alternatives) 12...h6 13 Bc2 exd4 14 cxd4 Nb4 15 Bb1 c5 16 d5 Nd7 17 Ra3 (intending to transfer the rook to kingside), and here both 17...c4 and 17...f5 have been played countless times. The theory is incredibly dense in this line and should really be avoided by players below master level; **(f) 9...Na5**, Black's most ambitious line. It bears the name of the Russian grandmaster Mikhail Chigorin, a world championship candidate in the 19th century.

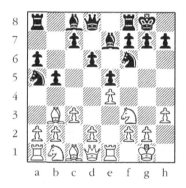

After 10 Bc2 c5 (the young Polish grandmaster Gregor Gajewski recently came up with the new gambit 10...d5!?) 11 d4 Qc7 (Black has several good alternatives in 11...Nd7, 11...Nc6 and 11...Bb7, each of which has its own considerable theory) 12 Nbd2 cxd4 (or 12...Nc6 after which both 13 dxc5 and 13 d5 deserve attention) 13 cxd4 Nc6

(Black can at this juncture consider moves such as 13...Rd8, 13...Bd7 and 13...Bb7) 14 Nb3 a5 15 Be3 a4 16 Nbd2, and the chances are approximately equal, though perhaps with a marginal edge for White.

Black's Second Move Alternatives

In this section, there is an incredible diversity of openings, from the very solid and sound, to the very sharp and unsound, along with a few things that fall betwixt and between.

The Petroff or Russian Game

This opening has been part of nearly every top grandmaster's repertoire over the last three decades. It combines the need for a solid opening that seeks equality as the primary goal, with the potential of playing for a win without taking unnecessary risks. However, thanks to the constant use by many of the world's best players, some of the lines are decidedly boring and can really only be of interest to those players who enjoy studying the finesses of dead-equal positions. Nevertheless, there are many opportunities for both sides to sharpen the game to increase the chances for a decisive outcome.

1 e4 e5 2 Nf3 Nf6

While this is the starting position of the Petroff, there are countless standard positions that occur later, even much later, and it is important to realize that in order to play the main lines of this opening successfully you will need to invest a serious amount of time to understand and play them well. Therefore if you are at a level where the material in this book is new to you, then you ought to stay well clear of the main lines and instead seek refuge in some of the numerous respectable sidelines that objectively offer chances that are just as good as anything you will come across in the main lines.

White has a couple of alternatives at this juncture. Of the lesser lines, 3 Bc4 immediately jumps to mind, intending 3...Nxe4 4 Nc3 Nxc3 5 dxc3, and here the theory usually continues with Black trying to hold on to the pawn with 5...f6 6 Nh4!? g6 7 f4 Qe7 8 f5 Qg7. White has compensation for the pawn, but Black can make it simpler by opting for either 5...c6 6 Nxe5 d5 7 0-0 Bd6 or 4...Nc6!?, after which 5 Nxe4 d5 6 Bd3 dxe4 7 Bxe4 Bd6 is not a problem for Black.

Another move is 3 Nc3, which will usually lead to the Four Knights when Black if 3...Nc6, since the alternative 3...Bb4 is considered to be slightly better for White and 3...d6 4 d4 is a Philidor's Defense, which is not to everybody's liking.

The two main moves are 3 Nxe5 and 3 d4, which will be covered in the next two sections.

3 Nxe5 Lines

If either of the two principal moves at this point is to be considered the main line, it is probably this move, which is seen slightly more frequently, but much depends on recent trends and these change frequently.

3 Nxe5 d6

3...Nxe4 is considered dubious because White picks up a pawn after 4 Qe2 Qe7 5 Qxe4 d6 6 d4 dxe5 7 dxe5 Nc6 8 Bb5 Bd7 9 Nc3, though matters aren't as clear and simple as they may appear, since Black does get some counterplay.

4 Nf3

The logical, but again, not the only move. The obvious alternative is 4 Nc4, though Black equalizes without too much difficulty after 4...Nxe4 5 d4 d5 6 Ne3 Qf6. However, if you are tactically inclined as White, you can also consider the brutally direct 4 Nxf7!?, which can cause Black trouble if he doesn't know how to conduct the defense after 4...Kxf7 5 d4!; White normally gets decent compensation for the piece in form of a space advantage with the pawns.

4...Nxe4 5 d4

White has other choices as well: **(a) 5 Qe2** aims to bore Black to death; former world champion Boris Spassky has played this line several times, though very rarely winning. The position after 5...Qe7 6 d3 Nf6 7 Bg5 Qxe2+ 8 Bxe2 Be7 is quite uneventful; **(b) 5 c4** is more interesting, though also considered to lead to equal chances; **(c) 5 Nc3** has in recent years enjoyed a lot of attention at top grandmaster level with even players like Anand, Topalov and Kramnik playing it several times and not without success. However, it now seems like Black has found adequate ways to defend after both 5...Nxc3 6 dxc3 Be7 7 Bf4 and 7 Be3. In both cases White continues with 8 Qd2 and 9 0-0-0.

5...d5 6 Bd3 Be7

Black's two main alternatives are: **(a) 6...Bd6** 7 0-0 0-0 8 c4 c6 9 cxd5 (two other good alternatives are 9 Re1 and 9 Qc2) 9...cxd5 10 Nc3 Nxc3 11 bxc3 Bg4 12 Rb1 Nd7 13 h3 Bh5 with a complicated game with chances for both sides; and **(b) 6...Nc6** 7 0-0 Bg4 8 c4 Nf6 9 Nc3 Bxf3 10 Qxf3 Nxd4 (Black wins a pawn, but White gets excellent compensation) 11 Qe3 Ne6 12 cxd5 Nxd5 13 Nxd5 Qxd5 14 Be4 Qb5 15 a4 Qa6 16 Rd1, and White has the initiative.

7 0-0 Nc6 8 c4

Another option at this juncture is 8 Re1, and now after 8...Bg4, White has to choose between the sharp 9 c3 f5 10 Qb3 0-0 11 Nbd2 Kh8 and the less sharp, but equally interesting 9 c4 Nf6 10 cxd5 Nxd5 11 Nc3 0-0, in both cases with more or less even chances.

8...Nb4

The exchange of the light-squared bishop will be an accomplishment for

Black, even at the cost of some time. One line now runs 9 cxd5 Nxd3 10 Qxd3 Qxd5 11 Re1 Bf5 with approximately equal chances.

9 Be2

White invests a tempo to avoid the exchange, even if it means retreating the bishop to a less active square, understanding that the b4-square will not be the final destination of the knight on b4.

9...0-0 10 Nc3 Bf5 11 a3 Nxc3 12 bxc3 Nc6 13 cxd4 Qxd5 and while opening theory calls this equal, there is obviously plenty of play in the position.

3 d4 Lines

White's principal alternative to 3 Nxe5 is 3 d4, which at times has been as popular, if not more so, than 3 Nxe5. It often leads to play that is quite different from 3 Nxe5, though in some lines the play closely resembles 3 Nxe5.

3 d4

A challenge is immediately issued in the center, forcing Black to decide what kind of game he wants.

3...Nxe4

All the center pawns are exchanged in another main line: 3...exd4 4 e5 Ne4 5 Qxd4 d5 6 exd6 Nxd6

Despite the symmetrical and unexciting pawn structure, White has a slight initiative because he has access to easier development and somewhat more active squares for his pieces. The fact that the queen has been developed so early helps keep Black relatively passive; this is one of the few cases where it pays to have the queen developed before the other pieces. The main line now runs: 7 Bd3 (or 7 Nc3 Nc6 8 Qf4 Nf5 9 Bb5 Bd6 10 Qe4+ Qe7 11 Bg5 f6 12 Bd2 Bd7 with approximately equal chances) 7...Nc6 8 Qf4 g6 (8...Be7 9 Nc3 Be6 10 Be3 Bf6 11 0-0-0 0-0 12 Rad1 leaves White with the initiative) 9 Nc3 Bg7 10 Be3 Be6 11 0-0-0, and White has the better chances.

4 Bd3

White occasionally experiments with 4 dxe5, when the tempting 4...Bc5 gives White a strong initiative after 5 Bc4!?, e.g., 5...Nxf2 6 Bxf7+ Kxf7 7 Qd5+, so Black will usually prefer 4...d5, which leads to approximately equal chances

after 5 Nbd2 Nxd2 6 Qxd2 and 6 Bxd2, but this line has not been explored much, leaving plenty of room to surprise an unsuspecting opponent.

4...d5

Surprisingly, Black can actually play 4...Nc6!?, for instance, 5 d5 Nc5 6 dxc6 e4 7 cxb7 Bxb7 or 5 Bxe4 d6 6 Bg5 (also 6 Nxe5 is played from time to time) 6...Qd6 7 dxe5 Qb4+ 8 Nc3 dxe4, in both cases Black wins back the piece, but in the latter example, White has the initiative as a result of the black queen wanderings, losing time, just to keep the position together.

5 Nxe5 Nd7

The main alternative for Black is 5...Bd6, e.g., 6 0-0 0-0, and here White has several moves available, but the main line runs forward with a long sequence of more or less pre-determined moves: 7 c4 Bxe5 8 dxe5 Nc6 9 cxd5 Qxd5 10 Qc2 Nb4 11 Bxe4 Nxc2 12 Bxd5 Bf5 13 g3 Bxg4 14 Bxe4 Nxa1. Black is up materially, but the knight on a1 is not going anywhere and in addition, White has the bishop pair. One line continues with 15 Bf4 f5 16 Bd5+ Kh8 17 Rc1 c6 18 Bg2 Rfd8, with approximately equal chances.

6 Nxd7

White has numerous alternatives, but this is the main move.

6...Bxd7 7 0-0 Qh4

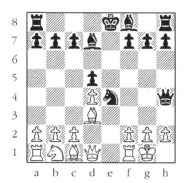

This is a very sharp continuation. Another option is 7...Bd6, e.g., 8 c4 c6, and now White can go pawn grabbing with 10 Qh5, which, after 10...0-0 11 Qxd5 Bc6 11 Qh5 g6 12 Qh3 Ng5, leaves Black with adequate compensation; or 10 Nc3 Nxc3 11 bxc3 0-0 with approximately even chances.

8 c4 0-0-0 9 c5 g5 10 Nc3 Bg7

With a complicated position and chances for both sides; this line requires very detailed and specific knowledge and should not be played by anyone from either side without proper preparation.

Minor Continuations

The "minor" continuations are indeed minor compared openings such as the Ruy Lopez and Italian, but at the club level, these openings appear quite frequently. However even grandmasters have been known to play the lines in this section with some frequency, and

some with a fair amount of success, showing you cannot ever really write these openings off altogether.

Philidor's Defense

The Philidor dates back to the 18th century and is named after the strongest player at the time, the Frenchman François-André Philidor.

1 e4 e5 2 Nf3 d6

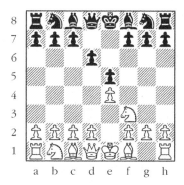

Black's original idea in the Philidor was to play an early ...f7-f5, but although advocated by English grandmaster Tony Kosten in a book in the early 1990s, it has never caught on; there were simply too many lines that didn't look promising for Black. Nevertheless, that book by Kosten gave the opening a new wave of popularity that is still going strong today. While it is certainly true that it isn't being played in every grandmaster tournament, it occurs often enough at that level and may even be found in the repertoires of some 2700+ rated players.

3 d4 Nf6

Aside from 3...f5, Black can also play 3...Nd7 and 3...exd4, but both moves are considered to lead to slightly better positions for White.

4 Nc3

White has an annoying alternative in 4 dxe5!?, which after 4...Nxe4 5 Qd5 Nc5 6 Bg5 Be7 7 exd6 Qxd6 8 Nc3 Qxd5 9 Nxd5 Bd6 10 0-0-0, leads to an initiative for White. For this reason, Black often adopts another move order to reach the Philidor: 1 e4 d6 2 d4 Nf6 3 Nc3 e5, and now 4 Nf3 transposes to our main line, whereas 4 dxe5 dxe5 5 Qxd8+ Kxd8, generally speaking, is fine for Black.

4...Nbd7

This is the so-called "Improved Hanham Variation," the original Hanham being 3...Nd7, which was advocated by Nimzowitsch and leads to a solid position. The alternative is 4...exd4, and after 5 Nxd4 (5 Qxd4 is also possible, but Black is fine after 5...Be7), Black has two alternatives: **(a) 5...g6**, the Larsen Variation, which is considered inadequate for equality by most sources, e.g., 6 Be3 Bg7 7 Qd2 0-0 8 0-0-0 Re8 (also 8...Nc6 is possible) 9 f3 a6, and a sharp position has arisen, where the slightest misstep from either side can cause serious problems; and **(b) 5...Be7**, named after grandmaster Vladimir Antoshin and is still played at grandmaster level by, among others, the Romanian grandmaster Liviu-Dieter Nisipeanu. One line runs 6 Bf4 (some sources give 6 Bc4 and 6 Be2 as leading to an advantage for White, but Black should be fine) 6...0-0 7 Qd2 c6 (other moves are also possible at this stage, e.g., 7...d5, 7...Nc6 and 7...a6) 8 0-0-0 b5 with a sharp game.

5 Bc4 Be7 6 0-0

Note that the tempting 6 Bxf7+ does not achieve much after 6...Kxf7 7 Ng5+ Kg8 8 Ne6 Qe8 9 Nxc7 Qg6, when 10 Nxa8? Qxg2 is quite bad for White; also after 6 dxe5 dxe5 7 Bxf7+ Kxf7 8 Ng5+ Kg6!, and here 9 Ne6 is answered with 9...Qg8, with an advantage for Black.

6...0-0 7 Re1

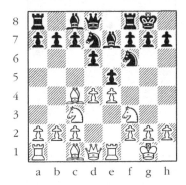

White can also play moves like 7 Qe2, 7 a4, 7 h3, in many cases transposing to our main line, but other moves are considered inadequate for an edge.

7...c6 8 a4 b6

The alternatives 8...a5 and 8...Qc7 are also playable, though they slightly favor White.

9 b3 a6 10 Bb2 Bb7 11 Qd2 Qc7

With a typical Hanham position where White has more space, but Black has a solid position.

Latvian Gambit

Though favored by a small crowd of fanatics, the Latvian Gambit is nowadays considered to offer White a fairly clear advantage, although it can be difficult to prove if White is not very familiar with the intricacies of this dubious gambit.

1 e4 e5 Nf3 f5?!

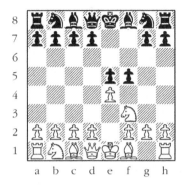

Like a Reversed King's Gambit, but White's extra tempo makes a world of difference.

3 Nxe5

Simple and best. White can also play 3 Bc4 and 3 exf5, but those moves are closer to what Black is hoping for.

3...Qf6

The sharp 3...Nc6 is also seen, inviting White to play 4 Qh5+, but the simple 4 d4 offers White a solid advantage.

4 Nc4

Or 4 d4 d6 5 Nc4 fxe4, and now 6 Nc3, 6 Be2 and 6 Nc3 all lead to a small advantage for White.

4...fxe4 5 Nc3 Qf7 6 Ne3 c6

Played in true gambit style; 6...Nf6 7 Bc4 Qg6 8 d3 is clearly better for White.

7 Nxe4 d5 8 Ng5 Qf6 9 Nf3 Bd6 10 d4 and Black doesn't have sufficient compensation for the pawn.

Center Game

This opening is quite rare, but it can lead to complications that Black may not be ready for unless he knows at least a little about it.

1 e4 e5 2 d4 exd4 3 Qxd4!?

It may seem a little strange that developing the queen before any of the other pieces can be a good idea, but if Black isn't careful he can get into trouble.

3...Nc6 4 Qe3 Nf6 5 Nc3 Bb4

This is Black's most aggressive response, but 5...Be7 is also playable.

6 Bd2 0-0 7 0-0-0 Re8

And Black has equalized, for now if White plays 8 Qg3, Black can play 8...Rxe4! after which White doesn't have quite enough compensation for the pawn.

Vienna Game

Unlike the other openings in this "Minor Continuations" section, the Vienna Game includes several widely diverse lines, some of which do not seem as if they could be the result of

White's apparently peaceful second move.

1 e4 e5 2 Nc3

This looks like White is ready for slow game, but black players beware, White may be up to something...

2...Nf6

On 2...Nc6, White can choose solid moves such as 3 g3 or 3 Nf3, taking the game to a Three Knights or Four Knights, depending on how Black follows up, but more importantly, White has the sharp Vienna Gambit available, viz., 3 f4!? *(D)* and one line runs 3...exf4 4 Nf3 g5 5 d4 g4 (5...Bg7 or other moves are too dangerous for Black, but you could say the same for the main line...) 6 Bc4! gxf3 7 Qxf3 with a gambit that somewhat resembles the Muzio Gambit, (cf. the King's Gambit). Here White has ample compensation for the piece; defending the black side of this gambit requires steady nerves and patient defense.

3 Bc4

White has a couple of other interesting moves at this juncture; both are seen

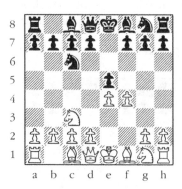

quite frequently at club level, though less commonly in grandmaster play: **(a) 3 f4** (this move resembles a King's Gambit, but Black cannot play 3...exf4 because of 4 e5, and the knight is already causing Black headaches. One of my childhood friends, international master Jan Sørensen, played this opening for years with very decent results) 3...d5 (4 fxe5 Nxe4 5 Nf3 – 5 d3 Nxc3 6 bxc3 is also fully playable – 5...Be7 6 Qe2 Nxc3 7 dxc3 (recapturing away from the center in order to keep the development fluid) 7...c5 8 Bf4 Nc6 (or 8...0-0!?) 9 0-0-0 Be6 with chances for both sides; **(b) 3 g3** Bc5 (just one of many options at this point; White doesn't mind 3...d5 4 exd5 Nxd5 5 Bg2 Nxc3 6 bxc3 Bd6 7 Nf3 (7 Ne2 can also be played) 7...0-0 8 0-0 Nd7, and the chances are approximately equal according to standard theory, but playing it for Black isn't without its problems.

3...Nc6

Black chooses the solid over the chaotic; here Black can let the game take an entirely different shape by playing 3...Nxe4

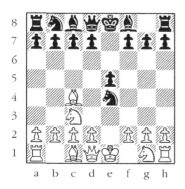

Now both 4 Nxe4 d5 and 4 Bxf7+ are inadequate for White, whereas 4 Nf3 takes us to the Petroff Defense, but if White knows the opening well, you may see 4 Qh5!? appear on the board. This leads to the so-called Frankenstein-Dracula Variation (named so by the Irish master and author Tim Harding) 4...Nd6 5 Bb3 (White can continue timidly with the drawish 5 Qxe5+ Qe7 6 Qxe7+ Bxe7, but after 4 Qh5!?, it is more a matter of honor to continue aggressively) 5...Nc6 (5...Be7 is decidedly more solid and also more advisable unless you like incredibly complicated positions, e.g., 6 Nf3 Nc6 7 Nxe5 g6 8 Nxc6 dxc6 9 Qf3 0-0 10 0-0 with fairly equal chances) 6 Nb5! (the central theme is the attack and defense of f7) 6...g6 7 Qf3 f5 8 Qd5 Qe7! 9 Nxc7+ Kd8 10 Nxa8, and we have a position on the board where Black is down a rook and has lost the right to castle. However, the knight on a8 is a lost cause, and Black has a lead in development along with a space advantage, giving Black good compensation for the material, e.g., 10...b6 11 Nxb6 axb6 12 Qf3 Bb7 13 d3 Nd4, and Black has the initiative, though theory claims the slightly better chances for White; this entire line should not be tested unless you really have studied these lines very carefully.

4 d3 Na5

Normally moving a piece twice this early in the opening is not advisable, but here it serves a specific purpose, eliminating the strong white bishop on c4. However, other moves such as 4...Bb4 and 4...Bc5 are also fully playable.

5 Nge2 Nxc4 6 dxc4 Bc5 7 0-0 d6 8 Qd3

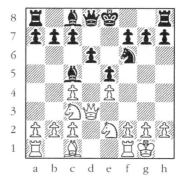

An odd-looking move, but one, as you will see, with a specific purpose in mind.

8...Be6 9 b3 0-0 10 Be3 Bxe3 11 Qxe3 with an interesting position where both sides have their share of the chances.

Bishop's Opening

Every now and then, a top grandmaster plays the Bishop's Opening; it was originally dusted off from obscurity by the Danish grandmaster Bent Larsen at the Interzonal in Amsterdam in 1964.

2 Bc4 Nf6

If Black simply copies White's moves, e.g., 2...Bc5 3 Nc3 Nc6, he will get a wake-up call after 4 Qg4!, after which 4...Qf6 doesn't work on account of 5

Nd5!: 5...Qxf2+ 6 Kd1, and now the threats against c7 and g7 makes Black's life untenable.

3 d3

The solid and sensible move, but Black also has to be ready for the much sharper 3 d4!?, which can cause Black serious headaches if he doesn't know what he is doing. The main line runs 3...exd4 4 Nf3 Nxe4 5 Qxd4 Nf6 6 Bg5 Be7 7 Nc3

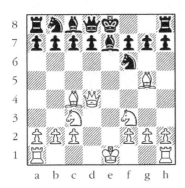

7...Nc6 (7...c6 8 0-0-0 d5 9 Rhe1 Be6 10 Bd3 Nbd7 looks more solid, but isn't a walk in the park either after 11 Qh4, with compensation for the pawn) 8 Qh4 d6 9 0-0-0 Be6 10 Bd3 Qd7 11 Bb5 0-0 with a sharp game where White has sufficient compensation for the pawn.

3...c6 4 Nf3 d5

Black can also play 4...Be7 with about even chances.

5 Bb3 Bd6

Note that 5...dxe4 isn't answered with 6 Nxe5?? on account of 6...Qa5+, winning the knight, but rather 6 Ng5!, forcing 6...Be7 7 Bxe6 fxe6 8 Nxe4 Nxe4 9 dxe4 Qxd1 10 Kxd1 with a slightly better endgame for White because of the superior pawn structure.

6 Nc3

White can also consider 6 exd5, but 6...cxd5 is considered to be sufficient for equality.

6...dxe4 7 Ng5 0-0 8 Ncxe4 Nxe4 9 Nxe4 and the chances are fairly level.

Gambits

One of the essential components in becoming a strong chess player is to understand dynamic compensation for sacrificed material. One way of acquiring such understanding is to play gambits, and the Open Games have quite a few of these as we have already seen in previous section, but I have left some of the more important fundamental gambits for last to round off this chapter.

Danish Gambit

Some gambits fell out of favor a long time ago, not because they are not playable, but simply because they fail to provide the kind of game the gambiteer is hoping for. The Danish Gambit is such a gambit, and it seems that its reputation is based on such misconceptions. Sure, Black has a couple of ways to obtain an equal game, but in all honesty, few Black players know how to play these lines well. Therefore this opening should be an excellent surprise weapon.

1 e4 e5 2 d4 exd4 3 c3 dxc3

3...d5!? is a good alternative, which will often transpose to the lines we will cover under the Göring Gambit (Declined).

4 Bc4!?

4 Nxc3 Nc6 5 Nf3 is a Göring Gambit by transposition.

4...cxb2 5 Bxb2

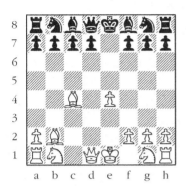

This is the starting position of the Danish Gambit. White has sacrificed two pawns for a solid lead in development. The white bishops look rather menacing and they can cause Black plenty of problems if he is not really careful. In praxis, Black usually gives up at least one of the two pawns in order to catch up a bit on development.

5...d5!?

5...Nf6 is also playable, intending to meet 6 e5 with 6...d5, which is known to lead to positions with approximately even chances.

6 Bxd5 Nf6 7 Nc3

White doesn't win Black's queen after 7 Bxf7+ Kxf7 8 Qxd8 because of 8...Bb4+. After 9 Qd2 Bxd2+ 10 Nxd2, the chances are considered to be about equal, but it isn't quite as simple as it may appear, and I have seen books where authors have claimed that White has the initiative and the better chances. The text move, 7 Nc3, is much sharper, keeping the opening a gambit.

7...Be7 8 Qe2 Nxd5 9 Nxd5

And White has enough compensation for the pawn.

Göring Gambit

Some gambits never get particularly popular, not because they are unsound, but because nearly everybody declines them and the resulting position is incredibly dull; such has been the fate of the Göring Gambit. In addition, the gambit in itself isn't all that dangerous, although it was played by some of the top Yugoslav players, such as Ljubojevic and Velimirovic, at the end of the 1960s and early 1970s.

1 e4 e5 2 Nf3 Nc6 3 d4 cxd4 4 c3

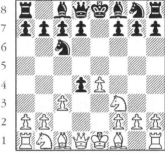

Now White hopes for 4...dxc3 5 Nxc3, which is the starting position of the gambit, but Black usually opts for 4...d5 5 exd5 Qxd5 6 cxd4 Bg4 (6...Nf6 is also fully satisfactory) 7 Be2 Bb4+ (Black can also play the sharper 7...0-0-0, keeping the isolated d-pawn in his sites, though the play is more like what White was aiming for when playing the gambit, sharp and unclear) 8 Nc3 Bxf3 9 Bxf3 Qc4! 10 Qb3 Qxb3 11 axb3, and now both 11...Nge7 and 11...Nxd4 12 Bxb7 Rb8 lead to equal positions.

4...dxc3 5 Nxc3

If White doesn't like the main line, then he can also consider 5 Bc4 in the style of the Danish Gambit, e.g., 5...d6 (taking the b2-pawn is too dangerous since the knight has already been developed to c6) 6 Nxc3 Nf6 7 Qb3, with compensation for the pawn.

5...Bb4 6 Bc4 d6 7 Qb3 Bxc3+ 8 bxc3 Qd7 9 Ng5 Nh6 with a position where White has adequate compensation for the pawn.

King's Gambit

Of all romantic openings, the one which shines the brightest is the King's Gambit. However, the King's Gambit is no longer considered a formidable weapon for White; Black simply has too many adequate answers to it, and currently there are not any grandmasters who play this opening with any regularity. Nevertheless, that has never been a deterrent for players at club levels.

1 e4 e5 2 f4

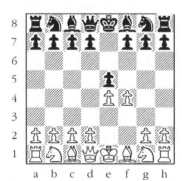

a b c d e f g h

After the Austrian grandmaster Rudolf Spielmann, romantic master of attack who was also known as the last knight of the King's Gambit, gave up on the opening, it really has not been seen much at top levels. It is true that players like Bronstein and Spassky have occasionally played it, and more recently grandmasters such as Gallagher and Fedorov have used it with some frequency, but the latter gave up on it after he lost amazingly fast against Shirov some years ago, and the former seemed to tire of throwing pawns away... Since then, no one has picked up and carried the mantle of this ancient opening into battle.

2...exf4

Accepting the gambit is obviously the critical reply, just as it is in most gambits, but Black actually has a couple decent alternatives: **(a) 2...Bc5** 3 Nf3 d6 4 Nc3 (also 4 c3 is playable, but it too leads to approximately equal chances) 4...Nf6 5 Bc4 Nc6 6 d3 Bg4 7 h3 Bxf3 8 Qxf3 exf4 9 Bxf4 Nd4 10 Qd1 c6, and the chances are about even; and **(b) 2...d5** (Black counters with a gambit of his own) 3 exd5 c6 (3...e4 is the Falkbeer Countergambit, which also works sufficiently well to ensure adequate play for Black: 4 d3 Nf6 5 dxe4 Nxe4 6 Nf3 c6 7 Nbd2 Nf6 8 dxc6 Nxc6 9 Bd3 Be7 10 0-0 0-0, and Black is considered to have sufficient counterplay for the pawn) 4 Nc3 exf4 5 Nf3 Bd6 6 d4 Ne7 7 dxc6 Nbxc6 8 Bc4 0-0 9 0-0 Bg4, with a complicated game and chances for both sides.

3 Nf3

This is the normal move, but again White has alternatives that deserve consideration: **(a)** 3. **Bc4** (the Bishop's Gambit) 3...d5!? (Black can also play 3...Nf6 4 Nc3 c6 5 d4 or 3...Qh4+ 4 Kf1 c6 5 d4 g5, in both cases with sharp positions and chances for both sides) 4 Bxd5 Qh4+ 5 Kf1 g5 6 Nc3 Bg7 7 d4 Ne7 8 Nf3 Qh5 with an unclear position; and **(b) 3 Nc3** (the Steinitz Gambit, which is generally considered to be overly provocative, but it is playable for White) 3...Qh4+ 4 Ke2 d5 5 Nxd5 Bg4 Nf3 Bd6 7 d4 Nc6 8 Kd3 Qh5 9 c3 0-0-0 10 Kc2, and the white king is finally somewhat safe. Needless to say, this line is quite dangerous for White if he doesn't know what he is doing.

3...g5

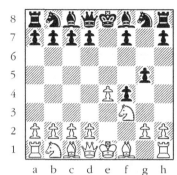

Black logically starts the defense of his recently gained pawn, yet several other moves are good alternatives: **(a) 3...d6** 4 d4 g5 5 h4 g4 6 Ng1 f5!? 7 Nc3 Nf6 with a sharp game; **(b) 3...Be7** 4 Bc4 Nf6 (4...Bh4+ is answered with 5 Kf1, and Black has simply lost time with the bishop) 5 e5 Ng4 6 Nc3 d6 7 exd6 Bxd6 8 Qe2+ Qe7 9 Qxe7+ Kxe7 10 Nd5+, and White wins the pawn on f4 back with fairly even chances; and **(c) 3...d5!?** (Black gives the pawn back right away for smoother development) 4 exd5 Nf6 5 Bc4 (or 5 Bb5+ c6 6 dxc6 Nxc6 7 d4 Bd6 is fine for Black) 5...Nxd5 6 Bxd5 Qxd5 7 Nc3 Qd8 8 d4 Be7 9 Bxf4 0-0 10 0-0, and while White has regained the pawn, Black should be quite pleased with the outcome of the opening, which leaves him with equal chances.

4 h4

In recent years, this continuation has been the preferred choice by White, but this has not always been the case. Some of the sharpest lines of the King's Gambit arise after 4 Bc4, and here Black's main choices are: **(a) 4...Bg7** 5 0-0 h6 6 d4 d6 7 c3 Nc6 with a complicated game and chances for both players; and **(b) 4...g4** 5 0-0 (the Muzio Gambit; White sacrifices his knight to get even further ahead in development) 5...gxf3 6 Qxf3 Qf6 7 e5 Qxe5 8 Bxf7+ (throwing more wood on the fire)

8...Kxf7 9 d4 Qxd4+ 10 Be3 Qf6 11 Bxf4 Ne7 12 Nc3, and White has sufficient compensation for the sacrificed material, but probably not more than that. This line is great fun to both play and analyze, and therefore it is a good variation to use as an analytical exercise with a couple of friends. See if you can find how to develop an adequate attack for White or a defensive setup for Black, and then play it against each other in 10- or 15-minute games. In this fashion, you will develop your attacking and defensive skills.

4...g4 5 Ne5

After 5 Ng5 h6, White does not obtain adequate compensation for the sacrificed piece, e.g., 6 Nxf7 Kxf7 7 Bc4+ d5 8 Bxd5+ Kg7 9 d4 f3!, and White's initiative will soon run out of steam.

5...d6

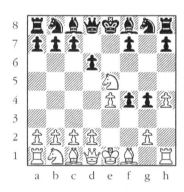

Or 5...Nf6 6 d4 d6 7 Nd3 Nxe4 8 Qe2 Qe7 9 Bxf4 Bg7 with equal chances.

6 Ng4 Nf6 7 Nf2 Nxf6+

White doesn't gain anything from 7 Nxf6+ either, e.g., 7...Qxf6 8 Nc3 Nc6 with an unclear position.

7...Rg8 8 d4 Bh6 9 Nc3 Nc6 10 Qd3 Bd7 and Black has at least equal chances.

Chapter 6

The Semi-Open Games

The openings we will cover in this chapter undoubtedly offer the greatest variety in styles and complexity of any in this book. On high, the Sicilian reigns with its many different variations and its huge popularity, but several others deserve serious attention too, for example the French Defense or the Caro-Kann Defense, while the majority of the other are relatively insignificant if judged by their current popularity. However, as you will see many of the less popular lines offer plenty of opportunity for creating interesting games too and should be explored.

The Sicilian Defense

One of the most interesting and versatile openings in all of chess is the Sicilian Defense. However, the variations of the Sicilian are so diverse that I think that calling it one opening is somewhat of a conceptual misunderstanding. The starting position of the Sicilian arises after

1 e4 c5

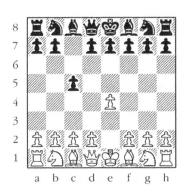

In an attempt to make sense of the many variations, they have been split into the following groups:

The Open Sicilians – Lines where White plays 2 Nf3, and in reply to 2...Nc6, 2...e6 or 2...d6, plays 3 d4 followed by 4 Nxd4.

The Offbeat Sicilians – Lines, where Black, after 2 Nf3, does not play 2...Nc6, 2...e6 or 2...d6.

The Anti-Sicilians – Everything else, including popular moves like 2 c3, 2 Nc3, as well as more exotic options.

The Open Sicilians

White's most popular answer to the Sicilian is also the most aggressive. White exchanges a his central pawns for Black's c-pawn, in return for easy development.

2 Nf3

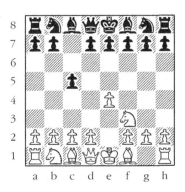

And here the coverage branches in three different directions: **(a) 2...Nc6**; **(b) 2...e6**; and **(c) 2...d6**.

While each has its own set of characteristics, there is still plenty of opportunity to transpose from one variation to another. Black has a number of other second moves available; these will be covered in the Offbeat Sicilians section.

The 2...Nc6 Sicilians

The oldest variations of the Sicilian have Black playing 2...Nc6. This, however, doesn't mean that the lines are old-fashioned. Several of the lines in this segment are still quite popular.

2...Nc6 3 d4 cxd4 4 Nxd4

Black main options are: **(a) 4...e5**; **(b) 4...Nf6 5 Nc3 e5** (Sveshnikov Variation); and **(c) 4...g6** (Accelerated Dragon).

As mentioned earlier, it is important to remember that Black has many other choices available, not just here, but also later. These additional lines can lead to transpositions to other lines or actually have independent significance. I will point out some of the more important transpositions, because some are rather obvious, whereas others are quite deep

and can be confusing to sort out. Aside from the above-mentioned moves, Black can play 4...e6 leading to a Taimanov Sicilian, which is covered in the 2...e6 section, 4...Nf6 5 Nc3 d6, the so-called Classical Sicilian, found under 2...d6, and the finally Black can also play 4...Qb6, a system by itself, in which Black intends to prove that forcing 5 Nb3 is worth spending a tempo on, as Black will later have to play ...Qc7.

4...e5 Lines

In one of the oldest games with the Sicilian, the 19th century French player Louis de Labourdonnais played the provocative move which is topic of this section. It was discredited for many years, but several strong players have injected new ideas and resulting in renewed popularity of these lines.

4...e5 5 Nb5

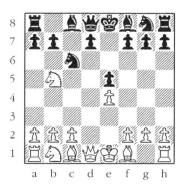

The only way for White to claim any sort of advantage against Black's fourth move is to attack the d6-square, which Black weakened with his 4th move. Now Black has a choice between two moves: **(a) 5...a6** (Löwenthal); and **(b) 5...d6** (Kalashnikov).

The Löwenthal Variation

In this line, Black continues as if White's 5th move is a bluff and forces that which White aimed to do in the first place.

5...a6 6 Nd6+ Bxd6 7 Qxd6 Qf6

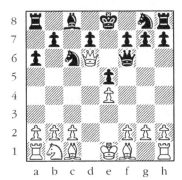

Black is already ahead in development, but at the cost of his dark-squared bishop. The absent bishop and the weakened dark squares force Black to play actively to keep the chances more or less even. In recent years it has mainly been the top Spanish grandmaster Francisco Vallejo-Pons who has taken on the responsibility of keeping this variation alive for Black.

8 Qd1

This move may seem surprising – White "un-develops" his queen. The argument White is trying to make is this square is in fact the ideal one for the queen to keep Black from developing counterplay based on ...d7-d5 and attacking in the center. However, according to current opening theory, 8 Qc7, 8 Qa3 or even 8 Qxf6 are also considered to be better for White.

8...Qg6 9 Nc3 Nge7

Black does best to continue his development, but the sharp 9...d5 is also seen; White has the better chances after 10 Nxd5 Qxe4+ 11 Be3, but it can be a mine field if Black knows what he is doing and White doesn't.

10 h4

Threatening to evict the queen from its ideal square.

10...h5 11 Bg5 d5 12 exd5 Nb4 13 Bxe7 Kxe7 14 d6+

And now the theoretical main line proceeds with 14...Kd8, which is supposed to leave White with a clear advantage after 15 Bd3 Nxd3+ 16 Qxd3 Qxd3 17 cxd3, but now rather than 17...Bf5, Black can obtain an even game with 17...Kd7 or 17...Be6. However, even better is 14...Kf8, and after 15 Bd3 Nxd3+ 16 Qxd3 Qxd3 17 cxd3, Black plays 17...Rh6 intending ...Rxd6, ...Bf5 and ...Rad8 with at least equal chances.

The Kalashnikov Variation

Despite its modern name, this line is older than the previous line, but it was given an overhaul by Russian grandmaster Evgeny Sveshnikov starting in the late 1980s after which it gained a fairly large following. It is in many ways similar to the Sveshnikov Sicilian with its pawn structure. However, White is given more freedom to choose his pawn set-up, allowing the option of the so-called Maroczy Bind structure.

5...d6 6 c4

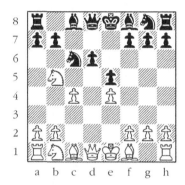

This must be considered the critical variation for White. Setting up with pawns on e4 and c4, White makes it more difficult for Black to accomplish the traditional ...d6-d5 and ...b7-b5 pawn breaks. However, Black in turn focuses attention on the kingside and realizing the ...f7-f5 break.

6...Be7 7 N1c3 a6 8 Na3 f5

Black can also play 8...Be6, and then after 9 Nc2 Bg5 exchange the dark-squared bishop, gaining control over the d4-square.

9 exf5 Bxf5 10 Bd3 Be6

Black cannot allow the exchange of the light-squared bishop.

11 0-0 Nf6 12 Nc2 0-0 and the chances are about equal.

The Sveshnikov Variation

The Sveshnikov Variation traces its origins back before the Russian grandmaster Evgeny Sveshnikov led the movement that brought the opening to the forefront of opening theory. Until quite recently, it seemed like all of the world's top players had the variation included in their repertoires, and therefore the volume of theory is quite large.

4...Nf6 5 Nc3 e5 6 Ndb5 d6 7 Bg5

White's 7th move is worth noting. Aside from some purely tactical reasons in this position, the main goal behind Bg5 is to exchange the knight on f6 to gain a better control over the d5-square. However, White also has other moves available, for example 7 a4, to restrain Black's queenside and prevent him for playing the active ...a7-a6 and ...b7-b5.

Another option is 7 Nd5, forcing 7...Nxd5 8 exd5, which gives White a pawn majority along with a space advantage on the queenside. This line isn't particularly difficult for Black to play against, and he should be able to obtain a decent position after the counter-intuitive 8...Nb8 (8...Ne7 is also seen, but the knight tends to get in the way of Black's own pieces and pawns when Black wants to develop the kingside) 9 c4 a6 10 Nc3 Be7 11 Be2 0-0 12 0-0 f5 13 f4 Bf6, with chances for both players.

7...a6 8 Na3 b5

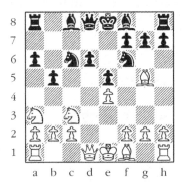

Formerly, Black frequently played 8...Be6, but nowadays this is considered inadequate on account of 9 Nc4 Rc8 10 Bxf6 gxf6 11 Ne3, even if Black does have some counterplay. The position we now have reached can rightfully be considered the starting position of the Sveshnikov Variation, because nearly all games in this opening reaches this particular position.

9 Bxf6

A major alternative for White is 9 Nd5, aiming to take control over the weakened d5-square. After 9...Be7, White normally exchanges on f6 to maintain his knight on d5: 10 Bxf6 Bxf6 11 c3 0-0 12 Nc2 Bg5, and Black gets

ready to start counterplay on the kingside: 13 a4 bxa4 14 Rxa4 a5 15 Bc4 Rb8 16 b3 Kh8 17 0-0 f5, with a complicated position where both sides have chances.

9...gxf6 10 Nd5 f5

A more recent try for Black is the so-called Novosibirsk Variation: 10...Bg7, and now 11 Bd3 Ne7 12 Nxe7 Qxe7 13 c3 f5 14 0-0 0-0 15 Nc2 Rb8 with another sharp position. However, 10...f5 remains the most popular option for Black.

11 c3

White has several other lines available at this juncture. 11 Bxb5 and 11 Nxb5 are two very sharp options for White, but Black should be fine, although the lines are very complicated and not particularly logical, for instance, 11 Bxb5 axb5 12 Nxb5 Ra4 13 Nbc7+ Kd7. Another main line is 11 Bd3 Be6 12 Qh5 Rg8 13 g3 Nd4 14 c3 fxe4 15 Bxe4 Bg4 16 Qxh7 Rg7 17 Qh6 Nf3+, with mutual chances.

11...Bg7 12 exf5 Bxf5 13 Nc2 0-0 14 Nce3 Be6

Despite White's already having established control over the d5-square, Black cannot afford to exchange his light-squared bishop as he may need it to evict the knight later. Furthermore, Black is getting ready to start his counterplay

15 Bd3 f5 16 0-0 Ra7 17 Qh5 Raf7 and again we have reached a double-edged position where both sides have chances.

> **Your pawn play and piece development should focus on and around the central squares.**

The Accelerated Dragon

A personal favorite of mine is the Accelerated Dragon.

4...g6 5 c4

The main consideration for Black between choosing the "normal" Dragon and the Accelerated Dragon is that White can employ the so-called Maroczy Bind against the Accelerated Dragon. This restraining setup – characterized by white pawns on c4 and e4 – ensures White a solid space advantage, but Black has a number of ways to deal with it. Black can aim for pawn breaks such as ...b7-b5 and ...f7-f5, but may also take a positional approach, trying to play against the dark squares White has weakened by placing the two central pawns on light squares.

White also frequently plays 5 Nc3 Bg7 6 Be3 Nf6 7 Bc4, and here Black has two options: **(a)** The positional **7...Qa5** 8 0-0 0-0-0 9 Bb3 (9 Nb3 Qc7 10 f4 d6 11 Be2 b6 12 Bf3 Bb7 is also possible, where Black, despite his passive-looking position, has sufficient counterplay) 9...d6 10 h3 Bd7 11 f4 Nxd4 12 Bxd4 Bc6 with approximately even chances; and

(b) the more tactical **7...0-0** 8 Bb3 a5 9 f3 d5 10 exd5 Nb4 11 Nde2 a4 12 Nxa4 Nfxd5 in which Black is supposed to have sufficient compensation for the pawn.

Other tries such as 6 Nxc6, 6 Be3 Nf6 7 Nxc6 or 6 Be3 Nf6 7 Be2 are also seen from time to time, but Black has nothing to worry about in these lines.

5...Bg7

A popular line for Black is the so-called Gurgenidze Variation, which arises after 5...Nf6 6 Nc3 d6 7 Be2 (White can also opt for 7 f3, but Black should be fine after 7...Nxd4 8 Qxd4 Bg7 9 Be3 0-0 10 Qd2 Be6 11 Rc1 Qa5 12 Nd5, and now not 12...Qxd2+ 13 Kxd2 Bxd5 14 cxd5 with a very uncomfortable game for Black, but 12...Qxa2 13 Nxe7+ Kh8 with a complicated middlegame) 7...Nxd4 8 Qxd4 Bg7, and in this position, White has numerous continuations available, one of which has been a source of irritation for Black: 9 Bg5 0-0 10 Qd2 Be6 11 Rc1 Qa5 12 f3 Rfc8 13 b3 a6 14 Na4 Qxd2+ 15 Kxd2 Nd7 16 g4 f6 17 Be3 f5, and, in this position which may be reached in a number of ways, Black is nearly equal, but the position is slightly easier for White to play.

6 Be3

White can also avoid the main line with 6 Nc2 d6 7 Be2 Nf6 8 Nc3 Nd7 9 Bd2 0-0 10 0-0 Nc5, and the chances are fairly even.

6...Nf6 7 Nc3 0-0

In the late 1980s, Larsen tried, with some success, to revive 7...Ng4; after 8 Qxg4 Nxd4 9 Qd1 Ne6 10 Rc1, and now 10...Qa5

11 Be2 b6 12 0-0 Bb7 13 f3 g5, and Black seeks to set up a bind on the dark squares; White is slightly better, but Black has counterplay.

8 Be2 d6 9 0-0 Bd7 10 Qd2

White also plays 10 Rc1 frequently, although play usually continues as in the main line.

10...Nxd4 11 Bxd4 Bc6 12 f3 a5 13 b3

Nd7 and here White has to decide whether to exchange the dark-squared bishops with 14 Bxg7 Kxg7 or retreat the bishop to e3 or f2. The latter is usually preferred. In both cases, White has more space, but Black's position is solid and Black should eventually generate sufficient counterplay.

The 2...e6 Sicilians

Of the three main continuations for Black on the second move (2...Nc6, 2...d6 and 2...e6), the 2...e6 Sicilian is currently the least popular. This has nothing to do with actual quality of the lines, particularly the Kan and the Taimanov, but more with the fact that neither line is a mainstay in the repertoires of the top players.

2...e6 3 d4 cxd4 4 Nxd4

And now we will split the coverage into three sections: **(a) 4...a6** (Kan Variation); **(b) 4...Nc6** (Taimanov Variation); and **(c) 2...e6 Specialties**.

The Kan Variation

Also known as the Paulsen, the Kan is an amazingly flexible variation in which both sides have a wide selection of moves.

4...a6 5 Bd3

This is just one of three main lines; each has its pros and cons. The play can move in very different directions, all depending on how Black decides to respond.

The first alternative is **5 c4**, but this is hardly the critical test of Black's choice of variation. If White likes this type of "bind" structure, **5 Bd3** followed by c2-c4 later is the proper order. After the immediate 5 c4, Black continues with 5...Nf6 6 Nc3 and now both 6...Qc7 and 6...Bb4 7 Bd3 Nc6 lead to a decent game for Black.

A much sharper continuation is **5 Nc3**, after which Black can choose between 5...b5 and 5...Qc7: **(a) 5...b5** 6 Bd3 (another interesting choice is 6 g3 Bb7 7 Bg2 Nf6, which leads to about equal chances) 6...Qb6 (6...Bb7 7 0-0 is also playable) 7 Be3 Bc5 8 Be2 Nc6 with a complicated game and approximately equal chances; and **(b) 5...Qc7** 6 Bd3 Nc6 7 Nxc6 dxc6 8 0-0 e5 9 f4 Nf6 10 Kh1 Bc5, and both sides have their share of the chances.

5...Nf6

Black usually plays this move, but another continuation has gained ground in recent years: 5...Bc5. This is another one of those moves that is a bit difficult to understand, because after the normal 6 Nb3, Black is forced to move the bishop once again. The idea is that the knight on b3 is not as well placed as the knight on d4. The variations after 5...Bc5 require a little thinking outside the box from Black, but he is generally fine.

After 6 Nb3, Black can choose between:

(a) 6...Ba7 (a bizarre-looking move which appears to leave the d6-square vulnerable, but White has difficulties taking advantage of this) 7 Nc3 Nc6 8 Qe2 d6 9 Be3 Nge7 10 0-0 e5, with a position that is at best slightly better for White; and **(b) 6...Be7** 7 Qg4 g6 (an ugly necessity. Black weakens his dark squares further, but both 7...Nf6 and 7...Bf6 are weaker alternatives) 8 Nc3 d6 9 f4 Nd7 10 Be3 Ngf6 11 Qe2 h5 12 0-0-0 Qc7, with a complicated position and more or less equal chances.

In addition, Black can also play the curious-looking 5...g6, which has been played by several grandmasters, but it requires thorough understanding by Black in order for the multiple weak dark squares not to have serious consequences.

6 0-0 d6

Alternatively 6...Qc7 can be played. One continuation is 7 Qe2 d6 8 c4 g6 9 Nc3 Bg7 10 Rd1 0-0 11 Nf3 Nc6, with approximately equal chances, where White has more space, but Black has a solid and flexible position, quite common for the Kan Variation.

7 c4 b6

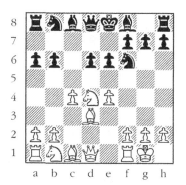

With this move Black aims for a "Hedgehog" setup, something which is primarily known from the Symmetrical English, but can be used by Black in a number of openings because it is both flexible and solid. If Black is not concerned about not reaching tactically complicated positions right away, but is satisfied with a strategically rich position where complications will usually only appear later on, this setup is a very good choice for Black.

Black can also play 7...g6, 7...Be7 and 7...Bd7, all of which should result in similar positions, but all have their own twists and turns.

8 Nc3 Bb7 9 Qe2 g6

It isn't really necessary for Black to choose this double fianchetto set-up, and alternatives include 9...Be7 and 9...Nc6, but our main line is the more flexible continuation.

10 b3 Bg7 11 Bb2 0-0 12 Rad1 Nbd7

And now Black continues with ...Qc7, ...Rfe8 and ...Rad8 with a balanced game. While the Kan looks strange and a little passive for Black, the plans are frequently similar, and the critical positions can be reached through a variety of move orders. Therefore it is also a good system to play because it offers plenty of opportunity to play for a win with careful play. White gains a space advantage that can be exploited, but White also has to understand these lines and the strategic nuances very well in order not to run into a well-timed counter-punch by Black.

The Taimanov Variation

Russian grandmaster Mark Taimanov is

91

frequently only remembered for his 6-0 loss against Fischer in the quarterfinals of the 1971 candidates matches, but he was for decades a very strong grandmaster and an important opening theoretician with many important lines and discoveries to his credit.

4...Nc6

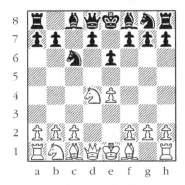

5 Nc3

While this is the more common continuation, another frequently played line is 5 Nb5, and then after 5...d6, White can choose between the sharp 6 Bf4 and the more positional 6 c4: **(a) 6 Bf4** e5 7 Be3 Nf6 (7...a6 8 N5c3 Nf6 9 Bg5 Be7 also leads to a complicated position) 8 Bg5 Be6 9 Bxf6 gxf6 10 Nd2 a6 11 Nc3 f5 with a sharp position and chances for both sides; **(b) 6 c4** usually leads to a Hedgehog type position after 6...Nf6 7 N1c3 a6 8 Na3 Be7 (Kasparov played the ultra-sharp gambit 8...d5!? twice against Karpov and scored 1½ points with it, and despite the passing of more than 20 years, the jury is still out) 9 Be2 0-0 10 0-0 b6 11 Be3 Ne5 (or 11...Bb7 12 Qb3 Nd7 with chances for both players) 12 f4 Ned7 followed by ...Bb7 and ...Qc7, after which Black has reached the normal Hedgehog setup.

5...Qc7

Black can also play 5...a6, which can transpose to our main line, but it also provides both sides with additional options such as 6 Be2 Nge7 and 6 Nxc6 bxc6 7 Bd3 d5 8 0-0 Nf6, both of which lead to approximately even chances.

6 Be3

The main line, but 6 Be2 and 6 g3 can also be played by White, though neither promises White any particular advantage.

6...a6 7 Be2

Another option is the more aggressive-looking 7 Bd3, but after 7...Nf6 8 0-0, Black can obtain a decent game in several ways, e.g., 8...Bd6, 8...b5, 8...Nxd4 9 Bxd4 Bc5 or 8...Ne5 9 h3 (otherwise the knight can often jump to g4 with annoying threats) 9...Bc5 10 Kh1 d6 11 f4 Ned7.

7...Nf6 8 0-0 Bb4 9 Na4!

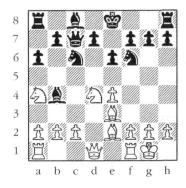

This move is both strong and surprising. Black appeared to be threatening to exchange on c3 and win the e4-pawn, but White sidesteps this plan by removing the knight. Black cannot take the pawn on e4 because of 9...Nxe4 10 Nxc6 Qxc6 11 Nb6 Rb8 12 Qd4 Bf8 13

Bf3 f5, and now 14 Rad1 leaves White with enormous compensation for the pawn. But the idea behind the move is even more surprising...

9...Be7

Black can also try other moves such as 9...Bd6 and 9...0-0, but the main line is the more flexible option.

10 Nxc6 bxc6 11 Nb6 Rb8 12 Nxc8

It is amazing that White invests this much time in exchanging a developed knight for an apparently bad bishop that is buried by its own pawns on a6, c6, d7 and e6. So why is that? There are several reasons: White gains the pair of bishops, a space advantage and generally an easier game. Yet, this line is considered adequate for Black after...

12...Qxc8 13 e5 Nd5 14 Bc1 Bc5 15 c4 Ne7 16 b3 Qc7

Black intends to play ...d7-d6 and then exchange the dark-squared bishops after which White risks being left with a bad light-squared bishop against a strong knight. However, the chances should be about equal. The Taimanov is a strategically complicated line which can be difficult to understand, particularly for Black.

2...e6 Specialties

In addition to these main lines, Black has a couple of variations that are seen with some frequency. After **3 d4 cxd4 4 Nxd4 Nf6 5 Nc3: (a) 5...Nc6** (the Four Knights Variation); and **(b) 5...Bb4** (the Pin Variation)

The Four Knights Variation

While not exactly the most popular line at grandmaster level, it is nevertheless still seen with some frequency.

5...Nc6

This position can of course also be reached after 2...Nc6 3 d4 cxd4 4 Nxd4 Nf6 5 Nc3 e6, whereas 5...d6 would take us to the Classical Sicilian.

6 Ndb5

Another popular option for White is 6 Nxc6 bxc6 7 e5 Nd5 8 Ne4, which looks at first glance rather problematic for Black, because the knight on d5 can be kicked with c2-c4, leaving Black with an apparent problem on the dark squares, in particular the d6-square. However, matters are far from simple: 8...Qc7!? 9 f4 Qb6 (even 9...Qa5+ 10 Bd2 Qb6 is playable) 10 c4 Bb4+ 11 Ke2 f5 12 exf6 Nxf6 is complicated but more or less even.

6...Bb4

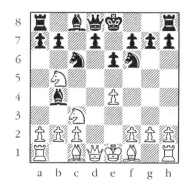

While this looks quite sharp, it is actually a very solid continuation.

7 a3

The sharpest continuation is 7 Bf4, which appears problematic, but Black doesn't have any serious problems after 7...Nxe4! 8 Qf3 (8 Nc7+ Kf8 9 Nxa8? Qf6! 10 Qf3 Nxc3 is very good for Black) 8...d5 9 Nc7+ Kf8 10 0-0-0 Bxc3 11 bxc3 g5, with a very complicated position.

7...Bxc3+ 8 Nxc3 d5

After this, Black takes on an isolated pawn, but he hopes that his more active piece play will compensate for this structural deficiency; in practice, this has more or less proven to be the case.

9 exd5 exd5 10 Bd3 0-0 11 0-0 d4 12 Ne2 Bg4

Black has taken an aggressive stance, taking on an isolated pawn even pushing it to d4. In addition, White has the bishop pair, which may lead you to think that White is comfortably better in this position. However, White doesn't have a lot of space for his pieces which makes it difficult to take advantage of his positional trumps. Theory assesses this variation as minimally better for White, but at all levels below grandmaster play, Black's active position easily provides Black with equal chances.

The Pin Variation

We have already seen how flexible and solid the 2...e6 lines can be, but Black also has a sharp and uncompromising line available: the Pin Variation.

5...Bb4 6 e5

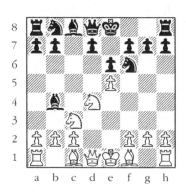

The only logical response for White, otherwise he will have to react much more passively, allowing Black to develop his pieces aggressively.

6...Nd5

Black can also play 6...Ne4?!, but after 7 Qg4 Nxc3 8 Qxg7 Rf8 9 a3, White gets a clear advantage.

7 Bd2 Nxc3 8 bxc3 Be7 9 Qg4 0-0 10 Bh6 g6 11 h4

White should not take the exchange as it allows Black counterplay on all the dark squares and against White's weak pawns. Now after 11 h4, on the other hand, Black is facing trouble on the kingside and doesn't have sufficient counterplay.

The 2...d6 Sicilians

The lines covered in this section have all at some point been very popular and therefore have very large bodies of theory attached to them, but there are many sidelines that makes it possible to take up these openings without having to memorize an endless amount of theory.

2...d6 3 d4 cxd4 4 Nxd4 Nf6 5 Nc3

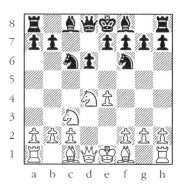

Now we have **(1) 5...Nc6** (Classical Variation); **(b) 5...g6** (Dragon Variation); **(c) 5...e6** (Scheveningen Variation); and **(d) 5...a6** (Najdorf Variation)

The Classical Variation

While not currently favored by many top players, the Classical Variation is perfectly playable and has over the years been an integral part of the repertoires of such players as Botvinnik and Kramnik, as well as many other top players.

5...Nc6

Develop knights before bishops is Tarrasch's old rule that Black seems to be following. It is a very flexible variation for Black, and depending on which main line White now chooses, Black has a wide variety of answers available. *(D)*

White has **(a) 6 Be2 e5** (Boleslavsky Variation); **(b) 6 Bc4** (Sozin Variation); and **(c) 6 Bg5** (Richter-Rauzer Variation)

The Boleslavsky Variation

The Boleslavsky is somewhat similar to its contemporary, the Classical Variation of the Najdorf Variation, 5...a6 6 Be2 e5. However, because the knight has already been developed to c6, Black's position is slightly less flexible, though just as solid.

6 Be2 e5

This is a fairly aggressive reaction to White's fairly dull response to the Classical Sicilian. Note that Black could, if he so desired, have played 6...g6 and entered the Classical Variation of the Dragon.

7 Nf3

Obviously White could also retreat his knight to b3, but that approach has been proven fairly harmless against Black's solid setup.

7...h6

A necessity, otherwise White will proceed with Bc1-g5xf6 and gain complete control over the position.

8 0-0 Be7 9 Re1

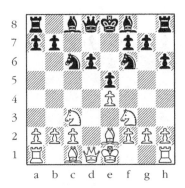

White's setup and plan of development look slow and non-threatening, but the idea is to prevent Black from playing ...d6-d5 by restraining the Black center without incurring any weaknesses of his own. At an opportune moment, White may play Nd5, offering to exchange a piece, but in return White will gain a pawn majority and a space advantage, both of which may be difficult for Black to handle.

9...0-0 10 h3 Be6 11 Bf1 Nb8!

Black's position is decidedly less flexible with the knight on c6 than it is on d7 (such as in the Najdorf Variation – see below for comparison). For instance, if White plays his knight to d5, with a black knight on c6, the d5-knight would only be able to be exchanged by the bishop, and not the f6-knight, because of the resulting c6/e6 fork.

12 b3 a6 13 a4 Nbd7 14 Bb2 Rc8 15 Nd2 Nc5 and the position is more or less even.

The Sozin Variation

One of White's most popular lines against the Classical is the sharp Sozin.

6 Bc4 Qb6

This move is the first choice if Black wants to maintain a pure Classical Sicilian, whereas 6...e6 will transpose to the lines we will cover in the section on the Scheveningen. The text move looks strange to the untrained eye. Why is Black willing to invest a tempo to force the knight back to b3 and then a few moves later retreat the queen to c7? Ideally White doesn't want his knight on b3; he wants to keep it on d4 where it can help apply pressure against e6 and the entire black kingside.

7 Nb3

White has tried a number of other moves at this juncture, e.g., 7 Nde2, 7 Ndb5, 7 Nxc6 and even 7 Be3, and while all of these continuations are interesting, Black essentially is fine after all of them, provided he knows what he is doing.

7...e6 8 0-0

Or 8 Bf4 Ne5 9 Be2 Bd7 9 Be3 Qc7, intending ...Nc4, and Black has more or less equalized.

8...Be7 9 Bg5 Ne5 10 Be2 Bd7 11 Be3 Qc7 12 f4 Nc4 13 Bd4 0-0 with an unclear position and chances for both sides. The Sozin Variation has a lot of theory, but is a fun line to play and is a good way to practice your attacking skills.

The Richter-Rauzer Variation

With the Classical Sicilian as a whole currently taking a backseat to other Sicilian lines, the Richter-Rauzer isn't seen as frequently as it once was.

6 Bg5 e6

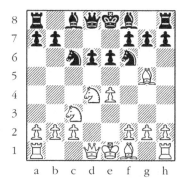

The normal move, not immediately allowing White to double Black's pawns though this in itself isn't necessarily a threat, and, as we will see below, there are several lines in which Black allows the doubled pawns anyway. Aside from the text move, Black can also play moves like 6...Qb6 and 6...Bd7, both of which carry a much smaller theoretical load and are considered fine, if a little passive, for Black.

7 Qd2

This and White's next move are part of the standard setup for White in the Richter-Rauzer. Then White will follow

up with either f2-f4 or f2-f3, depending on what Black plays.

7...a6

Currently this move is considered best because it is much more flexible than the other main line 7...Be7, in which White can claim a tiny edge after 8 0-0-0 0-0 9 f4 (a popular alternative is 9 Nb3 to avoid a possible exchange of knights on d4) 9...Nxd4 10 Qxd4 Qa5 11 Bc4 Bd7 (this looks like it loses a piece after White's next move, but Black has a clever point) 12 e5 dxe5 13 fxe5 Bc6 (if White now takes on f6, then the bishop is hanging on g5 with check) 14 Bd2 Bd7 15 Nd5 Qd8 16 Nxe7+ Qxe7 17 Rhe1, and White has the slightly better chances thanks to his space advantage and the fact that his dark-squared bishop is stronger than Black's light-squared bishop.

8 0-0-0 Bd7

Black also plays 8...h6 here, but Black has to be familiar with the theory; there is quite a bit of it and not all of it is easy to understand. White can retreat the bishop to both e3 and f4, both leading to complicated and double-edged positions.

9 f4 Be7

A sharp alternative is 9...b5, which can lead to lines that are quite typical of the Richter-Rauzer, e.g., 10 Bxf6 gxf6 11 Nxc6 Bxc6 12 Qe1 with chances for both sides, Black will keep the king in the center while trying to mobilize an attack on the queenside against the white king.

10 Nf3 b5 11 Bxf6 gxf6 12 Kb1 Qb6

A sharp position has arisen in which Black often also castles queenside because the kingside simply isn't safe enough to harbor the king.

The Richter-Rauzer offers both sides an amazing number of variations and sidelines, all of which require good understanding and excellent theoretical knowledge.

The Dragon Variation

The Dragon Variation is one of the very sharpest lines in the Sicilian Defense. It goes in and out of fashion and at the moment it is once again becoming popular thanks to the young Norwegian grandmaster Magnus Carlsen who is employs it regularly against top-rated grandmasters.

5...g6

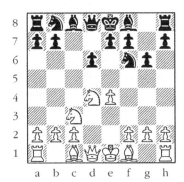

This move introduces Black's most aggressive setup; all of Black's pieces are developed with active counterplay in mind. The main continuations for White are: **(a) 6 f4** (Levenfish Variation); **(b) 6 Be2** (Classical Variation); and **(c) 6 Be3 Bg7 7 f3** (Yugoslav Attack). White has of course several other options available such as 6 g3 and 6 Bc4, to mention but a few.

The Levenfish Variation

White cannot expect to claim an edge against the Dragon if he sidesteps the Yugoslav Attack, but with the Levenfish, White can at least avoid the mountains of theory that exists in nearly all other lines, and thanks to the unbalanced the nature of the positions that arise, White will have good chances of success because so relatively few employ this line against the Dragon.

6 f4

White intends to follow up with a quick e4-e5 to exploit his easier access to development, but Black isn't without resources.

6...Nc6

This is the main line, but Black can also play 6...a6, 6...Nbd7 and even 6...Bg7.

7 Nxc6 bxc6 8 e5 Nd7!

With this clever move Black compels White to exchange the central pawns on Black's conditions rather than White's.

9 exd6 exd6 10 Be3

On 10 Qd4, Black simply plays 10...Nf6, and after 11 Be3 follows 11...Be7 12 Be2 0-0 13 0-0-0 d5 with chances for both sides.

10...Be7 11 Qd2 0-0 12 0-0-0 Nb6 13 Be2 d5

With a complicated struggle ahead.

The Classical Variation

Having played the Dragon extensively myself, I can safely say that the Classical Variation is one of Black's minor worries. The prolonged maneuvering that follows promises Black chances that are every bit as good as White's.

6 Be2 Bg7 7 Be3

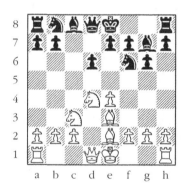

White can also opt for 7 0-0 0-0 8 Nb3 Nc6 9 Bg5, the so-called Karpov Variation; Black obtains adequate counterplay after 9...a6 10 f4 b5 11 Bf3 Bb7.

7...Nc6 8 0-0

A sharp alternative is 8 Nb3 0-0 9 f4 Be6, and now instead of 10 0-0, which will transpose to our main line, White can play 10 g4 after which Black has to be very careful, yet play actively at the same time, e.g., 10...Rc8 11 g5 Nd7 12 Qd2 Nb6 13 0-0-0 Nb4 with chances for both players.

8...0-0 9 Nb3

If White doesn't play this move, Black will be able to play the thematic ...d6-d5 counterthrust in the center with even chances.

9...Be6 10 f4 Rc8

Black can also safely play 10...Na5 and 10...Qc8, intending 11...Rd8 and ...d6-d5. The text move has only become popular more recently.

11 Kh1

On 11 f5, Black retreats the bishop to d7 followed by ...Ne5 with the threat of sacrificing the exchange on c3 followed by ...Nxe4.

11...a6

Also the immediate 11...Na5 is fully playable.

12 Qd2 Na5 13 Nxa5 Qxa5 and Black has a comfortable game.

The Yugoslav Attack

The line most Dragon players anticipate playing against is the Yugoslav Attack; it is also the most dangerous line to face. The Dragon Variation is not for the faint-hearted!

6 Be3 Bg7 7 f3 0-0

Black can also play 7...Nc6 and after 8 Qd2 play 8...Bd7 followed by ...Rc8 and ...Ne5 without castling, but this is not particularly problematic for White. Another, more recent attempt to deviate for Black is 7...a6, the so-called "Dragodorf," a combination of the Dragon and Najdorf. Black wants to play ...b7-b5 and take the game in a somewhat different direction than the usual Yugoslav Attack.

8 Qd2 Nc6

This is more or less the starting position of the Yugoslav Attack about which I have about a dozen books, which should give you a fair indication of just how comprehensive the theory is in these lines. Neither player should enter this variation without being thoroughly prepared and up-to-date with the latest developments.

9 Bc4

While this move is certainly the most popular, 9 0-0-0 is also both very interesting and frequently played. The main line is 9...d5 (9...Nxd4 and 9...Bd7 are the alternatives) 10 exd5 (White can also consider 10 Kb1 and 10 Qe1) 10...Nxd5 11 Nxc6 bxc6 12 Bd4 (12 Nxd5

cxd5 13 Qxd5 Qc7! 14 Qc5! Qb8! is fine for Black) 12...e5 13 Bc5 Be6 (Black doesn't mind giving up the rook on f8 for White's dark-squared bishop) 14 Ne4 Re8, and we have reached a position that is just the starting point in this variation.

9...Bd7 10 0-0-0

The exact move order of White's moves Bb3, h2-h4 and 0-0-0 is in most cases a matter of taste, but Black must stay very alert, because a setup that works against one move order doesn't necessarily work against another.

10...Rc8

It is has been established that this move in all likelihood is Black's best move, but it also has a tremendous amount of theory associated with it. This has made it attractive for Black to investigate other moves at this juncture. For instance, 10...Qc7 and 10...Qb8 have been played numerous times, but both appear to leave White with an advantage provided he knows what he is doing.

A more recent idea is the so-called Chinese Variation, 10...Rb8, which is still in the developmental phase, and is seeing a fair amount action at all levels. However, of Black's 10th move alternatives 10...Qa5 is both the sharpest and most attractive. At the moment, it is considered better for White in the Yugoslav *Encyclopedia of Chess Openings*, but the leading authority, English grandmaster Chris Ward, maintains Black has adequate chances if he knows what he is doing. One line runs 11 Bb3 Rfc8 12 h4 Ne5 13 Kb1 Nc4

14 Bxc4 Rxc4 15 Nb3 Qc7 16 Bd4 Be6 17 h5 a5 18 a4 b5! 19 Nxb5 Qb8 20 Nc3 Rb4, and Black has counterplay and compensation for the pawn. Note the sub-variations are something of a labyrinth and can be difficult to sort out, because they appear similar, but are in fact very different.

11 Bb3 Ne5 12 h4 h5

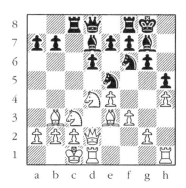

This is the so-called Soltis Variation. The other main line is 12...Nc4 13 Bxc4 Rxc4 which is still fully playable, but it allows White several forced draws and therefore isn't particularly attractive if Black is playing to win. Nevertheless, the total number of possible continuations is quite amazing. The main move is 14 h5 (14 g4 is also seen quite frequently), and after 14...Nxh5 15 g4 Nf6, White can choose between: 16 e5, 16 Kb1, 16 Nd5, 16 Nde2, 16 Nb3 16 Bh6, 16 b3 and even 16 Rdg1, all with their special characteristics and nuances that Black must know in detail; however, if he does, he is doing fine.

13 Bg5

The main alternatives at this juncture are the positional 13 Kb1 and the more confrontational 13 Bh6, which leads to

typical Dragon play: 13...Bxh6 (Black can also play 13...Nc4) 14 Qxh6 Rxc3! (a typical exchange sacrifice in the Sicilian and in particular in the Dragon) 15 bxc3, and here Black has to choose between 15...Qa5, 15...Qc7 and 15...Qc8, all of which should be adequate for Black.

13...Rc5!

It took a little time after this move was first played for it to establish itself. While it looks decidedly odd, it supports the advance of the black queenside pawns, helps to prevent a white e4-e5 and in many variations, the rook may be sacrificed for the white bishop on g5 or on d5, if White places a bishop or knight on that square.

14 Kb1

White can also play 14 f4 or the very sharp 14 g4, in both cases with approximately even chances, though both sides need to be very familiar with the theory.

14...b5 15 g4 a5

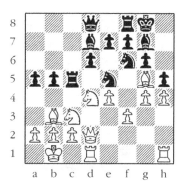

Black can also play 15...hxg4; one line runs 16 h5 Rxc3 17 bxc3 Nxf3 18 Nxf3 Nxe4 19 Qh2 Nxc3+ 20 Kb1 Qa5 with a very sharp position, in which Black has sufficient compensation for the sacrificed material.

16 gxh5 Nxh5 17 Nd5 Re8

And in this complicated position, both sides have their share of chances. Needless to say, the Dragon Variation is extremely complicated, and very entertaining, but you really need to know what you are doing if you are to enter the main lines of the Yugoslav Attack with either color.

The Scheveningen Variation

The Scheveningen is named after a Dutch town where one of the first games with the variation was played. Nowadays Black normally reaches the main lines via other move orders, such as from the Najdorf or the Taimanov Variations because the Keres Attack (6 g4 by White) is feared by many black players. Objectively speaking, however, Black should be fine if he knows what he is doing.

5...e6

The official starting position of the Scheveningen. Now White's main continuations are: **(a) 6 g4** (Keres Attack); **(b) 6 Be3** (English Attack); **(c) 6 f4** (Tal Variation); **(d) 6 Bc4**; (e) **6 Be2** (Classical Variation); and (f) **6 g3** (Fianchetto Variation).

The Keres Attack

As previously noted, the Keres Attack is quite feared; even Kasparov, when playing Black, avoided the traditional Scheveningen move order to stay clear of this variation.

6 g4

With this move, White makes his intentions clear from the outset: he wants to attack on the kingside and therefore Black is actively discouraged from castling there.

6...h6

Many things have been tried against the Keres Attack, but it seems that the text move is both the safest and best. The central counter-thrust 6...e5 is effectively met by 7 Bb5+ Bd7 8 Bxd7+ Qxd7 9 Nf5, and neither 6...Nc6 7 g5 Nd7 8 Be3 Be7 9 h4 0-0 10 f4 nor 6...a6 7 g5 Nfd7 8 Be3 b5 9 a3 Bb7 10 h4 is particularly attractive for Black unless you are ready to defend yourself from a positively scary attack on the kingside.

7 Rg1

Both 7 g5 hxg5 8 Bxg5 Nc6 9 Qd2 Qb6 and 7 h4 Be7 8 Rg1 d5!? have been played several times; in both cases the game is quite unclear.

7...Nc6 8 h4 h5!

This looks completely counterintuitive. Black provokes White into playing g4-g5 after just trying to prevent it. The idea is that White has weakened his light squares, and g4 in particular, when he played h2-h4, and therefore if White now plays 9 g5, then Black will continue with 9...Ng4! 10 Be2 g6! 11 Nxc6 bxc6 12 Bxg4 hxg4 13 Qxg4 Bg7 14 Bd2 Qb6, and Black has compensation for the sacrificed pawn.

9 gxh5 Nxh5 10 Bg5 Nf6 11 Qd2 Qb6

Black forces the white knight to a less active square.

12 Nb3 Bd7 13 0-0-0 a6 and the chances are more or less even in this complicated position.

The English Attack

Nowadays one of the most popular lines against the Scheveningen and the Najdorf is the English Attack which was almost unknown before 1980, but since the mid-1980s the volume of games and therefore theory has exploded.

6 Be3 a6

This position can of course also be reached via the Najdorf move-order 5...a6 6 Be3 and now 6...e6. However, that move order also allows Black the

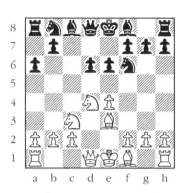

extra option of the traditional Najdorf move 6...e5 and the more provocative 6...Ng4. In many ways it seems like a slower version of Keres Attack, but at the same time it isn't, because it is far more flexible and not as committing.

7 Qd2 b5 8 f3 Nbd7 9 g4 h6

Just as is in the Keres Attack, it is in Black's interest to restrain White's kingside advance.

10 0-0-0 Bb7

Black can also play 10...b4 followed by 11...d5 with a complicated game.

11 h4 b4 12 Na4

It seems a little surprising that placing the knight on this vulnerable square is the best continuation for White, but current theory shows this to be better than the alternatives 12 Nb1 d5 and 12 Nce2 d5.

12...Qa5 13 b3 Nc5 14 a3! *(D)*

We have been taught that we shouldn't move the pawns in front of the king,

but here it is a necessity, and surprisingly the white king turns out to be rather safe.

14...Nxa4 15 axb4 Qc7 16 bxa4 d5 17 e5 Nd7 18 f4 with a complicated game ahead.

The Tal Variation

A third aggressive setup for White also makes White's intentions clear from the outset.

6 f4

6...Nc6

A major alternative for Black is 6...a6, with a position that may also be reached

via the Najdorf move order, 5...a6 6 f4 e6, but most Najdorf players will likely opt for 6...e5 instead, as the lines with 6...e6 tend to favor White slightly, e.g., 7 Qf3 (7 Bd3 and 7 Be3 are two popular alternatives) 7...Qb6 8 Nb3 Qc7 9 g4 b5 10 Bd3 Bb7 11 g5 Nfd7 12 Bd2 Nc5 13 0-0-0 Nxd3+ 14 Qxd3 Nd7 15 Rhe1, and White has the initiative and the better chances.

7 Be3 Be7 8 Qf3 Qc7 9 Bd3 0-0-0

White can also play 9 0-0-0 a6 10 g4 Nxd4 11 Bxd4 e5 12 fxe5 dxe5 13 Qg3 Bd6 with a sharp position.

9...a6 10 Nb3 b5 11 0-0 Bb7 12 Qh3 0-0 13 Rae1 Rfe8

And the chances are about even, though Black needs to be aware of and prepare for an eventual g2-g4-g5 pawn push by White.

The Bc4 Lines

The lines in this section are known by many names such as the Fischer Attack, the Sozin Attack, or the Velimirovic Attack, each with its own set of nuances. But they have a couple of things in common: the lines are sharp and there is a lot of theory to remember and work through.

6 Bc4 (D)

6...a6

6...Nc6 is another move which can transpose to our main line, resulting in a position that can also be arrived at via the Classical Sicilian, 5...Nc6 6 Bc4

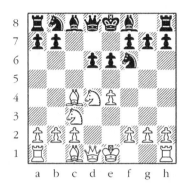

e6. Despite the likelihood of transposition, there are some nuances that should be noted, because, whereas in our main line White plays Bb3 right away, in the lines with an early ...Nc6, White often waits with the bishop retreat until later, keeping the option of Bd3 open as an alternative.

The so-called Velimirovic Attack arises after 6...Nc6 7 Be3 Be7 8 Qe2 0-0 (or 8...a6 9 0-0-0 Qc7 10 Bb3) 9 0-0-0. It was once considered very dangerous for Black, but several ways for Black to meet White's setup have been devised over the years, for instance: 9...a6 10 Bb3 Qc7 11 Rhg1 (or 11 g4 Nd7 12 Nf5 exf5 13 Nd5 Qd8 14 gxf5 Nf6 16 Rhg1 Nd5 17 exd5 Bf6 with chances for both sides) 11...Nd7 12 g4 Nc5 13 Nf5 b5 14 Bd5 Bb7 15 g5 Rfc8 16 Rg3 Bf8 17 Qh5 g6 18 Nh6+ Kh8, again with a double-edged position and approximately even chances. From these two examples it is clear that the lines are extremely complicated and careful study is required by both sides.

7 Bb3 Nc6

For those that have arrived at the position after White's 7th move via the Najdorf, with 5...a6 6 Bc4 e6 7 Bb3, 7...b5 might seem to be a more natural continuation. This is, of course, also entirely playable for Black. These lines are also known as the Fischer Attack. One main line runs 8 0-0 Be7 9 Qf3 (also 9 f4 is seen with some frequency) 9...Qb6 (or 9...Qc7 10 Qg3 0-0 11 Bh6 Ne8 with chances for both sides) 10 Be3 Qb7 11 Qg3 0-0 12 Bh6 Ne8 13 Rad1 Bd7 14 Rfe1 Kh8, and Black has deflected White's first wave of attack; the chances are balanced.

8 0-0 Be7 9 Be3 0-0 10 f4 Nxd4

This is the most common move, but Black can also enter less forced lines with 10...Qc7 11 Qf3 Nxd4 12 Bxd4 b5 13 a3 Qb7, with approximately even chances.

11 Bxd4 b5 12 e5 dxe5 13 fxe5 Nd7 14 Ne4 Bb7 15 Nd6 Bxd6 16 exd6 Qg5 17 Rf2 and the chances are about even, with both sides having their pieces on active squares.

The Classical Variation

The Classical lines at first glance look slow and positional, but as you will see, White can rapidly develop a kingside attack if Black isn't careful.

6 Be2 a6

A major alternative for Black is 6...Nc6, and since these lines can also be reached via the Taimanov Variation, it is one of the move order "tricks" Black can use to enter the Scheveningen without allowing the feared Keres Attack: 1 e4 c5 2 Nf3 e6 3 d4 cxd4 4 Nxd4 Nc6 5 Nc3 d6 6 Be2 Nf6. One of the main lines runs as follows: 7 0-0 Be7 8 Be3 Be7 9 f4 e5! 10 Nb3 exf4 11 Rxf4 Be6 12 Nd5 Bxd5 13 exd5 Ne5 with a sharp position with mutual chances.

7 0-0 Be7 8 f4 0-0 9 Be3 Nc6 10 a4

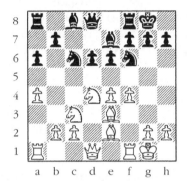

The big question for White at this juncture is whether to allow Black to play ...b7-b5 or not. The text move of course prevents it, but frequently White allows it and instead plays 10 Kh1 which aims to sharpen the game. The main line runs 10...Qc7 11 Qe1 (to transfer the queen to g3, targeting the black kingside and the g7-pawn in particular) 11...Nxd4 12 Bxd4 b5 13 a3 Bb7 14 Qg3 Bc6 15 Rae1 Qb7 16 Bd3 b4 with an unclear position and chances for both players.

10...Qc7 11 Kh1 Re8

You may wonder what the urgency is, i.e., why does Black prioritize placing his rook on e8 this quickly? The idea is to clear the f8-square for the bishop on e7, allowing it to assist in the defense of the g7-square, and sometimes even after...g7-g6 fianchettoing it on g7. Furthermore, on e8, the rook is ready to support applying pressure on White's center with ...e6-e5.

12 Bf3

This is considered the main move, but White has tried other moves, e.g., 12 Qe1, 12 Bg1, 12 Qd2, 12 a5, and 12 Bd3, just to mention some of the more important alternatives; in each line White has a particular set of objectives and Black has different ways to counter them. Needless to say, there is an abundance of theory to master and understand if you are considering taking up this opening with either color. But, as you may have realized already, this is a common theme for all the 2...d6 Sicilians.

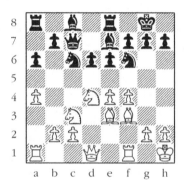

12...Bd7

Black has tried several other things here, but the text move is Kasparov's favorite and is considered best.

13 Nb3

Making the option 13...Nxd4 14 Bxd4 e5 impossible.

13...b6 14 g4 Bc8!

An excellent lesson: Don't look at what was played earlier, but which move is the best in a given position. White threatens g4-g5 and the knight on f6 needs a retreat square; the one on d7 is ideal for this purpose, allowing the knight to retreat further to f8 if necessary, or spring to life on c5.

15 g5 Nd7 16 Bg2 Bb7 17 Qh5 Nb4

The weakness White left behind when he played a2-a4 was the b4-square, which Black now utilizes for his knight.

18 Rf2 Bf8 19 Raf1 g6 20 Qh3 Bg7 and a sharp position has arisen, both sides have their chances and while White's position on the surface looks attractive with its extra space and attacking potential, Black's is solid and offers plenty of opportunity for active counterplay.

The Fianchetto Variation

While White's setup in this line seems a little slow at first, it in fact can turn out to be quite aggressive, once White has castled.

6 g3

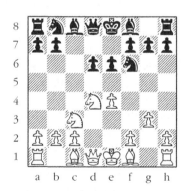

6...a6

Black often opts for 6...Nc6 7 Bg2 Bd7; one line runs 8 0-0 a6 9 a4 Be7 10 Nde2

Rb8 11 h3 Qc7 12 g4 h6 13 Ng3 g5, with an unclear position.

7 Bg2 Qc7 8 0-0 Be7 9 a4

White can also consider a number of other moves at this juncture, e.g., 9 f4, 9 Re1 and 9 Be3, all leading to unbalanced positions.

9...Nc6 10 Nb3 b6

Or 10...0-0.

11 f4 0-0 12 g4 Rc8 13 g5 Nd7 13 Be3 Bb7 with a sharp position and chances for both sides.

The Najdorf Variation

This opening was popularized by the Argentine world championship candidate Miguel Najdorf and has since been a favorite of numerous top players, most notably world champions Bobby Fischer and Garry Kasparov.

5...a6

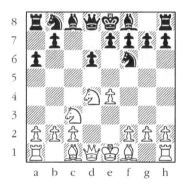

The Najdorf's trademark. What does Black achieve with his 5th move? It doesn't look like guarding the b5-square or preparing ...b7-b5 is a particularly noteworthy achievement. With the text move, Black prepares ...e7-e5, evicting the white knight from d4, without allowing it to go to b5. This is one of the fundamental ideas of the Najdorf, but in reality, many players as Black do not play ...e7-e5 when given the chance, but rather prefer to play the less committal ...e7-e6, in many cases transposing to a Scheveningen Variation. White's chief replies against the Najdorf are: **(a) 6 Be3** (English Attack); **(b) 6 Be2** (Classical Variation); **(c) 6 g3** (Fianchetto Variation); **(d) 6 f4**; and **(e) 6 Bg5**. White can also try 6 Bc4, but it transposes to lines already covered in the section on the Scheveningen.

The English Attack

This variation is often referred to as the Byrne Variation by purists, because American grandmaster Robert Byrne was the one to introduce this variation into practice.

6 Be3

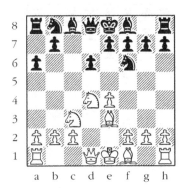

6...e5

Two common alternatives are 6...e6, which transposes to lines covered in

the Scheveningen section, and 6...Ng4, which looks strange and provocative, but it forces White to decide what to do with his dark-squared bishop. The normal move is 7 Bg5, but occasionally White plays 7 Bc1, and then Black can offer a repetition of moves with 7...Nf6. If, however, White isn't interested in a quick draw and still wants to play the English Attack, he could play 8 f3 first, followed by 9 Be3. After 7 Bg5, one main line runs 7...h6 8 Bh4 g5 9 Bg3 Bg7 10 Be2 h5 11 Bxg4 Bxg4 12 f3 Bd7 13 Bf3 Nc6, with approximately even chances.

7 Nb3

White can also play 7 Nf3, but in contrast to the Boleslavsky Variation where Nf3 is the better move, with the bishop already having committed to the e3-square, b3 is a better place for the knight.

7...Be6 8 f3 h5!?

You may wonder what makes Black weaken the kingside like this early in the opening, especially when castling queenside doesn't appear to be an option. With the text move, Black restrains White on the kingside and halts further pawn advances on this wing for some time to come. In fact, in many cases, Black eventually castles kingside, when White has focused his attention elsewhere. Other playable moves include the more normal-looking continuations like 8...Be7 and 8...Nbd7.

9 Qd2 Nbd7 10 0-0-0 Rc8 11 Kb1 Be7

Aside from ...h7-h5, everything has been standard developing moves. Now White has to choose a direction, usually between 12 Bd3 and our text move.

12 Nd5 Nxd5 13 exd5 Bf5 14 Bd3 Bxd3 15 Qxd3 Qc7 with a complicated struggle ahead.

The Classical Variation

Admittedly the Classical Variation looks rather tame for White, but for years it was Karpov's preferred line against the Najdorf and he scored several beautiful wins with it. This line demands a good understanding of the positional intricacies by both sides, because what appears to be careful maneuvering can actually turn out to be playing without a clear plan.

6 Be2 e5

6...e6 is a common way to transpose to the Scheveningen.

7 Nb3

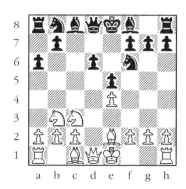

It has been determined that the knight is better placed on b3 than on f3 in this line; there are two main plans for White against Black's setup. In the first, White targets Black's kingside and wants to play f2-f4 quickly. In the other, White aims to exploit the weakness on d5, in some cases requiring the knight to proceed b3-c1-a2(d3)-b4.

7...Be7 8 0-0 0-0 9 Be3

Another popular continuation is 9 Kh1, after which Black has tried more than a half-dozen continuations: 9...Be6, 9...Bd7, 9...Qc7, 9...Nbd7, 9...Nc6, 9...b5 and 9...b6, several of which are considered adequate for equal chances.

9...Be6 10 Qd2

White often plays 10 f4 at this juncture, but Black is considered to be fine after 10...exf4 followed by 11...Nc6.

10...Nbd7 11 a4 Rc8

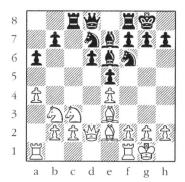

Initially, it can be difficult to spot where Black's counterplay will be coming from, because White seems to have everything neatly under control. Black, however, will be aiming to put pressure on White's queenside by preparing to play either ...d6-d5 or ...b7-b5, while controlling the c-file and the c4-square in particular.

12 a5 Qc7 13 Rfd1 Qc6

Black encourages White to place his bishop on the more passive f3-square, removing a guard for the c4-sqaure.

14 Bf3 Rfe8 15 Qe1 h6 16 Nc1

White begins one of the knight maneuvers that are so typical of this variation.

16...Ra8 17 Nd3 b5 18 Nb4 Qb7 and while White's position looks more comfortable, Black has an adequate game with a solid position.

The Fianchetto Variation

Never a very popular variation at top level, it has nevertheless seen steady support from grandmasters over the years, including the Americans Gata Kamsky and. Alexander Ivanov.

6 g3 e5

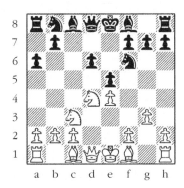

This is the principal challenge to the Fianchetto Variation, but Black can of course also consider 6...e6, which transposes to the Scheveningen Variation.

7 Nde2

The knight may initially look a little clumsily placed on e2, but the idea for White is continue with h2-h3, g3-g4 and then Ne2-g3, supporting a kingside attack. However, occasionally White also retreats the knight to b3, although this does not pose Black many problems.

7...b5 8 Bg2 Bb7 9 0-0 Be7 10 h3 0-0 11 g4

As previously noted, the plan of attack on the kingside.

11...Nbd7 12 Ng3 Nc5 13 Be3 Rc8 14 a3 g6 and the chances are more or less balanced.

The 6 f4 Variation

As a sharp alternative to 6 Bg5, but without the same tremendous amount of theory to master, 6 f4 has offered White players a good alternative. Nevertheless, Black should still be able to hold his own in this line too.

6 f4 e5

The best and most direct response to 6 f4. The main alternative is 6...e6, transposing to a Scheveningen, but 6...Nbd7 and 6...Qc7 are also seen with some frequency.

7 Nf3 Nbd7 8 a4 Be7 9 Bd3 0-0 (D)

This is more or less the standard setup for both sides in this variation.

10 0-0 Nc5

Black frequently plays 10...exf4, but

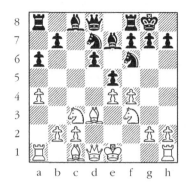

those lines are more complicated and make less sense.

11 Kh1 d5! 12 Nxe5 dxe4 13 Be2 Qc7 14 Qe1 b6 15 Qg3 Bb7 16 Be3 Rad8

Both Black and White have developed their pieces to attractive squares and the chances are fairly balanced.

The 6 Bg5 Main Lines

The only move for White that discourages Black from playing ...e7-e5 is White's Bg5, which has also long been established as the most critical response to the Najdorf. It also comes with an enormous amount of theory to master.

6 Bg5

With this move we enter a veritable labyrinth of complicated lines, incomprehensible moves, massive amounts of theory and everything else that lovers of opening theory will undoubtedly enjoy. Books have been written on several of the sub-variations that begin with this move and the consequences for even small mistakes can be immediate and disastrous. So for

the less experienced player, I recommend you play through the lines given below to gain a rudimentary understanding of the possibilities, but otherwise stay clear of them.

6...e6 7 f4

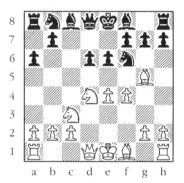

If White wants to avoid the main lines, then there are a couple of alternatives here, 7 Qd3 and 7 Qf3, but neither is particularly critical for Black.

7...Be7

This is a crucial junction in the main line Najdorf. Black has several other choices available, some of which are so complicated that I will actively discourage you from playing them unless you are a full-time chess player or really don't know what to do with you time.

Black can also consider 7...Nc6, 7...Nbd7 and 7...Qc7 in this position. Each of these moves has a reasonable reputation and has the added benefit of not having an overwhelming amount of theory.

The first of the ultra-sharp alternatives is 7...b5, the so-called Polugaevsky

Variation, which at first glance looks like mistake because it allows 8 e5 with an unpleasant pin on the knight. Black, however, can get out of the pin with 8...dxe5 9 fxe5 Qc7!.

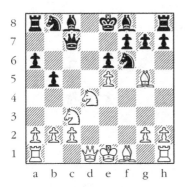

In this position, White has two main choices, both of which are in practice quite dangerous for Black, despite being theoretically satisfactory: **(a) 10 Qe2** Nfd7 11 0-0-0 Bb7 12 Qg4 Qxe5 with incredibly sharp play, where White has compensation for the pawn thanks to Black's almost non-existent development; and **(b) 10 exf6** Qe5+ 11 Be2 Qxg5 12 0-0 Ra7 13 Qd3 Rd7 14 Ne4 Qe5, and Black's position holds, but just barely. Only a very few grandmasters have played this variation with any regularity.

The second ultra-sharp continuation for Black is the so-called Poisoned Pawn Variation, where after 7...Qb6

the queen intends to take on b2 on the next move. Black does without normal developing moves in order to wreak havoc in White's position. This line is considerably more viable than the Polugaevsky Variation, but is still quite dangerous for Black, even though players like Fischer and Kasparov have played it several times, and a player like Latvian grandmaster Alexei Shirov claims that it is Black's best line against 6 Bg5! White has numerous lines to choose from, many quite dangerous, and one where he simply avoid immediate complications, i.e., 8 Nb3, not allowing Black to take the pawn on b2.

The main line is 8 Qd2 Qxb2 9 Rb1 (Spassky tried 9 Nb3 a couple of times against Fischer, but Black is should be fine after 9...Qa3 10 Bxf6 gxf6 11 Be2 Nc6) 9...Qa3 10 f5 (this is just one of many possibilities; White also gets adequate compensation after 10 Be2 and 10 Bxf6 gxf6 11 Be2) 10...Nc6 11 fxe6 fxe6 12 Nxc6 bxc6 13 e5 dxe5 14 Bxf6 gxf6 15 Ne4 Be7 16 Be2 h5 17 Rb3 Qa4 with an unclear position, where both sides need to play very accurately, but as you may have noticed, Black's setup is very artificial and demands very good knowledge of the theory to stay afloat in the ensuing complications.

8 Qf3 Qc7 9 0-0-0 Nbd7

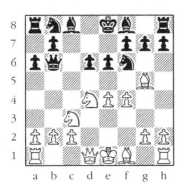

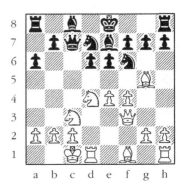

This position can be considered yet another basic starting point of the Najdorf Variation. White has a number of reasonable continuations available: 10 Qg3, 10 Be2, 10 Bd3, but the sharpest and best is our main line move.

10 g4 b5 11 Bxf6 Nxf6 12 g5 Nd7

White's pieces are actively placed and he has a large space advantage on the kingside, which should discourage Black from castling in that direction. All of this will probably make you wonder, why isn't Black just in serious trouble? This is a very good question, with no easy answer. However, Black's position is solid with relatively few weaknesses, and his pieces are developed on good squares.

13 f5

Sometimes White plays 13 h4 before proceeding with this pawn advance.

13...Bxg5+

Some years ago, this was considered inferior to 13...Nc5, but it has since been determined that White obtains a dangerous initiative with 14 f6 gxf6 15 gxf6 Bf8 16 Rg1, intending 16...Bg7 17 Rg7!.

14 Kb1 Ne5 15 Qh5 Qe7 16 Nxe6 Bxe6 17 fxe6 g6 18 exf7+ Kxf7 19 Qe2 and the position is rather unclear, but probably a little easier to play for White.

The Offbeat Sicilians

The lines covered in this section are less popular, but strictly speaking, they are fully playable though they pose White

fewer problems obtaining a good position. These are: **(a) 2...g6** (Hyper-Accelerated Dragon); **(b) 2...Nf6** (Nimzowitsch Variation); and **(c) 2...a6** (O'Kelly Variation).

The Hyper-Accelerated Dragon

If Black wants to reach the Accelerated Dragon, but doesn't want to allow White the opportunity to play 2...Nc6 3 Bb5, as covered below, Black has the option of playing 2...g6, which usually transposes to the desired variation, but it also allows White some extra options:

2...g6

3 d4

This is the normal continuation, but White can also play 3 c3, taking the play into lines similar to those of the 2 c3 Sicilian.

3...cxd4

Another line is 3...Bg7, but White gains the upper hand after 4 dxc5 Qa5+ 5 c3 Qxc5 6 Be3 Qc7 7 Bd4.

4 Qxd4

White can obviously take with the knight as well, but then 4...Nc6 takes us straight into the Accelerated Dragon as hoped for by Black.

4...Nf6 5 Nc3 Nc6 6 Qa4 d6 with a complicated position, where both sides have their share of the chances.

The Nimzowitsch Variation

A cousin of the Alekhine Defense, the Nimzowitsch Variation is even more provocative and is therefore rarely seen at any level of play, but in recent theoretical works some respectability has again been found in this opening.

2...Nf6

3 e5

If White wants to keep the play in normal lines, 3 Nc3 can be tried, after which Black can agree and return to normal theory with 3...d6 or continue along independent paths with 3...d5!? or 3...Nc6 4 d4 d5.

3...Nd5 4 Nc3 e6!?

Black also has the more solid option of 4...Nxc3, which leads to a marginally

better position for White after 5 dxc3 Nc6 6 Bf4 e6.

5 Nxd5 exd5 6 d4 Nc6

This leads to a sharpening of the play, but the alternative, 6...d6, is clearly better for White after 7 Bb5+ Nc6 8 0-0 Be7 9 c4.

7 dxc5 Bxc5 8 Qxd5 d6 9 exd6 Qb6

And Black has some if not entirely full compensation for the sacrificed pawn (the d6-pawn will be won back) thanks to the lead in development and White's vulnerable queen. Black's initiative can provide excellent winning chances, particularly at the club level.

The O'Kelly Variation

Named after the Belgian grandmaster Alberic O'Kelly de Galway, this line is somewhat more tricky than it appears at first glance.

2...a6 3 c4

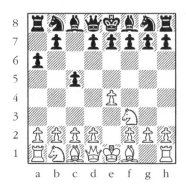

White can play 3 d4, but that helps to demonstrate the idea behind Black's second move: 3...cxd4 4 Nxd4 Nf6 5 Nc3

114

e5, and now unlike the Sveshnikov and Löwenthal, White doesn't have Nb5 available, and therefore after 6 Nf3 Bb4, Black is doing fine.

A better alternative for White is 3 c3, which resembles a sort of Alapin Variation, where 3...a6 isn't as useful as Black would like.

3...d6

Black should preferably play 3...e6, which after 4 d4 cxd4 5 Nxd4 leads to the Kan Variation.

4 d4 Bg4

Again Black should consider 4...cxd4, but even after the text, Black is only at a minimal disadvantage.

The Anti-Sicilians

With the large volume of theory involved with most of the lines we have looked at, it is not surprising that White often tries to avoid the main paths. There are quite of few anti-Sicilians, and therefore we will separate them into two categories: Lines without **2 Nf3**; and lines with **2 Nf3**.

Lines without 2 Nf3

There is quite a selection to choose from in this section, some are sharp gambits, others far more positional; **(a) 2 b4** (Wing Gambit); **(b) 2 b3**; **(c) 2 g3**; **(d) 2 d4** (Smith-Morra Gambit); **(e) 2 f4**; **(f) 2 c3** (Alapin Variation); **(g) 2 Nc3** with **f2-f4** (Grand Prix Attack); and **(h) 2 Nc3** with **g2-g3** (Closed Sicilian).

Wing Gambit

The Wing Gambit is hardly ever seen anymore by players of master level, but it is playable.

2 b4

The Russian Grandmaster Bezgodov devised a different version of the Wing Gambit: 2 a3 followed by 3 b4.

2...cxb4 3 d4

On 3 a3, Black plays 3...d5 4 exd5 Qxd5 5 Bb2 (note that 5 axb4?? is met by 5...Qe5+, winning the rook on a1) 5...e5 6 axb4 Bxb4 7 Na3 Nc6 8 Nb5 Qd8 9 Nf3 Nf6, and White has sufficient compensation for the pawn, but not more.

3...d5 4 e5 Nc6 5 a3 Qb6 6 Be3 Bf5 7 Bd3 Bxd3 8 Qxd3 e6 9 Ne2 Nge7 10 0-0 Nf5 and White has some compensation for the pawn, though I prefer Black.

> *It is usually a very good idea to wait a bit and only get the queen and rooks into play once the minor pieces have been developed and the king has been tucked safely away.*

The 2 b3 Sicilian

While seen infrequently, this variation does have regular support even by fairly strong players.

2 b3 d6 3 Bb2 Nf6 4 Bb5+ Nbd7

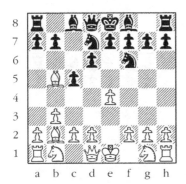

4...Bd7 5 Bxd7 Qxd7 6 Nc3 g6 7 Nd5 Bg7 8 Nxf6+ exf6 was played in a recent grandmaster game.

5 Qe2 a6 6 Bxd7+ Bxd7 7 f4 e6 8 Nf3 Bc6 9 d3 Be7 with chances for both sides.

The 2 g3 Sicilian

2 g3 d5

If Black plays 2...Nc6, the game can follow along the lines of the Closed Sicilian, but without the knight being developed to c3: 3 Bg2 g6 4 d3 Bg7 5 f4 d6 6 Nf3 e5 7 0-0 Nge7 8 c3 0-0 with a complicated struggle ahead.

3 exd5 Qxd5 4 Nf3 Bg4 5 Bg2 Qe6+ 6 Kf1 (D)

White has to give up the right to castle because 6 Qe2 Qxe2+ 7 Kxe2 Nc6 8 Nf3 Nf6 is very good for Black.

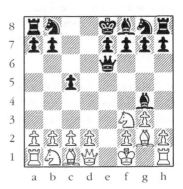

6...Nc6 7 h3 Bh5 8 Nc3 Nf6 9 d3 Qd7 and despite the fact White has lost the right to castle, the chances are approximately balanced.

The Smith-Morra Gambit

For good reasons the Smith-Morra Gambit is quite feared amongst lower-rated players; small mistakes on Black's part can lead to big problems, whereas White's moves are usually more principled.

2 d4 cxd4 3 c3 dxc3

Black can avoid the line entirely with 3...Nf6, and after 4 e5 Nd5, we have a position often reached from the Alapin Variation.

4 Nxc3

White's easy development and Black's lack of same gives White immediate compensation for the sacrificed pawn.

4...Nc6 5 Nf3 d6 6 Bc4 e6 7 0-0 Nf6 8 Qe2 a6 9 Rd1 Qc7 10 Bf4 Be7 11 Rac1 0-0 12 Bb3 Qb8

Black's position is passive and solid, White's aggressive with plenty of potential. White has compensation for the pawn and Black has to be very careful to keep the balance.

The 2 f4 Sicilian

This line of the Sicilian has more or less been abandoned in favor of the Grand Prix Attack where White plays 2 Nc3 before playing f2-f4.

2 f4 d5!

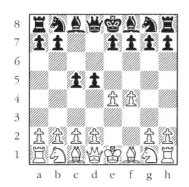

Black's only way to demonstrate the flaws in White's setup is this central counterthrust.

3 exd5 Nf6!

White doesn't mind 3...Qxd5 4 Nc3 Qd8 5 Nf3 Nf6 6 Ne5 e6 7 Qf3 Be7 8 b3 0-0 9 Bb2, and though the chances are supposed to be even, this is the kind of

position White has been hoping for. The text move introduces a gambit for which Black obtains sufficient compensation.

4 Bb5+

Or 4 c4 e6 5 dxe6 Bxe6 with a good game for Black because of the structural weaknesses in White's position.

4...Bd7 5 Bxd7+ Qxd7 6 c4 e6 7 Qe2 Bd6 8 dxe6 fxe6 9 d3 Nc6 10 Nf3 0-0 and Black has a good game with ample compensation for the pawn.

The Alapin Variation

Similar to what is now known as the Sveshnikov Sicilian, the Alapin Variation was not a particularly popular line for White against the Sicilian before Sveshnikov took up the variation. Nowadays it is the mainstay in the repertoires of a number of grandmasters.

2 c3

For many players on the black side of the Sicilian, this move is the closest thing to unsportsmanlike conduct you can get in opening play. Black doesn't get all the excitement and fun he is hoping for, but rather the course of the game is now mostly dictated by White, who is just looking for a tiny edge or maybe just the initiative.

2...Nf6

Black's main alternative is 2...d5, and then after 3 exd5 Qxd5, White plays 4 d4, inviting Black to isolate the White d-pawn. Black has to be very careful in this line, otherwise White will quickly generate an initiative that can take on dangerous proportions. The main line is 4...Nf6 5 Nf3, and now: 5...Nc6 6 dxc5 Qxc5 or 5...Bg4 6 Be2 e6 7 h3 Bh5 8 0-0 Nc6 9 Be3 cxd4 10 cxd4 Be7 11 Nc3 Qd6 or 5...e6 6 Bd3 (White has several alternatives such as, for example, 6 Na3 or 6 Be3 that are also seen quite frequently) 6...Nc6 7 0-0 cxd4 8 cxd4 Be7 9 Nc3 Qd6 10 Be3 0-0 in all cases with sharp positions and chances for both sides, though playing them requires a lot of precision and good understanding.

3 e5 Nd5 4 d4 cxd4 5 Nf3

Of course White can recapture with both the queen and the pawn on d4, but neither line is considered particularly dangerous for Black.

5...Nc6

Black can also play 5...e6, and then after 6 cxd4 either opt for 6...b6 or 6...d6, with interesting play to follow.

6 Bc4

The main alternative is 6 cxd4 after which 6...d6 7 Bc4 Nb6 8 Bb5 dxe5 9 Nxe5 Bd7 leads to a sharp game.

6...Nb6 7 Bb3 d6

Taking the pawn on c3 is very dangerous and cannot be recommended.

8 exd6 Qxd6 9 0-0 Be6 10 Na3 with a sharp position where Black needs to be very careful, as a slight mis-step can lead to a quick loss, but if he knows what he is doing, he should be fine.

The Grand Prix Attack

The Grand Prix was popularized by British players who developed the opening on the British Grand Prix circuit (weekend tournaments). The opening isn't as popular as it once was, but it is still to be found in the repertoires of some grandmasters, though still mainly British ones.

2 Nc3 Nc6 3 f4 *(D)*

A variation of this line is the odd-looking 3 Bb5, where White after 3...Nd4 4 Bc4 tries to show that Black has played his knight to d4 prematurely. The evidence isn't overwhelming, but the line is interesting.

3...g6 4 Nf3 Bg7 5 Bb5

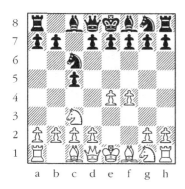

White can also play 5 Bc4. The text move has been recommended by, for example, Dzindzhichashvili on several of his DVDs and books. It certainly deserves attention, even if Black, objectively speaking, should be alright.

5...Nd4 6 Bd3 d6 7 Nxd4 cxd4 8 Ne2 Nf6 9 0-0 0-0 10 Qe1 Nd7 with a sharp game and chances for both sides.

The Closed Sicilian

A favorite among positional players such as Smyslov, Spassky and Adams, the Closed Sicilian is ideal for those who don't mind a lot of maneuvering and slowly built-up attacks. If Black isn't careful, the consequences can be quite dramatic as demonstrated in some of the games between the future world champion Spassky and his opponent in the candidates tournament, Efim Geller, where White won some exciting games that deserve careful study, even today.

2 Nc3 Nc6

Black can of course play 2...e6, 2...d6 or a number of other moves, but the text move is the main line, and the play will often transpose to this variation eventually.

3 g3 g6 4 Bg2 Bg7 5 d3 d6

Most games in the Closed Sicilian reach this position without much thinking from either player, and only now does the game start taking shape.

6 f4

The main alternative for White is 6 Be3, intending 7 Qd2 and 8 Bh6, which has been recommended in several repertoire books for White. Black should be fine, but it is important to know what you are doing and some of the lines are quite sharp.

6...e6

Black can also play 6...e5, but the text move is the main line.

7 Nf3 Nge7 8 0-0 0-0 9 Be3 Nd4 and in this position White usually chooses either 10 Bf2 or the sharper 10 e5, and in either case, the play leads to approximately even chances, but both sides have to know what they are doing.

Lines with 2 Nf3

There is an almost endless stream of Anti-Sicilians whose intention is to avoid the main lines of the Open Sicilian. In many ways the lines in this section offer White better chances than lines without 2 Nf3 do: **(a) 2...Nc6 3 Nc3**; **(b) 2...Nc6 3 Bb5** (Rossolimo Variation); **(c) 2...d6 3 c3** (Kopec Variation); **(d) 2...d6 3 Bb5+** (Moscow Variation); **(e) 2...d6 3 d4 cxd4 4 Qxd4** (4 Qxd4 Variation); and **(f) 2...e6 3 d3** (King's Indian Attack).

2...Nc6 3 Nc3

This line is mostly used by those players who, as White, want avoid the Sveshnikov Variation, but who do not mind other lines of the Sicilian. For instance, if Black plays 3...g6 or 3...e6, White will play 4 d4 and enter the Open Sicilian. If Black does not agree with that game plan he has a good alternative.

2...Nc6 3 Nc3 e5

3...Nf6 can lead to a line in the Nimzowitsch Variation – see above.

4 Bc4 Be7 5 d3 Nf6 6 Ng5 0-0 7 f4 exf4 8 Bxf4 d6 9 0-0 h6 and the chances are about even.

Rossolimo Variation

This variation used to be considered fairly harmless, but it has become increasingly popular.

2...Nc6 3 Bb5 *(D)*

White threatens to give Black doubled c-pawns, and while this may not look or sound like a serious threat, it can lead to an uncomfortable positional game for Black if he is not careful.

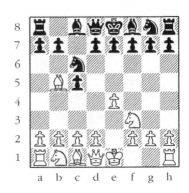

3...g6

3...e6 is a popular alternative: 4 0-0 (4 Bxc6 bxc6 5 0-0 Ne7 6 b3 Ng6 7 Bb2 is a worthwhile option for White too) 4...Nge7 5 c3 (5 Re1 and 5 b3 can also be tried) 5...a6 6 Ba4 b5 7 Bc2 Bb7 8 Re1 Rc8 with a complicated position.

4 0-0

An increasingly popular alternative is the immediate exchange on c6, e.g., 4 Bxc6 dxc6 5 h3 Bg7 6 d3 Nf6 7 Nc3 0-0 Be3 b6 with about even chances.

4...Bg7 5 Re1

White can also consider 5 c3.

5...Nf6

If Black tries 5...e5, White can consider the sharp 6 b4!? or the more positional 6 Bxc6, depending on White's taste.

6 c3

Or 6 e5 Nd5 7 Nc3 Nc7 8 Bxc6 dxc6 with a sharp game.

6...0-0 7 d4 cxd4 8 cxd4 d5 9 e5 Ne4 and the chances are about even.

Kopec Variation

Calling this the Kopec Variation is actually a bit inaccurate, because American international master Dan Kopec used to play the strange-looking 3 Bd3 first, and only then follow up with 4 c3. In fact, its roots go back at least to American grandmaster Arthur Bisguier who played it before Kopec was even born. While fully playable, it is less flexible than the immediate 3 c3, which reserves the right to develop the bishop to e2 or b5 as well as to d3. Additionally, White also has the options of 3 b3, 3 d3, 3 Bc4 and finally 3 Nc3; all being a matter of personal preference.

2...d6 3 c3 Nf6 4 Be2

White's main alternatives are 4 Bd3 and 4 h3, both leading to approximate equality.

4...g6 5 0-0 Bg7 6 Bb5+ Bd7 7 Bxd7+ Qxd7 8 Re1 0-0 9 d4 cxd4 10 cxd4 d5 11 e5 Ne8 and the chances are more or less even.

Moscow Variation

While considered less dangerous for Black than the Rossolimo Variation, the Moscow variation is still a good way for White to avoid the mountains of theory that exist after 3 d4. Several grandmasters play this variation frequently with very decent results, which of course is a good indication that it is perfectly playable at all levels.

2...d6 3 Bb5+

In this line White isn't necessarily trying to give Black doubled pawns and

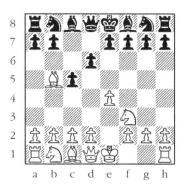

has no higher strategic agenda in mind, but rather hopes to get his pieces developed to reasonably good squares, while preventing Black from getting the usual active counterplay that is to be had in the Najdorf, the Scheveningen or the Dragon, which are the most common lines for Black after 2...d6.

3...Bd7

Not the only option, but the most logical one and also the one most frequently seen. Other choices include 3...Nd7, which is somewhat more ambitious, though not necessarily better, but it has a tendency to generate play that more resembles the Open Sicilian than the other lines after 3 Bb5+. 3...Nc6 leads to a position that can also be reached via the Rossolimo move order, 2...Nc6 3 Bb5 d6. One line runs 4 0-0 Bd7 5 c3 Nf6 6 Re1 a6 7 Bf1 (also 7 Ba4 and 7 Bxc6 can be considered) 7...Bg4 8 d3 e6 9 Nbd2 Be7 with chances to both sides.

4 Bxd7+ Qxd7

Black can also consider taking with the knight on d7, but recapturing with the queen is considered the main line.

5 c4

With this move, White takes the game into something similar to a Maroczy Bind, which isn't strictly necessary. For instance a good alternative can be found in 5 0-0 Nc6 6 c3 Nf6 7 Qe2 (7 Re1 leads to similar positions, but 7 d4 is a sharper option) 7...e6 8 d4 cxd4 9 cxd4 d5 10 e5 Ne4 11 Rd1 Rc8, and the game is more or less balanced.

5...Nf6 6 Nc3 Nc6 7 0-0 g6 8 d4 cxd4 9 Nxd4 Bg7 10 Nde2 0-0

White has more space and appears to have an easier game, but Black's position is both solid and flexible, and there are plenty of opportunities for counterpunches; the chances are equal.

4 Qxd4 Variation

This line presents White with another opportunity to avoid the theoretical main lines of the Open Sicilian.

2...d6 3 d4 cxd4 4 Qxd4

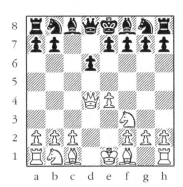

At grandmaster level, this line isn't seen particularly often because Black should equalize without too many problems, but at lower levels, it can be a dangerous weapon, because Black may not be familiar with the theory and will then often go wrong early, allowing White an easier game.

4...Nc6

The normal and logical move, but Black can also play 4...a6 or 4...Bd7 with the intention of following up with ...Nc6, but without allowing the pin and exchange of the knight on c6.

5 Bb5 Bd7 6 Bxc6 Bxc6

This looks fairly harmless for Black, but now White usually sharpens the game by castling queenside.

7 Nc3 Nf6 8 Bg5 e6 9 0-0-0 Be7 10 Rhe1 0-0 with a complicated position that is considered about even by theory, but where Black still has to be very careful.

King's Indian Attack

There are many different versions of the King's Indian Attack. One of the more popular lines is the one that arises from the 2...e6 Sicilian.

2...e6 3 d3

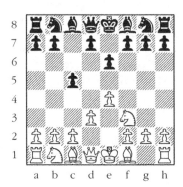

White has a number of alternatives at this juncture, such as 3 b3, 3 c3, 3 g3 as well as 3 Nc3, but none of these lines is considered particularly dangerous for Black.

3...Nc6

If Black plays 3...d5 here or on one of the next few moves, it takes us over to lines that are normally reached via the French.

4 g3 g6 5 Bg2 Bg7 6 0-0 Nge7 7 Re1 d6 8 c3 0-0 9 Nbd2 b6 10 Nf1 Bb7 and the chances are split approximately even.

The Pirc Defense

1 e4 d6 2 d4 Nf6 3 Nc3

White can also play 3 f3, which after 3...g6 4 c4 Bg7 5 Nc3 transposes to a Sämisch Variation of the King's Indian Defense. Another alternative is 3 Bd3.

3...g6

With this move we reach the starting position of the Pirc. Black intends to complete his development and see which setup White chooses before deciding on a line of action. Nowadays the Pirc isn't particular popular at the top of the chess hierarchy, but some years back the opening was championed by sharp creative players such as Jan Timman, Mikhail Gurevich and Yasser Seirawan.

Black also has other moves available at this juncture, e.g., 3...e5 4 Nf3 Nbd7 leads to a Philidor Defense, which is discussed in the chapter on the Open

Games. Another move is 3...c6, which Black intends to follow up with 4...Qa5 and 5...e5, which is called the Czech Defense. Both lines are considered slightly favorable for White. Now White has several different choices: **(a) 4 Nf3** (Classical System); **(b) 4 Be3** (150 Attack); and **(c) 4 f4** (Austrian Attack).

There are other moves too, for instance 4 Be2, 4 Bg5 and 4 Bc4 or even 4 g3, all have their supporters, even if they are not supposed to lead to any advantage for White.

The Classical System

4 Nf3

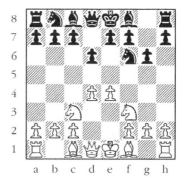

This setup aims for straightforward development with an eventual look to a slight plus thanks to a space advantage in the center.

4...Bg7 5 Be2 0-0 6 0-0 Bg4

This takes some of the dynamic potential out of White's game. Other tries include 6...c6, 6...c5 and 6...Nbd7.

7 Be3 Nc6 8 d5 Bxf3 9 Bxf3 Ne5 10 Be2 c6 11 f4 Ned7 12 dxc6 bxc6 and while White has more space, Black has a solid and flexible position. The chances are about even.

The 150 Attack

The name of this variation, the 150 Attack is actually a kind of joke. "150" comes from the English rating system and is equivalent to an ELO rating of 1800, thus indicating the line is not for very strong players. However, it has been recommended in a number of repertoire books for White because it is easy to learn and carries a punch if Black isn't careful.

4 Be3 Bg7 5 Qd2 c6 6 f3

6...b5 7 Bh6 Bxh6 8 Qxh6 Nbd7 with chances for both sides.

The Austrian Attack

The critical choice against the Pirc is the Austrian Attack, which grabs a space advantage and the initiative. While Black's situation by no means is threatening, White's position is usually a little easier to play. As always, if White is not careful, Black can take over the initiative.

4 f4 Bg7 5 Nf3 0-0

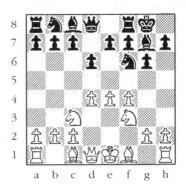

A main alternative for Black is the immediate 5...c5, where White can either take on c5 with 6 dxc5 after which Black plays 6...Qa5 7 Bd3 Qxc5 which leads to about even chances or 6 Bb5+ Bd7 7 e5 Ng4, and now after 8 e6!?, Black has two fascinating lines to choose between: 8...fxe6 9 Ng5 Bxb5 10 Nxb5 Qa5+ 11 c3 Qxb5 12 Qxg4 with an unclear position or 8...Bxb5 9 exf7+ Kd7! 10 Nxb5 Qa5+ 11 Nc3 cxd4 12 Nxd4 and again we have a position that has been played numerous times, yet is still considered unclear.

6 Bd3

White often plays 6 Be3 as well.

6...Nc6

Black has a number of alternatives is 6...c5, 6...Nbd7, 6...Bg4 and 6...Na6.

7 e5 8 fxe5 Nh5 9 Be2 Bg4 10 Be3 and White has perhaps a tiny edge, but Black's chances are considered fully adequate.

The King's Fianchetto ("Modern Defense")

Like the Pirc, the King's Fianchetto has been out of fashion for quite a while, but it is of course still fully playable and it is in fact a very flexible opening, and is a particular favorite of players with a creative flair.

1 e4 g6

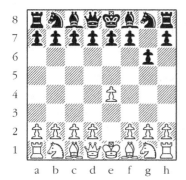

This opening can often transpose to the Pirc Defense if Black wishes, but Black can give the opening its own flavor by waiting to develop the g8-knight.

2 d4 Bg7 3 Nc3

White can also play 3 c4 taking the game to something that looks a bit like a King's Indian, but again Black can wait to develop the knight on g8, making it slightly different.

3...d6 4 f4

A good alternative is 4 Be3 followed by 5 Qd2.

4...c6 5 Nf3 Bg4 6 Be3 Qb6 7 Qd2 and White has the slightly better chances.

The French Defense

1 e4 e6

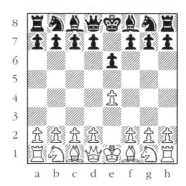

This is one of Black's oldest and most solid setups. Black wants to challenge White in the center with ...d7-d5, often followed by ...c7-c5. One of Black's main concerns is the light-squared bishop which is severely restricted by pawns on the e6 and d5. The second player often remedies this by playing ...b7-b6, ...Bd7-b5 or ...Bd7-e8 followed by ...f7-f6, and then the bishop may go to g6 or h5 via e8.

2 d4

White usually grabs the center squares when they are available, but occasionally he instead chooses the King's Indian Attack setups which can be reached with 2 d3 d5 3 Nd2 c5 4 Ngf3 Nc6 5 g3 Nf6 6 Bg2 Be7 7 0-0 b6 8 Qe2 Bb7 with chances for both sides. This line was an early favorite of Bobby Fischer, but isn't that popular these days in top level chess, while it is seen more often at lower levels because it is easy to learn and play and offers White excellent attacking chances.

2...d5

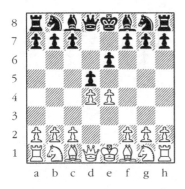

Now we have reached the first main fork in the road, where White can take the game in very different directions: **(a) 3 e5** (Advance Variation); **(b) 3 exd5** (Exchange Variation); **(c) 3 Nd2** (Tarrasch Variation); and **(d) 3 Nc3**.

The Advance Variation

3 e5

With this advance, White gains an immediate space advantage in the center and on the kingside. This move was popularized by Nimzowitsch and much later by Sveshnikov. These days this variation has gone through a renaissance and it is once again played frequently at top level.

3...c5

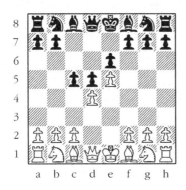

Black attacks White's center from the flank and will often follow it up with an initiative on the queenside. Occasionally Black will also open up the f-file with ...f7-f6.

4 c3 Nc6 5 Nf3 Qb6

Black puts pressure on White's center pawn on d4. If White now plays 6 Bd3, then Black has to be aware of the trap 6...cxd4 7 cxd4, and now Black cannot take the d-pawn with 7...Nxd4?? because of 8 Nxd4 Qxd4 9 Bb5+, and the black queen is lost. Instead, Black should play 7...Bd7, and then Black really threatens to take the pawn on d4, because the check on b5 is no longer available for White.

6 Be2 cxd4 7 cxd4 Nge7 8 Na3 Nf5 9 Nc2 Bb4+ 10 Kf1 Be7 11 h4 and White has a slightly better game because of his space advantage. The loss of the right to castle is not a big concern; White will play g2-g3 and place his king on g2.

The Exchange Variation

3 exd5 exd5

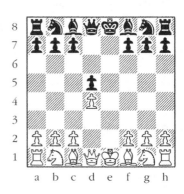

The exchange on d5 makes the position

completely symmetrical, and is usually perceived as an attempt by White to get a draw, but this is by no means a guaranteed result because all the pieces are still on the board.

4 Bd3 Bd6 5 c3 Nc6

Black can also play 5...c6 and keep the game symmetrical, but if Black wants to play for more than a draw, he can do so safely by developing his pieces actively.

6 Nf3 Nge7 7 0-0 Bg4 8 Re1 Qd7 9 Nbd2 and here Black can choose 9...0-0 and keep the game relatively quiet and even, or the sharp 9...0-0-0 where Black will follow up with a kingside attack, and White will attack with his pawns on the queenside. In either case, both sides have their chances.

The Tarrasch Variation

3 Nd2

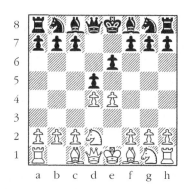

With this move, White aims for a solid setup in the center where he can support his d-pawn with c2-c3 at an opportune moment and then he can place his knights on f3 and e2.

Now Black can choose between three main continuations: **(a)** 3...c5; **(b)** 3...Nf6; and **(c)** 3...dxe4 (Rubinstein Variation).

Tarrasch with 3...c5

3...c5

This is Black's most aggressive option, he immediately challenges White's center.

4 exd5 exd5

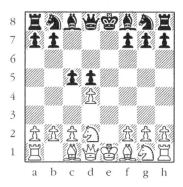

With this move Black accepts an isolated pawn, and in return he gets easy development for his minor pieces, including the c8-bishop which often gives Black headaches in the French. Black has an alternative in 4...Qxd5, which breaks one of the opening principles by developing the queen too soon. In this case, however, it is difficult for White to take advantage of it. One possible continuation is 5 Ngf3 cxd4 6 Bc4 Qd6 7 0-0 Nf6 8 Nb3 Nc6 9 Nbxd4 Nxd4 10 Nxd4 Bd7 11 b3 0-0-0 12 Bb2 Qc7 with a sharp position.

5 Ngf3 Nc6 6 Bb5 Bd6 7 dxc5 Bxc5 8 0-0 Ne7 9 Nb3 Bd6 10 Re1 0-0

Both sides are getting close to having finished their development, but White, thanks to his slightly better pawn structure (Black's isolated d-pawn) has a small advantage.

Tarrasch with 3...Nf6

3...Nf6 4 e5 Nfd7 5 Bd3

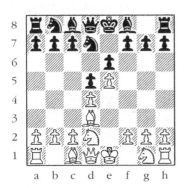

White can also consider the very sharp 5 f4 which leads to a complicated game after 5...c5 6 c3 Nc6 7 Ndf3 cxd4 8 cxd4 Qb6 9 g3 Bb4+ 10 Kf2 g5, and because of the pin of the d4-pawn, White cannot play 11 fxg5 because of 11...Ndxe5, and therefore often plays 12 Be3 g4 12 Nd2 f6, and both sides have to play carefully.

5...c5 6 c3 Nc6 7 Ne2 cxd4 8 cxd4 f6

Black doesn't want to allow White time to settle down and develop easily. By attacking White's center, Black gets to place his pieces on more active squares.

9 exf6 Nxf6 10 0-0 Bd6 11 Nf3 0-0 with a position that has occurred in many games. The chances are evenly split.

The Rubinstein Variation

3...dxe4 4 Nxe4

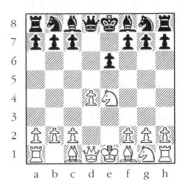

This variation can also arise after 3 Nc3 dxe4 4 Nxe4, which is why I have saved it for now. This is a solid, but slightly passive variation for Black, but it is often played if Black is satisfied with a draw as it is quite solid and flexible enough to ward off White's aggression.

4...Nd7 5 Nf3 Ngf6 6 Nxf6+

6 Bg5 Be7 will transpose to the Burn Variation which can be found in the next section.

6...Nxf6 7 Bg5 h6 8 Bxf6 Qxf6 9 Bb5+ c6 10 Bd3 Bd7 11 c3 Bd6 12 Qe2 c5 and with this counterpunch in the center, Black is ready to commence counterplay, transferring the light-squared bishop to the active c6-square. The chances are fairly even.

3 Nc3 Variations

Generally speaking, the 3 Nc3 lines lead to sharper play than 3 Nd2, although there are plenty of positional options for both sides.

3 Nc3

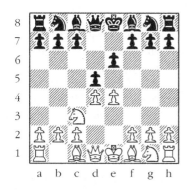

This is an invitation to some of the sharpest lines of the French: **(a) 3...Bb4** (Winawer Variation); and **(b) 3...Nf6** (Classical Variation).

Black has other options of course, including 3...dxe4 as noted above, but also 3...Be7 and 3...Nc6 as well as other more unusual lines. However, the two main lines mentioned above are by far the most popular, though very different.

The Winawer Variation

3...Bb4

With the pin on the c3-knight, White has to make a decision regarding the center.

4 e5

White closes the center and, as in the advance variation, White's game is often directed towards the kingside. Alternatively, White can play 4 exd5 and after 4...exd5, the game is a version of the Exchange Variation. Furthermore, White can also consider sharp continuations like 4 a3 and 4 Ne2; in either case Black should be fine, but careful play on both sides will still be required.

4...c5 5 a3 Bxc3+ 6 bxc3 Ne7

This is essentially the starting position of majority of the games in the Winawer. White can take the game into two very different directions: **(a) 7 Nf3** (Rauzer Variation); and **(b) 7 Qg4** (Poisoned Pawn).

The Rauzer Variation

7 Nf3

Thanks to the pawn structure, the plans for both sides are clearly defined: White will play on the kingside and Black on the queenside. With this in mind, it is surprising that the white king belongs on the kingside and the black king on the queenside.

7...Nbc6

Black has several alternatives, such as 7...Qc7 and 7...b6, but our chosen main line well illustrates the typical type of play in the Rauzer.

8 Be2 Qa5 9 Bd2 Bd7

Black may get tempted to play 9...cxd4 10 cxd4 Qa4, because 11 c3 Qxd1+ 12 Rxd1 Na5 13 h4 Bd7 leads to a comfortable game for Black, but 11 Rb1!? Nxd4 12 Bd3 Ndc6 13 Rb3 gives White a dangerous initiative for the pawn.

10 0-0 c4 11 Ng5 h6 12 Nh3 Ng6 13 Bh5 0-0-0 14 f4 and White has a slight initiative because he is somewhat further ahead with his plans than Black.

The Poisoned Pawn

7 Qg4

Again we see a move that appears to go against traditional opening principles. However, White is trying to take advantage of the absence of Black's dark-squared bishop. Black can only protect the pawn with 7...Kf8, which obviously isn't desirable, though it is playable, or play the very provocative 7...0-0, which has become a main line itself. Whole books have been devoted to this position, but one typical line runs 8 Bd3 Nbc6 9 Qh5 Ng6 10 Nf3 Qc7 11 Be3 c4 12 Bxg6 fxg6 with a complicated game, tending to favor the first player.

7...Qc7

With this move Black goes directly for counterplay along the c-file and in the center. Coupled with his lead in development, Black hopes this counterplay will offset White's material gains on the kingside.

8 Qxg7 Rg8 9 Qxh7 cxd4 10 Ne2 Nbc6 11 f4 dxc3 12 Qd3 Bd7

Black continues his development while White is trying to stabilize and consolidate his position.

13 Nxc3 a6 14 Rb1 Na5 15 h4 Nf5 with a complicated struggle and chances to both sides.

The Classical Variation

3...Nf6

Black tries to force White to close the center.

4 Bg5

White postpones the pawn advance for a short while, though the immediate 4 e5 is also very popular. One example is 4...Nfd7 5 f4 c5 6 Nf3 Nc6 7 Be3 cxd4 8 Nxd4 Bc5 9 Qd2 0-0 10 0-0-0 a6 11 h4 Nxd4 12 Bxd4 b5, with mutual chances.

4...Be7

This is one of a number of interesting continuations for Black, who may also consider 4...dxe4, similar to the Rubinstein Variation (3...dxe4) we looked at earlier, except this line, called the Burn Variation, is considered to offer Black better chances of equalizing, e.g., 5 Nxe4 Be7 6 Bxf6 Bxf6 7 Nf3 0-0 8 Qd2 b6 9 Nxf6+ Qxf6 10 Bd3 Bb7 with a solid position for Black. The surprising 4...Bb4, the MacCutcheon Variation, is also a valid try for Black, e.g., 5 e5 h6 6 Bd2 (White doesn't achieve anything after 6 Bh4 g5 7 Bg3 Ne4) 6...Bxc3 7 bxc3 Ne4 8 Qg4 g6 9 Bd3 Nxd2 10 Kxd2 c5 with a complicated struggle.

5 e5 Nfd7 6 Bxe7 Qxe7 7 f4 0-0 8 Nf3 c5 9 Qd2 Nc6 10 0-0-0 and in this line White's chances are considered preferable.

The Caro-Kann Defense

Although the Caro-Kann has always had a reputation as a solid opening and had the support of strong players in nearly all eras since it first appeared, including players such as Nimzowitsch, Botvinnik, Smyslov, Bronstein, Petrosian, and Larsen to mention some of the more recognizable names, it didn't truly become an everyday weapon for countless top grandmasters until world champion Anatoly Karpov made it his primary answer to 1 e4. Today it is regularly seen in the games of players such as world champion Viswanathan Anand, Veselin Topalov, Alexander Morozevich, Peter Leko and Vassily Ivanchuk, not to mention many other 2600+ rated players. However, it is also an opening that can be played by much lower-rated players because the strategies are simple to understand and follow, yet complex enough to offer something for the strongest players.

One benefit for Black is that in the main lines there are many options, and Black is able to dictate to a large extent in which direction the play will go.

1 e4 c6

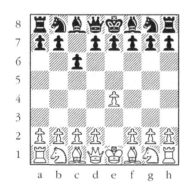

2 d4

White usually prefers this move, but there are other options that should not be discounted to easily:

(a) 2 c4, which can transpose into a Panov-Botvinnik Attack after 2...d5 (2...e5 is also possible) 3 exd5 cxd5 4 d4, but White can also opt for 4 cxd5. Black then usually continues with 4...Nf6

(4...Qxd5 5 Nc3 Qd8 6 d4 transposes to a variation in the Alapin Sicilian) 5 Bb5+ (the sharper 5 Nc3 and even 5 Qa4+ are also commonly seen) 5...Nbd7 6 Nc3 a6 7 Qa4 Rb8 8 Bxd7+ Qxd7 9 Qxd7+ Bxd7 10 Nge2 is about equal; **(b) 2 d3** is a version of the King's Indian Attack, though against the Caro-Kann, it isn't considered particularly dangerous, despite it being used frequently by particularly Ljubojevic. The play usually continues with 2...d5 3 Nd2 e5 4 Ngf3 Bd6 5 g3 Nf6 6 Bg2 0-0 7 0-0 Re8 8 Re1 Nbd7 with chances to both sides; and **(c) 2 Nc3** (2 Nf3 will usually lead to the same variation, but a line with a sting is 2...d5 3 exd5 cxd5 4 Ne5!?, but 4...Nc6 5 d4 e6 6 Bb5 Bd7 should be satisfactory for Black) 2...d5 3 Nf3, and we have reached the Two Knights Variation. Now Black can play 3...dxe4 4 Nxe4, but it should be followed by either 4...Bg4 or 4...Nf6 in this position, since 4...Bf5 only leads to headaches, e.g. 5 Ng3 Bg6?! (5...Bg4 is the only playable move) 6 h4 h6 7 Ne5 Bh7?! 8 Qf3 Nf6 9 Qb3 with simultaneous threats against f7 and b7. The main line is 3...Bg4 4 h3 Bxf3 (4...Bh5 5 exd5 cxd5 6 Bb5 Nc6 7 g4 Bg6 8 Ne5 Rc8 9 d4 e6 is also possible) 5 Qxf3 Nf6 6 d3 e6, and here White can choose between 7 Bd2 Nbd7 8 g4!? and the more solid 7 g3, in either case with chances for both sides.

2...d5

Here we have reached a major crossroad, where White has to choose between **(a) 3 f3** (Fantasy Variation); **(b) 3 exd5** (3 exd5 Lines); **(c) 3 e5** (the Advance Variation); and **(d) 3 Nc3** (Main Lines). **3 Nd2** is also seen rather frequently, but usually transposes to the lines after 3 Nxc3 with 3...dxe4 4 Nxe4.

The only exception is 3...g6, but White is better after 4 Ngf3 Bg7 5 h3 Nh6 6 Bd3 0-0 7 0-0.

The Fantasy Variation

White's sharpest option is undoubtedly the Fantasy Variation, which does not get as much recognition as it possibly deserves and therefore is often ignored by black players, but it can be quite dangerous if Black does not know what he is doing.

3 f3

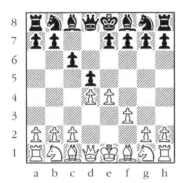

White intends to maintain a strong center by allowing himself the option of taking back on e4 with the f-pawn.

3...e6

Black must tread carefully in this line. There are several alternatives including 3...e5!?, 3...g6 and even 3...dxe4 4 fxe4 (4 Nc3 transposes to a version of the Blackmar-Diemer Gambit) 4...e5, in all cases with very sharp play. The text move is the most solid.

4 Nc3

4 Be3 dxe4 5 Nd2 exf3 6 Ngxf3 Nf6 7 Nc4 Nbd7 is odd version of a Blackmar-

Diemer Gambit, which should not cause Black too many problems.

4...Bb4 5 Bf4 Nf6 6 Qd3 b6 7 Nge2 Ba6 8 Qe3 0-0 9 0-0-0 c5

A very complicated position has arisen, both sides have their share of the chances.

3 exd5 Lines

The play can go in two very different directions in the lines in this section.

3 exd5 cxd5 4 c4

This is the starting position of the Panov-Botvinnik Attack. If White prefers a slower and more positional game, he can instead opt for the Exchange Variation, which arises when White refrains from 4 c4, but rather chooses 4 Bd3 (4 Nf3 and 4 c3 can also be played, transposing) 4...Nc6 5 c3. The position resembles an Exchange Variation of the Queen's Gambit Declined, but with the colors reversed. Black should be doing okay after 5...Nf6 6 Bf4 Bg4 7 Qb3 Qd7 8 Nd2 e6 9 Ngf3 Bxf3 10 Nxf3 Bd6 with more or less equal chances.

4...Nf6 5 Nc3 e6

Black has two good alternatives: **(a) 5...Nc6** 6 Nf3 (another good move is 6 Bg5, but 6...e6 will usually take the play to the main line after 5...e6) 6...Bg4 7 cxd5 Nxd5 8 Qb3 Bxf3 9 gxf3 e6 (Black can avoid the exchanges that follows by playing 9...Nb6, but 10 Be3 e6 11 0-0-0 followed by d4-d5 is pleasant for White) 10 Qxb7 Nxd4 11 Bb5+ Nxb5 12 Qc6+ Ke7 13 Qxb5 Qd7 14 Nxd5+ Qxd5 15 Qxd5 exd5 with an endgame that has been played many times. The current evaluation is that the position is equal, but there is a lot of play left in the position, despite the reduced material; and **(b) 5...g6** involves a pawn sacrifice for Black: 6 Qb3 Bg7 7 cxd5 0-0 8 Be2 Nbd7 9 Bf3 Nb6 10 Nge2 Bf5 11 0-0 Bd3, with a sharp game and chances for both sides; Black's active pieces compensate for the sacrificed pawn.

6 Nf3 Bb4

6...Be7 is a fully playable alternative.

7 cxd5

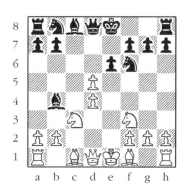

This is hardly White's only move, but the alternatives tend to transpose to other openings, e.g., 7 Bg5 h6 8 Bxf6 Qxf6 9 Qb3 leads to a line in the Queen's Gambit, and 7 Bd3 dxc4 8 Bxc4 0-0 9 0-0

leads to a position that may originate either from Queen's Gambit Accepted or a number of lines in the Nimzo-Indian Rubinstein Complex.

7...Nxd5 8 Bd2 Nc6 9 Bd3 Be7 10 0-0 0-0 11 Qe2 Nf6 and although this position is considered about equal, there is a wealth of play ahead, and very good understanding is required of both players, but Black will need to be particularly vigilant.

The Advance Variation

This variation was for many years considered quite harmless, despite it being played by Tal against Botvinnik in the 1960 world championship match. However, a number of ideas for White, first in the 4 Nc3 lines in the 1980s, and much later in several other lines, gave this line a newfound popularity it had never previously enjoyed.

3 e5 Bf5

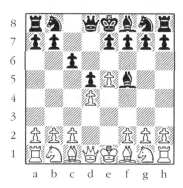

The only alternative for Black is 3...c5, which is best answered by the illogical-looking 4 dxc5 as discovered by Tal.

4 Nf3

Although this line was used countless times before English grandmaster Nigel Short refashioned and refined the strategies behind this move, the variation now bears his name. However, White has many of alternatives at this juncture, the main ones being: **(a) 4 h4** – 4...h5 5 c4 dxc4 6 Bxc4 e6 7 Nc3 Nd7, with a sharp position and about equal chances; **(b) 4 Be3** – 4...e6 5 Nd2 Nd7 6 Be2 c5 7 Ngf3 Rc8 with a sharp battle ahead; **(c) 4 Nd2** looks completely illogical, but became popular after Kramnik used it to defeat Leko in the last, must-win game of their world championship match, allowing Kramnik to level the match score and thus keep his title. Now follows 4...e6 5 Nb3 Nd7 6 Nf3 Ne7 7 Be2 Nc8 (allowing the bishop on f8 to develop) 8 0-0 Be7, and Black will now continue with ...0-0 and then prepare the ...c6-c5 advance, against which White can try to find a suitable plan. The ideas for White include a4-a5, and Nf3-e1-d3. While White has more space, Black's position is solid and he has a clearly defined plan; and **(d) 4 Nc3** – White's sharpest move. It experienced a surge of popularity in the beginning of the 1980s, and while it isn't played as much now as it once was, it remains a popular option for those who like complex and unclear positions. Now 4...e6 (playable alternatives include 4...Qd7, 4...Qb6, 4...a6 and 4...h5) 5 g4 Bg6 6 Nge2 c5 (Black can also consider 6...f6 and 6...Ne7) 7 h4 **(D)**

7...cxd4 (7...h5 8 Nf4 Bh7 9 Nxh5 Nc6 and 7...f6 8 Nf4 Bf7 are considered fine for Black) 8 Nxd4 h5 9 f4 hxg4 10 Bb5+ Nd7 11 f5 Rxh4 12 Rf1, with incredible complications and chances for both sides.

4...e6 5 Be2 Nd7

Black's main alternatives are 5...Ne7 and 5...c5, both of which are fully playable.

6 0-0 Ne7

Here Black has also played 6...Bg6 and 6...h6 with success.

7 Nbd2 Ne7 8 Nb3 Nc8 9 a4 Be7 with another strategically complex line with mutual chances.

Main Lines

With the resurgence of popularity of the Caro-Kann Defense, the volume of theory attached to the main lines has exploded by leaps and bounds, but it is still possible to find minor lines that suit just about any type of player.

3 Nc3 dxe4

As with 3 Nd2, Black can also play 3...g6 at this point, but here too, White obtains the better chances: 4 Nf3 (4 e5 Bg7 5 f4 is also possible) 4...Bg7 5 h3 (preventing a possible ...Bg4) 5...dxe4 (other moves include 5...Nf6 and 5...Nh6) 6 Nxe4 Nd7 7 Bd3 Ngf6 8 0-0.

4 Nxe4

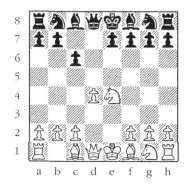

The starting position of the main line Caro-Kann. Play may now go in many directions, each leading to its own type of game.

Nimzowitsch's 4...Nf6

In this line, Black offers to take on a doubled pawn in return for dynamic play. It isn't seen as often as it once was, but it is still fully playable, even if the theory claims a small advantage for White.

4...Nf6 5 Nxf6+

White can also decline the offer to double pawns with 5 Ng3, but then Black has no worries at all.

5...gxf6

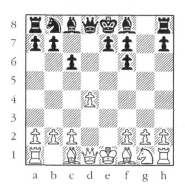

Nimzowitsch also played 5...exf6, which is best met by 6 c3 Bd6 7 Bd3 0-0 8 Qc2 Re8+ 9 Ne2 h6 with chances for both sides. The text move is named the Bronstein-Larsen Variation after the two dynamic players who did a lot to promote this move.

6 c3 Bf5 7 Nf3 e6

Black can also consider 7...Qc7 and 7...Nd7, the former planning queenside castling, the latter kingside castling.

8 g3

Other moves have proved inadequate for an advantage.

8...Qd5 9 Bg2 Qc4 10 Be3 Nd7 11 Nh4 Bg6 12 Nxg6 hxg6 and while Black has prevented White from castling at the moment, the black queen is susceptible to being pushed around a bit. Theory considers White's chances somewhat more favorable.

The Smyslov Variation

Though named after world champion Vassily Smyslov, it was another champion, Anatoly Karpov, who brought it back to the limelight, and it has since been used by many grandmasters, most notably Anand.

4...Nd7 5 Ng5

This move was not played until the late 1980s, but it is currently the main line. Other continuations include 5 Nf3 Ngf6 6 Ng3 e6 7 Bd3 c5 with chances for both players, and the former main line 5 Bc4 Ngf6 6 Ng5 e6 7 Qe2 Nb6 (White threatened 8 Nxf7) 8 Bd3 (8 Bb3 is also possible, e.g., 8...h6 9 N5f3 a5 with about equal chances) 8...h6 9 N5f3 c5 10 dxc5 Bxc5 11 Ne5 Nd7 12 Ngf3 Bc5 with a complicated and approximately equal position.

5...Ngf6 6 Bd3 e6

Black has to be a little careful, e.g., 6...h6 is met by 7 Ne6!.

7 N1f3 Bd6 8 Qe2 h6 9 Ne4 Nxe4 10 Qxe4 Nf6

Another option is 10...Qc7, allowing 11 Qg4, but Black should be fine after 11...Kf8 12 0-0 c5.

11 Qe2 Qc7 12 Bd2 b6 13 0-0-0 Bb7 14 Kb1 0-0-0 and the chances are approximately equal.

The Classical Main Line

Currently this perennial favorite is at its peak of popularity. As with other solid openings, such as the Petroff or the French lines with ...dxe4, White obtains a slight initiative and more space with which to work, but Black's position is solid and full of resources and as such is a perfect way to start a game.

4...Bf5 5 Ng3

White sometimes experiments with Bronstein's 5 Nc5, but Black is fine after 5...b6 6 Nb3 e6 7 Nf3 Bd6.

5...Bg6 6 h4

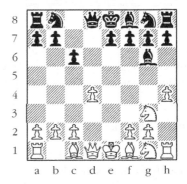

White uses the somewhat exposed position of Black's light-squared bishop to gain some space. He can allow himself to do this because he frequently will castle queenside, and even if the white king ends up on the kingside, the knight on g3 will protect the pawn once it has reached h5.

Other alternatives can be considered by White in this position: **(a) 6 N1e2** (6 Nh3 usually leads to the same position) 6...Nf6 7 Nf4 e5 8 Nxg6 hxg6 9 Be3 Nbd7 is about even; **(b) 6 f4** e6 7 Nf3 Bd6 8 Be2 Ne7, intending ...c5, is also fine for Black; and **(c)** Tal's old favorite **6 Bc4** e6 7 N1e2 was for some time used by both Tiviakov and Rublevsky, but it has been established that Black should be fine, even if the positions become quite complex: 7...Nf6 8 Nf4 Bd6 9 c3 Nbd7 10 Qf3 Nb6 11 Bb3 a5, with chances for both sides.

6...h6 7 Nf3 Nd7

Conventional wisdom suggested that Black should play this move to prevent White from playing his knight to e5 on the next move, but in recent years, Black has with some frequency allowed White that possibility with 7...Nf6!?, hoping to prove that White overextends himself after 8 Ne5 Bh7 9 Bc4 (or 9 Bd3 Bxd3 10 Qxd3 e6 11 Bd2 Nbd7 11 f4 Be7 12 0-0-0 0-0 with a sharp battle ahead) 9...e6 10 Qe2 Nd5 (White threatened 11 Nxf7) 11 Bd2 Nd7 12 0-0-0 Nxe5 13 dxe5 Qc7 14 f4 0-0-0, with another complex position where both sides can expect to play for a win.

8 h5 Bh7 9 Bd3 Bxd3 10 Qxd3 Qc7

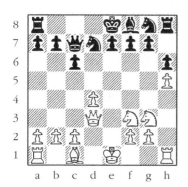

This is not mandatory; Black often plays either 10...e6 or 10...Ngf6, but the lines usually transpose to our main line, e.g., 10...Ngf6 11 Bf4 Qa5+ 12 Bd2 Qc7 (12..Bb4!? provoking 13 c3 Be7 is also playable), reaching a position in the main line, but with an extra move played by each side.

11 Bd2 e6 12 0-0-0 Ngf6 13 Ne4 0-0-0 and we have reached a typical position that has been tested in hundreds of games in the Classical Main Line of the Caro-Kann Defense. White has perhaps a slight advantage, but Black's position is resilient and his long-term prospects are fine. If White overreaches in an attempt to push for a win, Black is poised to strike back.

The Alekhine Defense

The Alekhine is a somewhat provocative, but mostly an ambitious opening, where Black hands over the center and initiative to White at the very beginning of the game, only to start chipping away at it and eventually working to equalize or even take over the initiative. It has never been particularly popular at any level of play, but for those who knows the opening reasonably well, it can be a faithful servant, such as it has been for grandmaster and three-time U.S. Champion Lev Alburt.

1...Nf6 2 e5

If White doesn't want to discuss the Alekhine, then 2 Nc3 is a reasonable alternative, after which 2...d5 keeps the game in the Alekhine, whereas 2...e5 transposes to the Vienna Game.

2...Nd5 3 d4

The "Hunt" variation, 3 c4 Nb6 4 c5 Nd5 4 Bc4, gives Black an adequate position after both 4...e6 and 4...c6, but Black needs to know the theory to stay out of trouble.

3...d6 4 Nf3

This is the solid and sane main line, but White has a couple of interesting alternatives. After 4 c4 Nb6, White can take the game in two different directions:

(a) 5 f4, the Four Pawn Attack, which may look attractive, especially to the inexperienced player. White gains an amazing space advantage, but Black's position is solid, and White's isn't all it appears to be: 5...dxe5 6 fxe5 Nc6 7 Be3 Bf5 8 Nc3 e6 9 Nf3 Be7 with a sharp position and approximately even chances.

(b) 5 exd6 cxd6 (5...exd6 is also playable, leading to a fairly balanced game) 6 Nc3 g6 7 Be3 Bg7 8 Rc1 0-0, with mutual chances.

4...Bg4

Black has several alternatives here. The great Danish grandmaster Bent Larsen provoked the former world champion Mikhail Tal with 4...dxe5 5 Nxe5 Nd7!?, inviting the tactical wizard to sacrifice on f7. Now 40+ years later, the consequences are still unclear. While this line has been seen with some frequency, a more popular line for Black is 5...c6, which was popularized by the British grandmaster Tony Miles, and has been taken up by several grandmasters including the Norwegian grandmaster and *wunderkind* Magnus Carlsen. Black intends to follow up with ...Nd7 with a solid position. While theory gives

White a slight nod, the black position is fully playable.

Some years ago 4...g6 was a much more popular alternative, but White appears to get the better chances after 5 Bc4 Nb6 6 Bb3 Bg7 7 a4 a5 8 Qe2.

5 Be2 e6

Another option is 5...c6.

6 0-0 Be7 7 c4 Nb6 8 h3 Bh5 9 Nc3 0-0 10 Be3 and White has the better chances thanks to his more space and easier mobility of the pieces.

The Scandinavian Defense

1 e4 d5

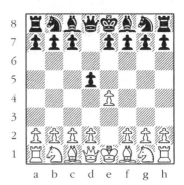

Along with the Alekhine Defense, the Scandinavian Defense, also known as the Center Counter, is one of the most provocative answers to 1 e4.

2 exd5 Qxd5

This is the more popular move. Black exposes his queen to an attack from the knight on b1, but Black claims that the exchange of the central pawns and his easier development compensates for the loss of time spent moving the queen in the opening. Less frequently, Black plays 2...Nf6, hoping to recapture the pawn on d5 with the knight. If White now plays 3 c4, Black can play 3...c6! (3...e6 4 dxe6 Bxe6 5 Nf3 is a sharp, but ultimately unsound gambit), and here 4 dxc6 Nxc6 followed by ...e7-e5 is pleasant for Black thanks to his easy development and control over the d4-square. Therefore White usually plays 4 d4, and after 4...cxd5, we have arrived, by transposition, to a Panov-Botvinnik Attack in the Caro-Kann. White does best to play 3 d4, and after 3...Nxd5 4 Nf3 g6 5 c4 Nb6 6 Nc3 Bg7 7 Be2 0-0 8 0-0 Nc6 9 d5, White has the slightly better chances thanks to his space advantage, but Black's position is solid.

3 Nc3

Attacking the queen makes the most sense, but White frequently plays 3 d4 as well; Black meets this with either 3...Nc6 or 3...e5, both of which lead to approximately equal chances.

3...Qa5

Of Black's available choices, this one remains the most popular, although 3...Qd8 and in particular 3...Qd6 have gained popularity in recent years. One illustrative line runs as follows: 3...Qd6 4 d4 Nf6 5 Nf3 c6 (also 5...a6 and 5...g6 are played in this position, but the text move is a favorite of Dutch grandmaster Sergei Tiviakov, one of the greatest specialists in this line) 6 Ne5 (White often plays 6 g3, but after 6...Bg4 7 Bg2 e6, Black has a solid position) 6...Nbd7 7 Bf4 (or 7 Nc4 Qc7 8 Qf3 Nb6 9 Bf4 Qd7 with, for this variation, a typically strange position where both sides set aside the most fundamental principles

of opening play) 7...Nd5 8 Nxd5 Qxd5 with mutual chances.

4 d4 Nf6 5 Nf3 c6

Black can also play 5...Nc6 or 5...Bg4, both of which are considered insufficient for equal chances, whereas 5...Bf5 usually can be substituted for 5...c6, because these lines tend to transpose.

6 Bc4 Bf5 7 Bd2 e6 8 Qe2

Nowadays White often opts for 8 Nd5 or 8 Ne4, and after 8...Qd8 9 Nxf6+, Black has the opportunity to take back with either the pawn or the queen. In either case, the theory ever-so-slightly favors White, but Black's position is of course fully playable and is indeed seen quite frequently in games between grandmasters.

8...Bb4 9 0-0-0 Nbd7 10 a3 Bxc3 11 Bxc3 Qc7 12 Ne5 Nd5 with more or less even chances.

The Nimzowitsch Defense

This invention of the Danish grandmaster Aron Nimzowitsch has never been particularly popular and, in all fairness, it never will be. However, that doesn't make it a bad opening and there have been many players at nearly all levels of play who have made use of the opening on a regular basis.

1...Nc6 (D)

2 d4

Despite the opening's inferior

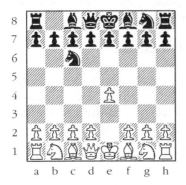

reputation, many players as White opt for 2 Nf3 to steer the game back into normal lines, simply because they don't know the theory. Black can then either choose to play 2...e5, transposing into a classic Open Game; 2...e6, which after 3 d4 d5 will lead to a line in the French; or keep it offbeat, by playing 2...d6, e.g. 3 d4 Nf6 4 Nc3 Bg4 followed by ...e7-e6, which is slightly better for White according to the theoretical manuals, but obviously Black can easily play this without too many headaches.

2...d5

Nimzowitsch himself played this move, but Black can also opt for 2...e5, which is slightly less provocative and was used by the late English grandmaster Tony Miles. White can then choose 3 d5 Nce7 4 Nf3 Ng6, which looks bizarre, but is playable, or 3 dxe5 Nxe5 4 Nf3 Bb4+ 5 c3 Nxf3+ 6 Qxf3 Bc5, and White is at best slightly better.

3 e5

3 Nc3 is a good alternative for White since both 3...dxe4, 3...e5 and 3...Nf6 all lead to a solid plus for White, and therefore Black may have to choose the passive-looking 3...e6, which takes us

to an offbeat line of the French, somewhat favorable for White, yet playable for Black.

3...f6 4 f4 Bf5 5 Ne2 e6 6 Ng3 fxe5 7 fxe5 Qd7 and White has the slightly better chances. There are good several books on the Nimzowitsch Defense, and playing this opening can be lots of fun if you know you way around. Studying it isn't very hard work because the amount of important theory on this opening is very limited.

Unusual Responses to 1 e4

Only rarely played unusual openings remain for us to examine, yet this doesn't mean that they are not being played, even at grandmaster level.

1...a6 was once used by Miles to beat then world champion Anatoly Karpov at the European Team Championship in 1980, but White obtains the better chances with simple, natural moves: 2 d4 b5 3 Bd3 Bb7 4 Nf3 e6 5 Qe2 Nf6 6 a4 with a slightly better game.

1...b6 is called Owen's Defense, and is seen far more frequently than 1...a6. It has been a pet variation of a few contemporary grandmasters. White is considered to be slightly better, because Black's setup is somewhat passive and isn't as flexible as perhaps the Pirc or some of the more solid lines in the Sicilian, but Black's game is fully playable. If Black knows the opening reasonably well, he can easily play it on a regular basis, even against strong opposition. One line runs: 2 d4 Bb7 3 Bd3 (or 3 Nc3 e6 4 a3 Nf6) 3...Nf6 4 Qe2 e6 5 Nf3 c5 6 c3 Be7 with perhaps a tiny edge for White, but certainly nothing to cause Black major concern.

> *Don't look at what was played earlier, but which move is the best in a given position.*

Chapter 7

The Closed Games

The openings that begin with **1 d4 d5** fall into the category of the "Closed Games," yet the name, as was the case with the "Open Games," does not accurately and fairly describe the openings and variations that fall into this category, because they can be just as open, complicated, tactical or closed and boring as the openings in any other category. However, the name is still used as a common label for this group of openings.

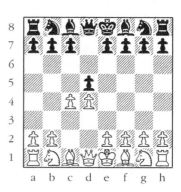

The majority of what follows falls within the Queen's Gambit, arising after **1 d4 d5 2 c4**.

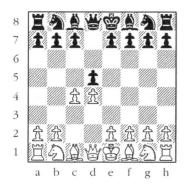

We will sort the material as follows: **(a)** The Queen's Gambit Declined (1 d4 d5 2 c4 e6); **(b)** The Slav (1 d4 d5 2 c4 c6); **(c)** Other Queen's Gambits; **(d)** The Catalan; and **(e)** Offbeat Variations

The Queen's Gambit Declined

1 d4 d5 2 c4

Its designation as a "gambit" notwithstanding, the Queen's Gambit is not really a gambit, because, if White wants the pawn back, it is almost impossible for Black to hold onto it after 2...dxc4. We will discuss the repercussions of the Queen's Gambit Accepted in the third section of this chapter (Other Queen's Gambits).

2...e6

This is the classical answer to White's second move. Black supports the center with the e-pawn, opening the way for the dark-squared bishop, thus getting one step closer to developing the kingside pieces and castling. However, one of the main implications of Black's second move is the fact that the pawn on e6 blocks the path of the c8-bishop, something we have also discussed in the chapter on the French Defense. Depending on the particular line, Black may deal with the issue of the light-squared bishop in a number of ways. Black can play ...b7-b6 and fianchetto the bishop, or, at a later stage, try to break the center open with ...e6-e5, re-opening the diagonal. More about that later.

3 Nc3

Frequently White plays 3 Nf3 first. Often this will only amount to a transposition to lines we will cover after 3 Nc3, but there are a few exceptions. If White wants to play the Catalan, Nc3 is usually avoided, because the knight may not fit into White's plans as we will see later. However, there are also other lines in which this move can wait if White does not like the prospect of facing ...Bb4 from Black or wants to make Black think that the knight may be developed to d2. There can be many reasons for this.

Here we reach the first fork in the road: **(a) 3...c5** (Tarrasch Defense); and **(b) 3...Nf6** (Queen's Gambit Declined, Main Line)

Other moves include 3...c6, which we will cover below in the sub-chapter on the Slav, and 3...Bb4, which is quite rare, whereas 3...Be7 can be used as a transpositional tool to avoid certain lines of the Exchange Variation, while still allowing for the main lines.

The Tarrasch Defense

The German world championship contender and theoretician Siegbert Tarrasch was a man of many principles and in his opinion there was only one correct way to counter the Queen's Gambit, and that was of course with the variation that carried his name.

3...c5

This sharp response immediately challenges White to an all-out battle for the center. It also allows White the opportunity to give Black an isolated

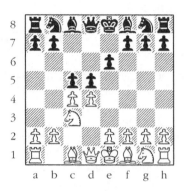

center pawn on d5. It was the opinion of Tarrasch that Black receives fully adequate counterplay as a result of the easy development of his minor pieces. This opening is not as popular as it used to be in the early 1980s when the young Kasparov played it quite frequently.

4 cxd5

The only way for White to truly challenge Black in this variation is to immediately force Black to recapture, creating an isolated d-pawn. Tarrasch, on the other hand, claimed that the natural and best continuation was 4 e3 Nf6 5 Nf3 Nc6 with an equal game, an evaluation which is still valid a century after he introduced this line.

You would now think Black only has one response in this position, but in fact, there are two: the sharp **4...cxd4** (Schara-Hennig Gambit) and the obvious **4...exd5**, recapturing the pawn.

The Schara-Hennig Gambit

This sharp gambit can be very dangerous if White is not properly prepared, as the white queen is drawn out early while the black minor pieces are able to develop rapidly.

4...cxd4 5 Qxd4

Another move is 5 Qa4+, but it will lead to the same position after 5...Bd7 6 Qxd4 exd5 7 Qxd5 Nc6.

5...Nc6 6 Qd1 exd5 7 Qxd5 Bd7

Obviously Black cannot allow White to exchange queens just yet, because with White having already invested three moves with the queen to win a pawn (and it will be forced to move again) Black can gain tempos by developing pieces while at the same time attacking the white queen.

8 Nf3 Nf6 9 Qd1 Bc5 10 e3 Qc7 11 a3 0-0-0 12 Qc2 Kb8

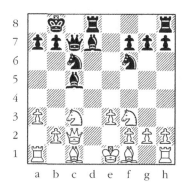

with a sharp, unbalanced position. White's chances are normally considered to be better, but because of Black's lead in development, White has to be quite careful.

The Tarrasch Defense, Main Line

Returning to the main lines of this variation, Black's natural response is...

4...exd5

This position is similar to that of the Panov-Botvinnik Attack in the Caro-Kann Defense, but with colors reversed.

5 Nf3

White has other options such as 5 e4 and 5 dxc5, but neither should pose great problems for Black.

5...Nc6 6 g3

The Polish Grandmaster Akiba Rubinstein first introduced this move. Despite its vintage – it dates back more than 80 years – this variation is considered White's best against the Tarrasch. White aims to block Black's isolated pawn on d5 with a knight on d4 and then target the "weak" pawn on d5 with the knight on c3, the bishop on g2 and heavy pieces on the d-file.

White plays 6 e3 less frequently, reaching a position from the 4 e3 move order mentioned above.

6...Nf6 7 Bg2 Be7 8 0-0 0-0 9 Bg5

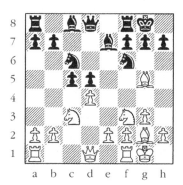

In contrast to the Panov-Botvinnik Attack in the Caro-Kann, White has more aggressive moves available, and Black has to be aware of some defensive considerations. Another popular way for White to play is 9 dxc5 Bxc5 10 Bg5 d4 11 Bxf6 Qxf6 12 Nd5 Qd8 13 Nd2, though it is considered about equal.

9...cxd4 10 Nxd4 h6 11 Be3

Wait a minute, doesn't the bishop block the e-pawn? Sure it does, but for the time being the e-pawn does not need to move because the light-squared bishop is well-placed on g2 and it is far more important that the knight on d4 is supported as it blocks the isolated d-pawn.

11...Re8 12 Rc1 Bf8 13 Nxc6 bxc6 14 Na4 Bd7 15 Bc5

This position has been played many times at grandmaster level, and it is considered a tiny bit better for White because of the blockade of Black's hanging pawn pair on c6 and d5. However, this is the type of position Black has to be willing to play if he wants to sharpen the battle with a Tarrasch Defense.

Queen's Gambit Declined, Main Line

The natural continuation of Black's development is...

3...Nf6

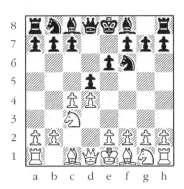

And here White may take the game in several different directions: **(a) 4 cxd5** (the Exchange Variation); **(b) 4 Nf3**; and **(c) 4 Bg5**.

The Exchange Variation

In many openings, exchange variations are considered somewhat boring and perhaps even drawish. Such is the case, for example, in the French Defense, the Ruy Lopez and the Slav. But in the Queen's Gambit Declined, the Exchange Variation is actually a sharp and critical continuation. Its main drawback is that it is not as strategically complex as some of the other main lines, but it can be an effective weapon in the hands of dynamic players and it has enjoyed the support of players with diverse styles, such as Botvinnik, Kasparov and Karpov to mention but a few.

4 cxd5

Some players prefer to wait with this exchange until after the development of some of the minor pieces, but the immediate capture opens for some added possibilities for both sides.

4...exd5 5 Bg5 Be7

Black can also play 5...Nbd7 and 5...c6, both usually transposing to our main line, but there are some finesses such as 5...Nbd7 6 Nf3 Bb4 or 5...c6 6 e3 Bf5, taking the play away from more standard Exchange Variation paths.

6 e3 c6 7 Qc2

This looks a bit odd – why develop the queen so early? The answer lies in the variation 7 Bd3 Ne4 8 Bxe7 Qxe7 with

144

equal chances for Black, whereas after 7 Qc2 Ne4, White wins a pawn after 8 Bxe7 Qxe7 9 Nxd5 because 9...cxd5 allows 10 Qxc8+.

7...Nbd7 8 Bd3 0-0 9 Nf3

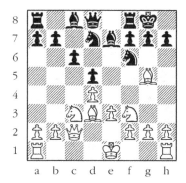

White also has a sharper option available at this point, 9 Nge2 Re8, and now White can choose between castling short, 10 0-0, followed by f2-f3 and eventually e3-e4, or 10 0-0-0 with a pawn storm on the kingside in mind.

9...Re8 10 0-0

Remember White can also consider castling queenside in this line, leading to pawn storms against the respective kings.

10...Nf8

White has played an amazing variety of moves in this position: 11 Rab1 and 11 a3, to start a minority attack on the queenside with b2-b4-b5; 11 Ne5 and 11 Rae1 to play in the center; or 11 h3 to play on the kingside, just to mention some of the most popular continuations. The chances in each of these variations are considered fairly even, but a good understanding of the small differences

and subtleties of each line is very important.

4 Nf3 Variation

White's fourth move in this continuation will often transpose to lines covered below, but there are a couple of variations that are specific to this move order.

4 Nf3 Bb4

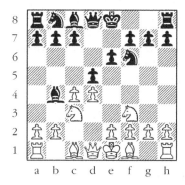

This is the Vienna or Ragozin Variation, depending on how the game continues. Another popular move is 4...Be7, after which 5 Bg5 will take us to the main lines below, but White can play 5 Bf4, which leads to a different type of game, for instance, 5...0-0 6 e3 c5 7 dxc5 Bxc5 8 Qc2 Nc6 9 Rd1 Qa5 10 a3 Be7 with a complicated game and chances for both sides.

5 cxd5

The Vienna Variation is reached after 5 Bg5 dxc4 6 e4 c5. It is very complicated and demands extensive theoretical knowledge. One of the main lines run 7 Bxc4 cxd4 8 Nxd4 Bxc3+ 9 bxc3 Qa5 10 Bb5+ Nbd7 11 Bxf6 Qxc3+ 12 Kf1 gxf6 and White has good compensation for the pawn, but I really recommend against playing lines like this as Black until you have studied the line carefully.

5...exd5 6 Bg5

Note that White does not accomplish anything with 6 Qa4+ Nc6 7 Ne5, as Black can play 7...Bd7, and on 8 Nxc6, Black has 8...Bxc3+ 9 bxc3 Bxc6 available, with a solid position.

6...Nbd7 7 e3 c5 8 Bd3 c4 9 Bf5 Qa5 10 Qc2 0-0 11 0-0 Re8 with an interesting battle ahead. White will primarily try to play in the center and on the kingside, whereas Black will try to control the e4-square and advance his queenside pawns.

Queen's Gambit Declined, Main Line (continued)

4 Bg5 Be7

In the endless sea of variations we will also find that after 4...Nbd7

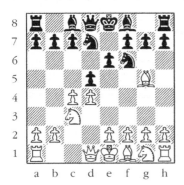

there are independent continuations. First we need to dispel the notion that White will win a pawn after 5 cxd5 exd5 6 Nxd5. This is actually a well-known trap that costs White a piece after

6...Nxd5! 7 Bxd8 Bb4+, and White has no choice but to block the check with his queen, 8 Qd2, and then 8...Bxd2+ 9 Kxd2 Kxd8 follows. Therefore White will usually play 5 e3, and then 5...c6 6 Nf3 Qa5

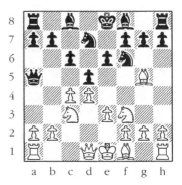

leads to the Cambridge Springs Variation. After 7 cxd5 (after 7 Nd2 bxc4, White has to remember that his bishop on g5 is threatened by the queen on a5) 7...Nxd5 8 Qd2 Bb4 9 Rc1 0-0 10 Bd3 h6 11 Bh4 e5 with chances to both players.

5 e3 0-0 6 Nf3

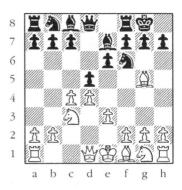

Here Black can go in two directions, the first being a little old fashioned and not seen that often anymore, but it was once very popular: **(a) 6...Nbd7** (Orthodox Variation); **(b) 6....h6** (Neo-Orthodox Variation)

In addition, there are versions of lines that are covered in the Neo-Orthodox section in which Black does not play 6...h6. These lines are 6...b6 and 6...Ne4, and while they are playable, they are considered somewhat more passive than the 6...h6 variation and therefore they are seen much less frequently.

Orthodox Variation

In the first part of the 20th century, the most popular response to the Queen's Gambit was the so-called Orthodox Variation. Black usually does not play ...h7-h6 until later and instead continues with solid development.

6...Nbd7

Black's setup in this variation looks quite passive, but the idea is that Black, at some point, will break in the center with ...dxc4 followed by either ...c6-c5 or ...e6-e5, which Black hopes will result in some exchanges and a good game. However, things are rarely that simple.

7 Rc1

The classical continuation, but White can try to sharpen the game with 7 Qc2. The idea is to castle queenside. If Black now plays 7...h6, then White can consider the piece sacrifice 8 h4!?. Therefore Black usually plays 7...c5, and here White can play 8 0-0-0 with a sharp game, or the more positional 8 cxd5 cxd4 9 Nxd4 Nxd5 10 Bxe7 Nxe7 11 Be2 Nf6 12 0-0 Bd7 with a solid position and perhaps a slight initiative for White because of somewhat more active pieces.

7...c6

Part of the waiting game in this variation; Black wants to play ...dxc4 followed by ...e5 at some point, but wants to wait with the exchange on c4, until White has moved the light-squared bishop to d3. This jousting can be continued if White now plays 8 Qc2, Black replies 8...a6, and then 9 a4 Re8, and only then will White have run out of productive moves and will have to play 10 Bd3.

8 Bd3 dxc4 9 Bxc4 Nd5

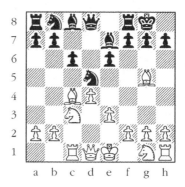

This is named after Capablanca. Black's idea is to exchange the f6-knight for White's knight on c3, and also exchange the dark-squared bishops, making the central break ...e6-e5, easier to accomplish and more effective.

10 Bxe7 Qxe7 11 0-0

Alekhine, who encountered this variation several times as White, occasionally tried 11 Ne4 to avoid the exchange of knights, but nowadays this is not considered a problem for Black.

11...Nxc3 12 Rxc3 e5

Finally Black has achieved the much desired pawn break in the center.

13 dxe5

White can also sharpen the game with 13 Qc2, accepting an isolated pawn after 13...exd4 14 exd4, but 14...Nb6 15 Re3 Qd8 16 Bb3 Nd5 is considered solid, leading to more or less equal chances.

13...Nxe5 14 Nxe5 Qxe5 15 f4 Qe4

This position has been played many times. White will chase Black's queen away with his bishop and then try to advance his e- and f-pawns, whereas Black will create counterplay down the d- and e-files. The chances are considered more or less even, perhaps with a slight pull for White.

Neo-Orthodox

Nowadays Black prefers to play in a more flexible fashion and that includes challenging the white bishop on g5, simultaneously creating a breathing hole for the castled king.

6...h6 7 Bh4

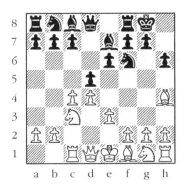

Usually White retreats his bishop, but 7 Bxf6

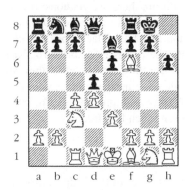

also has been played many times. The type of position that arises is more similar to the Orthodox lines previously discussed: 7...Bxf6 8 Rc1 c6 9 Bd3 Nd7 10 0-0 dxc4 11 Bxc4 e5 12 h3 cxd4 13 exd4 Nb6 14 Bb3 Bf5 15 Re1 Re8 16 Rxe8+ Qxe8 17 Qd2 Qd7 18 Re1 with chances for both sides – Black has the better pawn structure, White the better light-squared bishop. Black now has the choice between two good moves: (a) **7...Ne4** (Lasker Variation); and (b) **7...b6** Tartakower Variation).

The Lasker Variation

This is actually the "Improved" Lasker Variation, because Lasker used to play his line with 6...Ne4 directly.

7...Ne4

The idea behind this move is not unlike Capablanca's method we saw in the section on the Orthodox; Black wants to exchange a pair of knights and the dark-squared bishops.

8 Bxe7 Qxe7 9 cxd5

The exchange on e4 does not accomplish much for White: 9 Nxe4 dxe4

10 Nd2 f5 11 Rc1 Nd7 12 Qc2 c6 13 c5 e5 with chances for both sides. Another and more popular option is 9 Rc1 c6 10 Bd3 Bxc3 11 Rxc3 dxc4 12 Bxc4 Nd7 13 0-0 e5 with a balanced game.

9...Nxc3 10 bxc3 exd5 11 Qb3 Rd8

White has a pawn advantage in the center, but Black has a solid position and the opportunity to develop his pieces to good squares.

12 c4 dxc4 13 Bxc4 Nc6 14 Be2 b6 15 0-0 Bb7 with chances for both sides.

The Tartakower Variation

A dear child has many names, and that is certainly the case for this variation, which is also known as the Bondarevsky System and Makagonov Variation.

7...b6

Rather than waiting for a chance to break in the center with ...e6-e5, Black decides to fianchetto his bishop on b7 or even put it on a6 in some variations. This line is quite solid, but also offers Black a good position from which he can play for a win, if White is not careful.

It has been included in the repertoires of numerous grandmasters and even world champions, including both Karpov and Spassky, who lost a famous game in this variation in his 1972 match against Fischer.

8 Be2

This is just one of many continuations available to White; other options include 8 Bxf6, 8 Qc2, 8 Qb3, 8 Rc1, 8 Bd3 and 8 cxd5.

8...Bb7 9 Bxf6

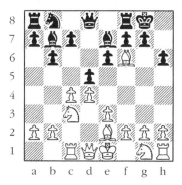

Sometimes chess openings seem quite contradictory, and this certainly falls into that category. Why did White play Bh4 a few moves ago only to exchange the bishop voluntarily a couple of moves later? Circumstances decide which moves are better, and the position has changed considerably since White retreated the bishop on move 7; the point behind this move will soon become evident.

9...Bxf6 10 cxd5 exd5

White played 9 Bxf6 to force Black to play this move. If White had not exchanged on f6, but instead played 9 cxd5, Black would have played 9...Nxd5 with a pleasant position. Now, on the other hand, the pawn on d5 limits the scope of the light-squared bishop on b7.

11 b4 c6

What is the point of this move? As if the d5-pawn were not already restricted enough, Black now puts another pawn on the diagonal. Black wants to play ...a7-a5 to challenge the white pawn on b4, but the immediate 11...a5 is met by 12 b5 with a better game for White, as he can apply pressure on the c-file against Black's backward c-pawn.

12 0-0 Re8 13 Qb3 a5 14 bxa5 Rxa5 with a balanced game and chances for both players.

The Slav

In recent years, many of the openings covered in this section have become among the most popular lines in all of chess opening theory, and as a result several lines have developed with breathtaking speed. The Slav has been a popular opening for decades; for example it was the battleground in the 1935 world championship match between Alekhine and Euwe and again as recently as the 2006 world championship match, where it almost seemed like there was a rule that the players had to play the Slav!

1 d4 d5 2 c4 c6

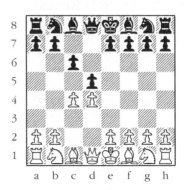

In many ways this is the most solid response for Black against the Queen's Gambit. Now White has a number of very different choices: **(a) 3 cxd5 cxd5** (The Exchange Variation); **(b) 3 Nf3 Nf6 4 Nc3 dxc4** (The Main Line Slav); **(c) 3 Nf3 Nf6 4 Nc3 e6 5 e3** (The Meran); **(d) 3 Nf3 Nf6 4 Nc3 e6 5 Bg5** (The Semi-Slav and Anti-Meran)**;** and **(e) Slav Specialties**.

The Exchange Variation

Many chessplayers who play the Slav as Black dread facing the Exchange Variation. It can be excessively boring if White so desires, but the other hand, if both sides play for a win, it can rapidly develop into an interesting battle.

3 cxd5 cxd5 4 Nc3

As someone who has played this opening regularly, I think this move is more accurate than 4 Nf3, because 4 Nc3 limits Black's options somewhat and adds some extra possibilities for White.

4...Nf6

On the immediate 4...Nc6, White can consider 5 e4!? with a sharp game.

However, in a similar fashion, Black can also consider the sharp 4...e5 at this juncture.

5 Bf4

Again it is a matter of taste which move is better here. On 5 Nf3, players like Kramnik have tried 5...Ne4, and in other lines Black can play ...Bg4, pinning the knight on f3. Therefore the development of the bishop is the normal move for White.

5...Nc6 6 e3 a6

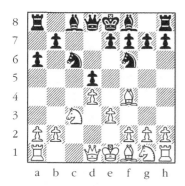

Another main line is 6...Bf5 7 Nf3 e6, and if White lacks ambition to play for a win, he can play as many others have done in the past, 8 Bd3 Bxd3 9 Qxd3 Bd6 10 Bxd6 Qxd6, and a draw is usually soon agreed. However, both 8 Ne5 and 8 Bb5 are worthwhile continuations with interesting possibilities for both players.

7 Bd3 Bg4 8 f3!?

This is the reason why White held back the knight on g1. Now the bishop has to move again and White will play Nge2, working for a central break, a kingside attack or even infiltration on the queenside. This is the reason why the Slav Exchange Variation is more popular than many other exchange variations: it is far more than just a one-trick pony.

8...Bh5 9 Nge2 e6 10 Rc1 Bg6 11 0-0 Be7 and both sides have chances in the battle ahead.

The Main Line Slav

1 d4 d5 2 c4 c6 3 Nf3 Nf6 4 Nc3 dxc4

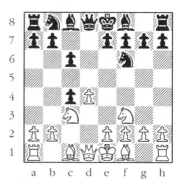

While Black is certainly better equipped to protect the pawn in this position than in the Queen's Gambit Accepted, White can still regain the pawn with ease. However, White will have to make a positional concession which compensates Black for having conceded White a pawn majority in the center.

5 a4

The so-called Alapin Variation. With the last move, White prevents Black from playing ...b7-b5, holding on to the c4-pawn. In the sharp Geller Gambit, 5 e4, White intends to prove that the broad center is more valuable than the pawn on c4. Current praxis does not support White's claim after 5...b5 6 e5 Nd5 7 a4 e6 8 axb5 Nxc3 9 bxc3 cxb5 10 Ng5 Bb7

151

11 Qh5 g6 12 Qg4 Be7 13 Be2 Bd5, and Black has stabilized his position, retaining the extra pawn.

Another option is 5 e3, which also allows Black to play 5...b5, but here White can regain the pawn after 6 a4 b4 7 Na2 e6 8 Bxc4 Bb4, and the chances are about even.

5...Bf5

This was established as Black's main move a long time ago, but nevertheless Black has two good and solid alternatives: 5...Na6 6 e4 Bg4 7 Bxc4 e6 8 Be3 Be7 9 0-0 and 5...Bg4 6 Ne5 Bh5 7 g3 e6 8 Bg2 Bb4 9 0-0 0-0 10 Nxc4, in both cases with at best a tiny advantage for White.

6 e3

After this move, the players will head for a solid position that has been played thousands of times. But White has a much sharper alternative in 6 Ne5!?.

White wants to recapture the c4-pawn with the knight and also play f2-f3 and e2-e4, creating a broad center and harassing the bishop on f5. These lines have received a lot of attention over the last couple of decades. Now Black can take the game in two directions. In the first, Black sacrifices a piece after 6...e6 7 f3 Bb4 8 e4 Bxe4 9 fxe4 Nxe4 10 Bd2 Qxd4 11 Nxe4 Qxe4 12 Qe2 Bxd2+ 13 Kxd2 Qd5+ 14 Kc2 Na6 15 Nxc4 0-0-0 with a complicated game. Black has three pawns for the piece and the white king has yet to find a safe place to settle. The second option is 6...Nbd7 7 Nxc4 Qc7 8 g3 e5 9 dxe5 Nxe5 10 Bf4 Nfd7 11 Bg2, and now Black can choose between the ultra-sharp 11...g5 and the somewhat more solid 11...f6 12 0-0 Nc5 13 Ne3 Bg6, and in either case the players really need to have studied the theory and the latest developments carefully.

6...e6 7 Bxc4 Bb4 8 0-0 0-0 9 Qe2

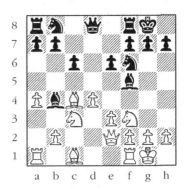

White can also consider eliminating Black's light-squared bishop with 9 Nh4, but 9...Nbd7 10 Nxf5 exf5 11 Qc2 g6 is considered fine for Black.

9...Nbd7 10 e4 Bg6 11 Bd3 Bh5 12 e5 Nd5

White has once again managed to establish a nice looking center and a spatial advantage, but Black's position is solid and should not be a cause for concern.

The Meran

The variations covered in this and the following section are currently extremely popular.

3 Nf3 Nf6 4 Nc3 e6

One of the strongest players in the world before World War I was the Polish grandmaster Akiba Rubinstein, who introduced this opening for Black in 1924 in a tournament in Merano, Italy, and from there it has retained its name.

5 e3

White protects his pawn on c4, before continuing his further development. As we will see in the following section, Black will otherwise take the pawn and hold on to it. White can also play 5 Qb3, but this is normally considered fine for Black after 5...dxc4 6 Qxc4 b5 7 Qd3 Nbd7 8 g3 Bb7.

The sharp 5 Bg5 is covered in the next section.

5...Nbd7 6 Bd3

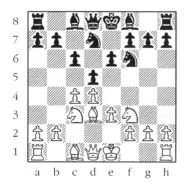

While this is the most popular move for White, another move, 6 Qc2, has also received a lot of attention. The idea is to stay clear of the heavily-analyzed main lines and just play chess. However, because of the popularity of the Meran, these lines have also seen a lot of top-level games. Black now usually plays 6...Bd6, after which White can consider the sharp 7 g4 with the idea 7...Nxg4 8 Rg1 and White will win the g7-pawn. Also worth consideration are the more normal continuations such as 7 Be2, 7 Bd2, 7 b3 and 7 Bd3. There is quite a bit of theory for all of these lines and the chances are considered more or less even, although there is plenty to study.

6...dxc4

As we saw in the Orthodox Queen's Gambit Declined, Black is ready to make this exchange once White has developed bishop to d3. Black can also play 6...Bd6 or 6...Be7, but these lines are a little more passive and not seen as frequently.

7 Bxc4 b5 8 Bd3

This square is undoubtedly the best for the bishop because from d3 it can support the advance of the e-pawn, even if the knight on c3 should get kicked away when Black plays ...b5-b4. Two other moves which also deserve attention are 8 Bb3 and 8 Be2, both of which get played from time to time, but are considered less critical.

8...a6

Black supports the b5-pawn one more time in order to prepare the ...c6-c5 counter-stroke against White's center. Other moves include 8...b4, 8...Bb7 and 8...Bd6.

9 e4 c5

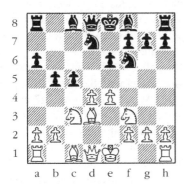

Black has to strike back in the center immediately. When the battle gets so intense so early in the game, with both sides not yet fully developed and both kings are still in the center, the complications are bound to be considerable and rather confusing.

10 d5

Another popular continuation is 10 e5 cxd4 11 Nxb5 Nxe5 (it is possible to capture the knight on b5: 11...axb5, but after 12 exf6 Qb6 13 0-0 gxf6 we have another complicated position) 12 Nxe5 axb5, and here one continuation runs 13 Bxb5+ Bd7 14 Nxd7 Qa5+ 15 Bd2 Qxb5 16 Nxf8 Rxf8 with a double-edged position. The text move, 10 d5, has superseded 10 e5 in popularity, but this can of course change again.

10...c4 11 dxe6 fxe6

The alternative is 11...Bxd3 12 exd7+ Qxd7 13 0-0 Bb7 14 Re1 Be7 15 e5 Nd5 16 Ne4 0-0 with complications and chances for both players.

12 Bc2 Bb7 13 0-0 Qc7 14 Nd4 Nc5 15 Be3 e5 and here White has tried both

16 Nf5 and 16 Nf3 several times in top grandmaster games. It appears that Black is doing fine in these lines, though it should be noted that the theory runs several moves deeper and the game quickly becomes even more complicated.

The Semi-Slav – Anti-Meran

One of the most eagerly debated and most complicated openings of today is the Anti-Meran. In these lines, both sides seem eager to sacrifice material, mostly pawns, for different types of dynamic compensation. Venturing into these lines unprepared against a knowledgeable opponent is asking for trouble.

1 d4 d5 2 c4 c6 3 Nf3 Nf6 4 Nc3 e6 5 Bg5

White is daring Black to take the pawn on c4, the capture of which would be answered by e2-e4 with a strong center for White.

5...dxc4

Black does it anyway. It was Botvinnik who first determined that Black can get away with this indiscretion. The main alternative for Black is the more solid 5...h6,

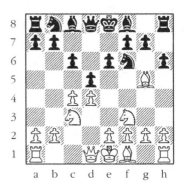

the Moscow Variation. After 6 Bxf6 Qxf6 7 e3 Nd7 8 Bd3 dxc4 9 Bxc4 g6 10 0-0 Bg7 11 Rc1 0-0, the position reminds us somewhat of a regular Orthodox Queen's Gambit. Black has a solid, but somewhat passive position, and the chances are considered more or less equal. Therefore in recent years a sharp alternative has been revived for White, 6 Bh4, the so-called Anti-Moscow Gambit. It is constantly being re-evaluated, so it is difficult to say who currently holds the theoretical upper hand, but one line runs 6...dxc4 7 e4 g5 8 Bg3 b5 9 Be2 Bb7 10 0-0 Nbd7 11 Ne5 Bg7.

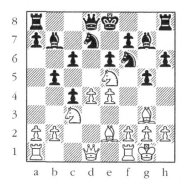

Now the main line continues 12 Nxd7 Nxd7 13 Bd6 a6 with complications where White has adequate compensation for the pawn on account of Black's king not having a safe home and White having a nice pawn center.

It is worth noting, that the Moscow Variation and the Anti-Moscow Gambit are primarily played by very strong players; their popularity has yet to trickle down to the level of club players.

6 e4 b5 7 e5

At first glance, this looks problematic for Black, but there is a solution to the problem...

7...h6 8 Bh4 g5

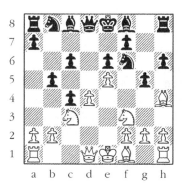

9 Nxg5

White often plays 9 exf6 as well, e.g., 9...gxh4 10 Ne5 Qxf6 with chances for both sides.

9...hxg5 10 Bxg5

Thanks to the pin, White immediately wins the piece back.

10...Nbd7 11 exf6 Bb7

Black isn't necessarily interested in taking the pawn back on f6 since it only renews the pin on the diagonal, and Black should normally be able to regain the pawn later anyway.

12 g3 c5 13 d5 Nxf6

Needless to say, this position is very sharp with mutual chances.

Slav Specialties

In addition the many main lines just discussed, there are a number of other lines that have also been popular with players who are not inclined to engage in a duel over the latest cutting-edge theory in super-sharp lines. In this section, we will take a brief look at some of these lines:

1 d4 d5 2 c4 c6

And now we look at: **(a) 3 Nf3 Nf6 4 Nc3 a6** (The Chebanenko Variation); **(b) 3 Nf3 Nf6 4 e3 Bf5**; **(c) 3 Nc3 e6 4 Nc3 dxc4** (The Noteboom Variation); and **(d) 3 Nc3 e6 4 e4** (The Marshall Gambit)

The Chebanenko Variation

Two decades ago, this line was almost unknown, but it has gained a lot of popularity and is now regularly featured in the repertoires of some of the strongest players. One of its main attractions is that it still is relatively unknown and unusual compared to the main variations of the Slav, despite the fact that entire books have been devoted to this line.

3 Nf3 Nf6 4 Nc3 a6

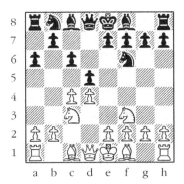

This peculiar looking move has gone from being completely unknown before the 1970s to becoming one of the most popular answers to the Queen's Gambit. Black's idea is to play ...b7-b5 and grab space on the queenside, while at the same time, White has be aware of the

possibility of Black playing ...dxc4 when the supporting move ...b7-b5 can result in Black winning a pawn. Other versions of the ...a6 Slav arise after 1 d4 d5 2 c4 c6 3 Nf3 Nf6 4 e3 a6 and 1 d4 d5 2 c4 c6 3 Nc3 Nf6 4 e3 a6.

5 c5!?

You should usually refrain from playing moves like this, because once your opponent plays ...e7-e5 (or e2-e4 with the colors reversed), the pawn center can become very loose and weak. However, in this case, it has been established that White can normally prevent Black from making the pawn break. Aside from the main move, White has played just about every other legal move in this position, though only a few are considered challenging for Black: 5 a4, 5 e3 and 5 Ne5, with all of them having a fairly large body of theory to support them.

5...Nbd7 6 Bf4

As mentioned above, White has to careful to prevent Black from play ...e7-e5.

6...Nh5 7 Bg5 h6 8 Bd2 Nhf6 9 Qc2

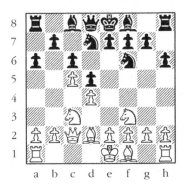

White can also play 9 Bf4 again, and after 9...Nh5, the bishop will go to e5: 10 Be5 Nxe5 11 Nxe5 Nf6 12 e4 Be6 with a complicated game and chances for both sides.

9...Qc7 10 e4 dxe4 11 Nxe4 Nxe4 12 Qxe4 Nf6 13 Qc2 Be6 14 Bd3 and White is considered to be slightly better in this line, but it is a line which is in continuous development and therefore the evaluation is in a constant state of flux.

The 4 e3 Bf5 Variation

The solid 4 e3 prevents the Slav lines with ...dxc4, but restricts the development of the dark-squared bishop.

4...Bf5

With the knight on f3, this line is considered a solid choice, but note that after 3 Nc3 Nf6 4 e3, 4...Bf5 is considered dubious: 5 cxd5 cxd5?! (5...Nxd5 is considered safer, but also better for White) 6 Qb3 Bc8 (6...Qb6 loses a pawn to 7 Nxd5 and 6...Qd7 7 Nf3 Nc6 8 Ne5 Qc7 9 Bb5 is very good for White) 7 Nf3 e6 8 Ne5 Be7 9 Bd3 and White is clearly better. Black can also consider 4...a6, 4...e6, 4...Bg4 and even 4...g6.

5 Nc3 e6 6 Bd3 (D)

Rather than offering the even exchange of bishops, White can also try 6 Nh4, though Black can meet it with 6...Bg4, 6...Bg6 or 6...Be4.

6...Bxd3 7 Qxd3 Nbd7 8 0-0 Be7 9 e4 dxe4 10 Nxe4 Nxe4 11 Qxe4 0-0 and though White has more space, the chances are fairly even.

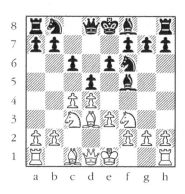

The Noteboom Variation

The sharp Noteboom is an attempt by Black to unbalance the game right from the outset.

3 Nc3 e6 4 Nf3 dxc4

For the time being Black wins a pawn, but it cannot be safely held.

5 a4 Bb4 6 e3 b5 7 Bd2 a5 8 axb5 Bxc3 9 Bxc3 cxb5 10 b3

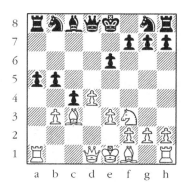

The consequences of Black's opening play – only developing the dark-squared bishop and otherwise making pawn moves – now becomes evident. White wins the pawn back, has more central pawns and a lead in development. Yet

157

matters are not entirely clear as Black has two connected passed pawns on the queenside.

10...Bb7 11 bxc4 b4 12 Bb2 Nf6 13 Bd3 Nbd7 14 0-0 0-0 with a complicated struggle ahead.

The Marshall Gambit

Rather than allowing the Noteboom Variation, White has a sharp response, sacrificing a pawn.

3 Nc3 e6 4 e4!?

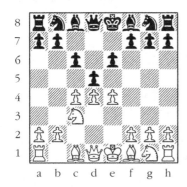

White takes advantage of Black's knight not yet being developed to f6.

4...dxe4 5 Nxe4 Bb4+ 6 Bd2 Qxd4 7 Bxb4 Qxe4+

Black has won a pawn, but at the same time, Black's position has been weakened by the absence of the dark-squared bishop. This often means that castling kingside is out of the question. White will try to show that Black's early queen sortie along with other undeveloped pieces creates an unsafe situation for the black king. Black on the other hand has won a pawn and will try to develop pieces, get his king to safety, possibly on the queenside, and then start consolidating.

8 Be2 Na6 9 Bc3 Ne7 10 Bxg7 Rg8 11 Bf6 Qf4 12 Bxe7 Kxe7 and White has won his pawn back and the game remains complicated. This line can be very dangerous for both sides and should be studied carefully by both players as otherwise the consequences could be disastrous.

Other Queen's Gambits

1 d4 d5 2 c4

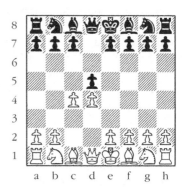

In addition to the Queen's Gambit Declined lines already discussed, there are several other options, sharp and solid, that are playable for Black: **(a) 2...dxc4** (Queen's Gambit Accepted); **(b) 2...e5** (Albin Counter Gambit); **(c)**

2...Bf5 (Baltic Defense); and **(d) 2...Nc6** (Chigorin Defense).

Queen's Gambit Accepted

By accepting the Queen's Gambit, Black does not have any illusions about actually being able to hang on to the pawn. For starters, White can win it back immediately with 3 Qa4+, though this move is considered harmless for Black.

1 d4 d5 2 c4 dxc4

The Queen's Gambit Accepted is Black's most solid alternative to the main lines, and has been used by a number of the strongest players over the years, including Kramnik, Kasparov and Karpov, to mention but a few.

3 Nf3

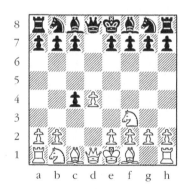

White can continue in a number of ways, but this is the most common. An obvious alternative is 3 e4, which lays claim to the center. Black can meet this move in several ways, for example 3...e5 (other popular moves are 3...Nf6 and 3...Nc6; both are considered to lead to approximately even chances) 4 Nf3 exd4

5 Bxc4 Bb4+ 6 Nbd2 Nc6 7 0-0 Nf6 8 e5 Nd5 9 Nb3, and White will soon win the d-pawn back with perhaps a slightly better game.

3...Nf6

Again Black can consider the alternatives: 3...c5 4 d5 Nf6 5 Nc3 e6 6 e4 leads to a complicated position, which is a bit better for White. Then there are the attempts to hold the pawn: 3...b5 4 a4 c6 5 e3 e6 6 axb5 cxb5 7 b3 (this move was also seen in the Noteboom Variation as a method to win back the pawn – keep it in mind) 7...Bb4+ 8 Bd2 Bxd2+ 9 Nbxd2 a5 10 bxc4 b4, and with his good center, White is slightly better; or 3...a6 4 e4 b5 5 a4 Bb7 6 axb5 axb5 7 Rxa8 Bxa8 8 Nc3 e6 9 Nxb5 Bxe4 10 Bxc4 Nf6 with chances for both players.

4 e3 e6 5 Bxc4 c5 6 0-0

Another popular option for White is 6 Qe2, aiming for a different type of game, e.g., 6...a6 7 dxc5 Bxc5 8 e4 Nc6 9 0-0 with sharp play.

6...a6 7 Qe2

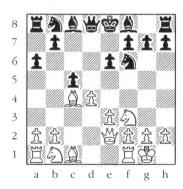

If White is not keen on allowing Black

queenside expansion with ...b7-b5, White can play 7 a4, which however, weakens the b4-square considerably; after 7...Nc6 8 Qe2 cxd4 9 Rd1 Be7 10 exd4 0-0 11 Nc3 Nd5 12 Bd3, a sharp position has arisen with chances for both sides.

7...b5 8 Bb3

This is the more common move for White, but 8 Bd3 is also fully acceptable, for instance, 8...cxd4 9 exd4 Be7 10 a4 bxa4 11 Rxa4 0-0 12 Nc3 Bb7 13 Rd1 with a double-edged position.

8...Bb7 9 Rd1

9 a4 b4 10 Nbd2 Be7 can also be considered.

9...Nbd7 10 Nc3 Qc7 with mutual chances.

The Albin Counter-Gambit

One of the sharpest answers to Queen's Gambit is the Albin Counter-Gambit. It has never had a large following at the highest levels, but a strong player like Morozevich has used it as a surprise weapon on several occasions.

1 d4 d5 2 c4 e5

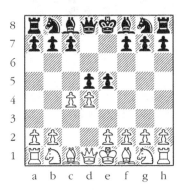

A full-blown charge against White's center, trying to show that White has weakened his position with 2 c4!

3 dxe5 d4!

Black takes the c3-square away from White's knight, making Bb4+ more potent at a later stage.

4 Nf3 Nc6 5 g3 Bg4 6 Bg2 Qd7 7 Nbd2 0-0-0 8 0-0 and White is supposed to be better, though it is worth remembering that Black has some compensation for the pawn as a result of the possibility of a potential kingside attack, and Black may in fact be able to win back the gambit pawn with ..Ng8-e7-g6. White should focus on getting a queenside attack rolling as soon as possible.

The Baltic Defense

This line enjoyed a brief popularity in the late 1980s and early 1990s, but is still seen as a surprise weapon in some strong players' repertoires.

1 d4 d5 2 c4 Bf5

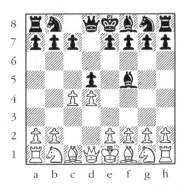

A somewhat safer version for Black is 2 Nf3 Bf5 3 c4, where White does not have some of the sharper continuations available. After 3...e6 4 Nc3 Nc6 (4...c6 takes the game to a variation of the Slav Defense that is also fully playable for Black) 5 Bf4 Nf6 6 e3, and now both 6...Be7 and 6...Nb4 7 Rc1 dxc4 8 Bxc4 c6, intending 9...Nbd5 is playable for Black, though somewhat better for White.

3 cxd5

Another option is 3 Nc3 e6, and now 4 Qb3 and 4 cxd5 exd5 5 Qb3 are both met by the sharp response ...Nc6 with chances for both sides. Similarly 3 Qb3 can be answered by 3...e5 leading to hair-raising complications that should not be entered unless studied carefully before a game.

3...Bxb1

This is necessary because if 3...Qxd5, there follows 4 Nc3 and e2-e4 with a clearly better game for White.

4 Qa4+!

The intermediary check helps to take the sting out of Black's counterplay although 4 Rxb1 has been played by several grandmasters too, but 4...Qxd5 5 a3 Nc6 6 e3 seems fine for Black.

4...c6 5 Rxb1 Qxd5 6 Nf3

White can also consider the sharp 6 f3, intending e2-e4, and the developing 6 e3.

6...Nd7 7 a3

And White intends to continue development with 8 e3, develop the kingside bishop to e2 and then initiate queenside

play. Black's play is a little awkward thanks to the early development of the queen.

The Chigorin Defense

Even more provocative than the Albin is the Chigorin Defense is the Chigorin, named after its inventor, the Russian grandmaster Mikhail Chigorin, one of the strongest players of the late 19th century.

1 d4 d5 2 c4 Nc6

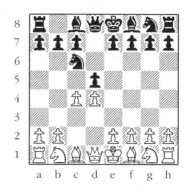

Black aims for quick development of his pieces at the cost of conceding the center and in many lines, the bishop pair to White.

3 Nf3 Bg4 4 cxd5 Bxf3 5 gxf3 Qxd5 6 e3 e5 7 Nc3 Bb4

Necessary.

8 Bd2 Bxc3 9 bxc3 exd4 10 cxd4 and White has the slightly better chances.

The Catalan

Some openings are seen quite often at top level, but hardly ever at lower levels of play. The Catalan is one such opening.

1 d4 d5 2 c4 e6 3 g3

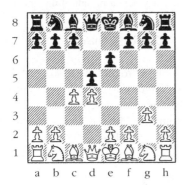

Another move order is 1 d4 Nf6 2 c4 e6 3 g3 d5. White aims to put pressure on Black's queenside restricting Black's development. Now we have **(a) 3...Nf6 4 Nf3 dxc4** (The Open Variation); and **(b) 3...Nf6 4 Nf3 Be7 5 Bg2 0-0 6 0-0** (The Closed Variation).

The Open Variation

The line usually preferred by top players is the Open Variation, which allows Black a number of options, including trying to hang on to the pawn.

3...Nf6 4 Nf3 dxc4

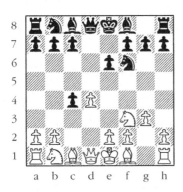

As in the Queen's Gambit Accepted, Black should not hope to keep the pawn just captured, although it may be held if White allows it.

5 Bg2 Be7

Black has a number of other continuations available, e.g., 5...c5 6 0-0 Nc6, 5...a6, 5...Nc6, 5...Bd7, 5...Nbd7 and 5...Bb4+ to mention some of the more usual moves.

6 0-0 0-0 7 Qc2 a6 8 Qxc4

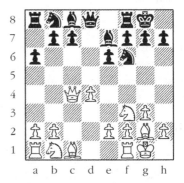

White can also try to restrict Black with 8 a4, but after 8...Bd7 9 Qxc4 Bc6 10 Bg5 Bd5 11 Qd3 c5 the chances are approximately even.

8...b5 9 Qc2 Bb7 10 Bd2 Be4

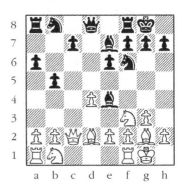

Over the years, this move has been

established as the main line, but Black frequently also plays 10...Nc6 11 e3 Nb4, or even the peculiar-looking 10...Ra7, intending 11 Rfc1 Be4.

11 Qc1 Nbd7

Black can also invite a draw by repetition with 11...Bb7, and now of course 12 Qc2 Be4 is the path to splitting the point, but usually White goes in for 12 Bf4 or 12 Rd1 and the game continues.

12 Ba5 Rc8 13 Nbd2 Ba8 with chances for both sides.

The Closed Variation

While the Open Variation can lead to over-analyzed lines, the Closed Variation leads to a slower maneuvering game, where the player with the better understanding of the game often prevails.

3...Nf6 4 Nf3 Be7 5 Bg2 0-0 6 0-0

As in the Orthodox Queen's Gambit, Black has to find a way to develop the light-squared bishop. This is usually accomplished by fianchettoing it to b7.

6...Nbd7 7 Qc2 c6 8 Rd1 b6 9 Bf4 Bb7 10 Nc3 Rc8

Black prepares to break in the center with ...c6-c5. This position and ones like it are more or less equal, but there is plenty of play, as well as room for mistakes for both sides.

Offbeat Variations

Many of the lines discussed below can also arise via various move orders.

1 d4 d5

And now we have quite a choice of lines, from the unsound, to the sharp, and to solid: **(a) 2 e4** (Blackmar-Diemer Gambit); **(b) 2 Nf3 Nf6 3 e3** (Colle System); **(c) 2 Bg5** (Pseudo-Trompowsky); and **(d) 2 Nc3**.

The Blackmar-Diemer Gambit

There are some openings that are quite feared at lower levels, and this is one of them. At the higher levels, it is not regarded as equalizing for White.

1 d4 d5 2 e4 dxe4 3 Nc3 Nf6 4 f3

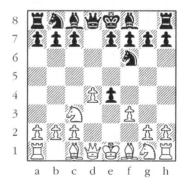

This is the starting position of the Blackmar-Diemer Gambit. Several books have been written about this opening, but generally by enthusiasts who are not particularly strong and therefore the coverage is heavily biased in favor of White's chances.

4...exf3 5 Nxf3

The so-called Ryder Gambit 5 Qxf3? is just bad after 5...Qxd4 6 Be3 Qg4! 7 Qf2 e5, and Black has two extra pawns and White no real compensation.

5...e6 6 Bg5 Be7 7 Qd2 0-0 8 Bd3 c5 9 Qf4 cxd4 10 Qh4 and here Gallagher has recommended 10...g6! 11 Nxd4 Nd5 12 Bxe7 Qxe7 13 Qxe7 Nxe7, and White does not have sufficient compensation for the pawn.

The Colle System

In its original form, the Colle is fairly harmless, but in some of its incarnations, it carries a bit more of a punch.

1 d4 d5 2 Nf3 Nf6 3 e3

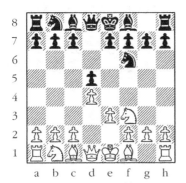

This does not appear either logical or particularly dangerous for Black. But if the move order is somewhat different, it can be both, e.g., 1 d4 Nf6 2 Nf3 e6 3 e3 c5 4 Bd3 Be7 5 0-0 Nc6 and now both

6 c3 and 6 b3 have been played, even at fairly high levels of competition

3...e6

Black can also try to take advantage of White's slow setup and play 3...Bf5.

4 Bd3 c5 5 b3

The original Colle System had White playing 5 c3, but Black is fine after 5...Nc6 6 Nbd2 Bd6 7 0-0 0-0 8 Re1 e5.

5...Nc6 6 Bb2 Bd6 7 0-0 0-0 8 Nbd2 b6 9 Ne5 Bb7 10 a3 Ne7 11 f4 Ne4 with mutual chances.

The Pseudo-Trompowsky

With the Trompowsky gaining popularity by leaps and bounds, Black needed to find a good way to play against 1 d4 d5. With the Pseudo-Trompowsky, White may have found a new wrinkle.

1 d4 d5 2 Bg5

White plays the bishop to g5, attacking the "shadow" of the black knight. This line has been developed by several English grandmasters, primarily Julian Hodgson, after whom this line is often

named. Black has established several ways to obtain a pleasant position.

2...h6 3 Bh4 c6 4 e3 Qb6 5 Qc1

White often also plays 5 b3, but Black can use the same method as in our main line to get a good game: 5...Bf5 6 Nf3 e6 7 Bd3 Bxd3 8 Qxd3 Nd7 9 0-0 Be7 10 Bxe7 Nxe7, and Black has nothing to worry about.

5...Bf5 6 Nf3 e6 7 Be2 Nd7 8 Be2 Be7 9 Bxe7 Nxe7 10 c4 0-0 with a solid position and fairly even chances.

2 Nc3 Variations

The lines in this section are decidedly unorthodox in the sense that the knight on c3 blocks the advance of the c-pawn, contradicting conventional opening wisdom. While perfectly playable, the lines don't enjoy a widespread popularity at the higher levels of play, but they are seen frequently at lower levels.

1 d4 d5 2 Nc3 Nf6

and now **(a) 3 Bf4**; and **(b) 3 Bg5** (Richter-Veresov Attack).

The 3 Bf4 System

This variation tends to lead to a setup called the Barry Attack.

3 Bf4 g6 4 Nf3

The starting position of the Barry Attack has been reached. Black can obviously play other third moves such as 3...Bf5 and 3...c6, with even chances.

4...Bg7 5 e3

5 Qd2 is also a popular alternative.

5...0-0 6 Be2 c6

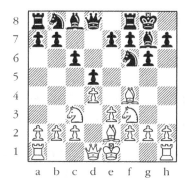

Black can also consider 6...c5 and 6...b6.

7 h3 Nbd7 8 a4 a5 9 0-0 b6 10 Bh2 Bb7 11 Ne5 e6 with mutual chances.

The Richter-Veresov Attack

While overall less popular than the 3 Bf4 line, the Richter-Veresov has been covered more frequently in monographs. As with the previous line, Black has several adequate answers.

> *You should not automatically play the rooks the d- and e-files because the pawn structure may dictate something entirely different.*

165

3 Bg5 Nbd7

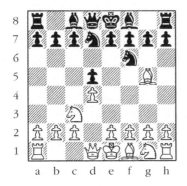

Other popular replies include 3...c5 and 3...Bf5, both of which are fully adequate to obtain even chances.

4 Nf3

4 e3 and 4 f3 are also possible, but offer Black excellent chances. The text move is more solid.

4...h6 5 Bf4

White has a sharp alternative in 5 Bh4 e6 6 e4 g5 7 Bg3 Nxe4 8 Nxe4 dxe4, which is very complicated and requires careful study from both players, but in the end is considered fine for Black.

5...a6 6 e3 e6 7 Bd3 c5 8 0-0 Be7 9 Re1 b5 and Black has a pleasant game.

The German theoretician Siegbert Tarrasch wrote that, as a rule of thumb, knights should be developed before bishops. This is nearly always the case and worth keeping in mind, though there are of course many exceptions.

It is quite common to play either h3 or ...h6, giving the king some "room to breathe," but if the opponent has yet to castle or has castled queenside, this innocent move can constitute an immediate weakness that the opponent can target by launching a kingside attack.

Chapter 8

The Semi-Closed Games

In this chapter we will examine all the openings that start with 1 d4, but where White doesn't answer 1...d5. This includes all the popular Indian Defenses, such as the Nimzo-Indian, King's Indian and Queen's Indian, but also sharp and provocative openings like the Modern Benoni, the Benko Gambit, the Dutch Defense, as well as many less popular defenses. We will also have a look at some of the so-called Anti-Indian Openings, such as the Trompowsky, the Torre Attack and the London System.

The Nimzo-Indian Defense

Of all the openings we will cover in this chapter, the Nimzo-Indian is undoubtedly the most respected. It is the brainchild of Aron Nimzowitsch, but since his adventures with it in the early decades of the 20th century, it has been played by just about every world champion since.

1 d4 Nf6 2 c4 e6 3 Nc3 Bb4

With the pin on White's knight, Black restrains White from playing e2-e4,

threatens to double White's c-pawns and take control over the center.

White can now take the game in several directions: **(a) 4 a3** (Sämisch Variation); **(b) 4 Bg5** (Leningrad Variation); **(c) 4 Nf3** (Flexible Variation); **(d) 4 Qc2** (Capablanca Variation); and **(e) 4 e3** (Rubinstein Complex).

The Sämisch Variation

White's sharpest and most direct response to the Nimzo-Indian is the Sämisch; White forces a resolution in regards to the pin of the knight on c3.

4 a3

A related line is 4 f3, which immediately leads to very sharp play, e.g., 4...d5 5 a3 Bxc3+ 6 bxc3 c5 7 cxd5 Nxd5 8 dxc5 (8 Qd3 b6 is the alternative, which is supposed to be fine for Black) 8...Qa5 with an unclear position.

4...Bxc3+ 5 bxc3 0-0 6 e3 c5

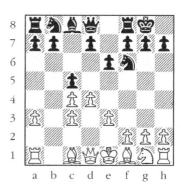

Black has several other options available here, but this is generally considered the critical line; the doubled c-pawns are fixed, and Black will start applying pressure against them, whereas White will start developing an initiative in the center and on the kingside.

7 Bd3 Nc6 8 Ne2 b6 9 e4 Ne8

This odd-looking move is standard. Black wants to avoid the pin with Bg5 and also reserves the option of playing ...f7-f5, when White plays f2-f4.

10 0-0 Ba6 11 f4 f5

This is more or less a necessity because otherwise White's initiative on the kingside gains too much momentum after f4-f5.

12 Ng3 g6 with a sharp position with which Black should be pleased.

The Leningrad Variation

If White likes sharp play, but doesn't necessarily enjoy the theory-heavy main lines, White can opt for the Leningrad, which has been a favorite of Spassky and Bareev.

4 Bg5

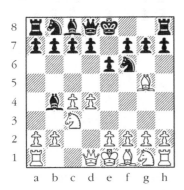

The pin isn't a major concern for Black, but at least White has developed the bishop outside the pawn structure d4-e3 which is so typical in the Nimzo-Indian.

4...c5

Black can also play 4...h6, but it usually only leads to a transposition to the main line after 5 Bh4 c5 6 d5.

5 d5 h6 6 Bh4 Bxc3+

An enjoyably sharp alternative is 6...b5!? which can end up resembling a Blumenfeld Gambit after 7 dxe6 fxe6 8 cxb5 d5.

7 bxc3 d6 8 e3 e5 9 Bd3 Qe7 10 Ne2 g5 11 Bg3 Nbd7 and the chances are about even.

The Flexible Variation

White's most non-committal move is 4 Nf3, after which the game may take a number of different directions.

4 Nf3 c5

Black's main alternative is 4...b6, after which 5 Bg5 transposes to a line you will find under the Queen's Indian, 4 Nc3 Variation, but 5 Qb3 is also a plausible continuation, e.g., 5...c5 6 Bg5 Bb7 7 a3 Ba5 8 0-0-0 with an interesting game. Should Black opt for 4...d5, then 5 e3 leads to the Rubinstein Nimzo-Indian, while 5 Bg5 is a Ragozin Queen's Gambit. There is little doubt why this line is called the Flexible Variation.

5 g3

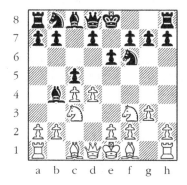

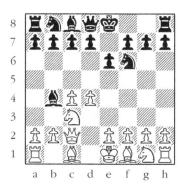

With this move we transpose to a Fianchetto Variation or Romanishin Variation as it is also known, when White has played Nf3. Alternatively White can also play 5 e3, which transposes to the Rubinstein, covered below.

5...cxd4 6 Nxd4 0-0

5...Ne4 is also possible.

7 Bg2 d5 8 cxd5 Nxd5 9 Bd2 Nxc3 10 bxc3 Be7 11 Rb1 Nd7 and the chances are approximately balanced.

The Capablanca Variation

Also known as the Classical Variation, 4 Qc2 for many years lived a life in relative obscurity until the line, in the 1980s, was taken up by a number of the strongest players including Kasparov and Karpov. Nowadays this line, along with 4 e3, is considered the most critical response to the Nimzo-Indian.

4 Qc2 (D)

White wants to avoid the doubling of the c-pawns and hopes that gaining the bishop pair will compensate for the loss

of time involved with this maneuver. The related line, 4 Qb3 is less critical, because the queen is less well-placed when Black avoids the exchange on c3, e.g., 4...c5 5 dxc5 Nc6 6 Nf3 Ne4 (if the queen had been on c2, this move would not have been possible) 7 Bd2 Nxd2 8 Nxd2 Bxc5 with equal chances.

Of Black's many available continuations, the main ones are: **(a) 4...d5**; **(b) 4...c5**; and **(c) 4...0-0**.

The Capablanca Variation, 4...d5

If Black wants to unbalance the game quickly, the best option is undoubtedly 4...d5.

4...d5 5 a3

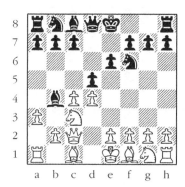

The main alternative is 5 cxd5 after which Black can play 5...exd5 6 Bg5 h6 7 Bh4 (7 Bxf6 is safer) 7...c5 8 dxc5 g5 9 Bg3 Ne4 10 e3 Qa5 11 Nge2 Bf5 with an unclear position, or 5...Qxd5 6 Nf3 (6 e3 c5 7 Bd2 Bxc3 8 Bxc3 cxd4 9 Bxd4 Nc6 is more or less equal) 6...Qf5!? 7 Qxf5 (White can avoid the exchange with 7 Qd1) 7...exf5 8 a3 Bd6 9 g3 Be6 10 Bf4 Nd5 11 e3 Nxf4 12 gxf4 c6 13 0-0-0 Nd7 and the chances are almost level, perhaps only with slight edge for White.

5...Bxc3+ 6 Qxc3 Ne4

Black can also consider 6...dxc4 7 Qxc4 b6 or 6...c5 7 dxc5 d4.

7 Qc2 c5 8 dxc5 Nc6 9 e3

Or 9 cxd5 exd5 10 e3 Bf5 leads to unclear play.

9...Qa5+ 10 Bd2 Nxd2 11 Qxd2 dxc4 12 Bxc4 Qxc5 and Black has equalized.

The Capablanca Variation, 4...c5

The solid 4...c5 is also a popular choice for Black.

4...c5 5 dxc5 0-0 6 a3 Bxc5 7 Nf3 b6 8 Bf4

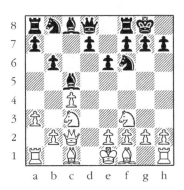

8 Bg5 can also be considered.

8...Bb7 9 Rd1 Nc6 10 e3

Or 10 b4 Nh5 11 Bc1 Be7 12 e4 Rc8 13 Be2 Qc7 14 Nb5 Qb8 15 Rxd7 Nf6 16 Rd1 Ne5, and Black has an excellent game.

10...Nh5 11 Bg5 Be7 12 Bxe7 Nxe7 13 Be2 Nf6 14 0-0 a6 15 Qd2 d5 with approximately equal chances.

The Capablanca Variation, 4...0-0

4...0-0 5 a3

After 5 e4 d5 6 e5 Ne4, Black is doing fine.

5...Bxc3+ 6 Qxc3 b6

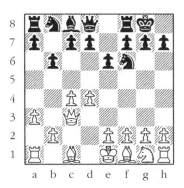

Other options for Black include 6...Ne4, 6...d6 and the gambit 6...b5!?, intending 7 cxb5 c6 with compensation for the pawn.

7 Bg5

White often plays 7 Nf3, but Black is okay after 7...Bb7 8 e3 d6 9 Be2 Nbd7 10 0-0 Ne4 11 Qc2 f5 with chances for both sides.

7...Bb7 8 e3 d6 9 Nge2 Nbd7 10 Qc2

Sometimes White also places the queen on d3, but it is matter of taste.

10...c5 11 Rd1 Qe7 12 Nc3 h6 13 Bh4 cxd4 14 Rxd4 Rfd8 and this position is considered almost equal, though White, thanks to the pair of bishops has a tiny edge, which he surprisingly often manages to convert.

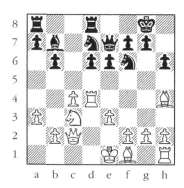

The Rubinstein Complex

Named after the Polish grandmaster Akiba Rubinstein, this flexible approach remains one of White's most popular continuations. The volume of theory attached to this complex of variations is enormous. A few years back I wrote 320 packed pages on this variation, and I had to make significant cuts in the material to make it fit. A testament to its enduring popularity is that many of the subvariations carry the names of many of the strongest players in chess history.

4 e3

A flexible setup which allows White to choose a number of piece configurations, depending on Black's choice of line.

Now Black can take the game in several different directions: **(a) 4...b6**; **(b) 4...c5**; and **(c) 4...0-0** (Main Line). 4...d5, 4...Nc6, 4...d6 and even 4...Ne4 can also be tried for Black in this position, though these options tend to offer White the better chances.

The Rubinstein, 4...b6

This dynamic move was a Fischer favorite. The bishop can be developed to both a6 and b7.

5 Ne2

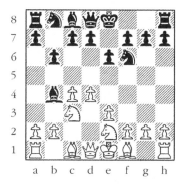

On 5 Bd3, Black can react à la the Classical Dutch: 5...Bb7 6 Nf3 Ne4 7 0-0 f5 8 d5 Bxc3 9 bxc3 Nc5 10 Ba3 Nba6, which, after 11 Re1 or 11 Nd4 leads to a slightly better game for White, or he can try 6...0-0 7 0-0 c5, after which White should play the awkward looking 8 Na4, and then 8...cxd4 9 exd4 Re8 10 a3 Bf8 11 b4 followed by Bb2 leaves White with more space and the slightly better chances.

5...Ba6

A popular alternative is 5...Ne4 6 Bd2 (also 6 Qc2 Bb7 7 Nf4 0-0 8 Bd3 f5 is possible) 6...Nxd2 7 Qxd2 Ba6 8 a3 Bxc3

9 Nxc3 d5 10 b3 Nc6 with chances for both players. 5...Bb7 is also seen with some frequency, but 6 a3 Be7 7 d5 0-0 8 Ng3 d6 9 Be2 leaves White slightly better. Finally, Black has the very provocative 5...c5, which after 6 a3 Ba5, looks like Black is going to get his bishop trapped, but after ...Qe7 and ...Na6 Black normally doesn't have any problems.

6 Ng3 Bxc3+ 7 bxc3 d5 8 Ba3

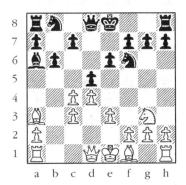

Or 8 Qf3 0-0 9 cxd5 Qxd5 10 e4 Qa5 with a sharp position and chances for both players.

8...Bxc4 9 Bxc4 dxc4 10 0-0 h5 11 Qf3 Qd5 12 e4 Qg5 and White has compensation for the pawn but not more than that.

The Rubinstein, 4...c5

5 Bd3

White can obviously also play 5 Ne2 in this line, which leads to interesting play, for instance, 5...cxd4 6 exd4 d5 7 c5 (or 7 a3 Be7 8 c5 0-0 9 g3 b6 with chances for both players) 7...Ne4 8 Bd2 Nxd2 9 Qxd2 a5 10 a3 Bxc3 11 Nxc3 a4 12 Bd3 b6, and Black is doing fine. Also note that 5...b6 transposes to the line mentioned under 4...b6.

5...Nc6 6 Nf3 Bxc3+ 7 bxc3 d6 (D)

This is the so-called Hübner Variation. Black closes the center to shut down White's initiative and complete his development.

8 0-0

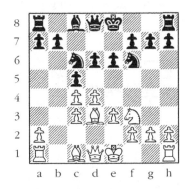

Black has fewer problems after the more conventional 8 e4 e5 9 d5 Ne7 10 Nh4 h6 11 f3 Qa5 12 Bd2 Ng6.

8...e5 9 Nd2 0-0 10 Re1

White still avoids closing up the center, which is what Black is striving for.

10...cxd4 11 cxd4 exd4 12 exd4 Bg4 13 f3 Bh5 14 Nb3 and White has the somewhat better chances.

The Rubinstein, Main Line

4...0-0 5 Bd3 (D)

White plays 5 Nf3, reserving the option of developing the knight to e2. Also possible is 5 Ne2, the so-called Reshevsky Variation; after 5...d5 6 a3 Be7 7 cxd5 Nxd5 (7...exd5 is also playable) 8 Qc2 Nd7 9 e4 Nxc3 10 Nxc3 c5, with chances for both sides.

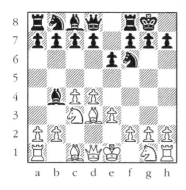

5...d5 6 Nf3

6 a3 is also possible, taking the game to a Sämisch type of position after 6...Bxc3+ 7 bxc3, whereas 6 Ne2 is the Modern Variation, when 6...dxc4 7 Bxc4 c5 8 0-0 cxd4 9 exd4 Nc6 is considered adequate for Black.

6...c5

There are numerous side lines in the Rubinstein. 6...b6 is an interesting alternative for Black, e.g., 7 0-0 b6 8 a3 Bd6 9 b4 dxc4 10 Bxc4 Nbd7, and the chances are about balanced.

7 0-0 Nc6

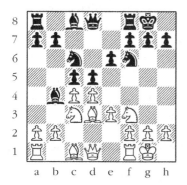

A major alternative for Black is 7...dxc4 8 Bxc4 cxd4 9 exd4 b6, the so-called

Karpov Variation, which can also be reached via the Panov Attack in the Caro-Kann or the Queen's Gambit Accepted. White takes on an isolated pawn in return for easy development and active piece play. One line runs 10 Bg5 Bb7 11 Ne5 Bxc3 12 bxc3 Nbd7 13 Nxd7 Qxd7 14 Bxf6 gxf6, with an unclear position. Black can also consider 8...Qe7, 8...Nbd7 or 7...Nbd7, each of which carry its own volume of theory.

8 a3 Bxc3

Black can also play 8...dxc4 9 Bxc4 cxd4 10 exd4 Be7 11 Re1 b6 12 Bd3 Bb7 with a sharp position.

9 bxc3 dxc4

Even without this exchange, 9...Qc7 is an interesting option.

10 Bxc4 Qc7

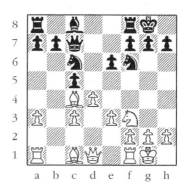

In this position, White has played nearly every reasonable move available, e.g., 11 Be2, 11 Bd3, 11 Ba2, 11 Bb5, 11 Qc2, 11 h3, 11 a4, 11 Re1 and the move we will use for our main line...

11 Bd3

Deciding which move is the better line

is a matter of taste, but this, 11 Ba2, and 11 Bb2, are usually given preference by White.

11...e5 12 Qc2 Re8

Threatening ...e4 with a fork.

13 dxe5 Nxe5 14 Nxe5 Qxe5 15 f3 Bd7 16 a4 Bc6 with a strategically complicated position where both sides have chances.

The Queen's Indian Defense

The second brainchild of Nimzowitsch is the Queen's Indian, which even today is one of the most important defenses for Black against 1 d4.

1 d4 Nf6 2 c4 e6 3 Nf3 b6

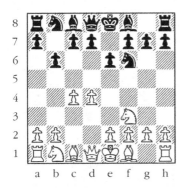

White now has several different ways to meet this opening; the main ones are: **(a) 4 a3** (Petrosian Variation); **(b) 4 Nc3**; and **(c) 4 g3** (Fianchetto Variation).

The Petrosian Variation

This line was first bought into focus by the late world champion Tigran Petrosian and the line carries his name. Again it became very popular in early 1980s when Kasparov used it frequently.

4 a3

The idea behind this move is to prevent Black from playing ...Bb4 when White follows up with 4 Nc3.

4...Bb7

Black can also consider 4...Ba6 forcing White to protect the c-pawn rather than following the standard plan. White's normal moves are either 5 Nbd2 or 5 Qc2, in both cases with interesting play to follow.

5 Nc3 d5 6 cxd5 Nxd5

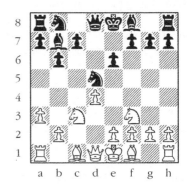

A somewhat more solid, yet also slightly more passive continuation is 6...exd5, e.g., 7 g3 Be7 8 Qa4+ c6 9 Bg2 0-0 10 Ne5, with a slight pull for White.

7 e3

Another popular continuation is 7 Qc2 Nxc3 8 bxc3 Be7 9 e4 0-0 10 Bd3 c5 11 0-0 Qc8 with approximately even chances for the contestants.

7...Be7 8 Bb5+ c6 9 Bd3 Nxc3 10 bxc3

White appears to have a nice pawn center, but Black's pieces develop easily, and if White isn't very careful, the white pawns will just become weak.

10...c5 11 0-0 Nc6 12 Qe2 0-0 13 Bb2 Rc8 14 Rad1 cxd4 15 cxd4 Bf6 and the chances are about even.

4 Nc3 Variation

This line is very dynamic and had its heyday in the 1980s when many of the top players took on this line with either color.

4 Nc3 Bb7

4...Bb4 can transpose to the Nimzo-Indian.

5 Bg5 Bb4

This can lead to one of the sharpest positions in the entire Queen's Indian. If Black is more solidly inclined, then 5...Be7 is a good alternative.

6 e3 h6 7 Bh4 g5 8 Bg3 Ne4 9 Qc2 Bxc3+ 10 bxc3 d6 11 Bd3 Nxg3 12 fxg3 Qe7 with a complicated game and chances for both sides.

Fianchetto Variation

A perennial favorite in top level chess is the Fianchetto Variation, which has numerous sidelines that can lead all types of positions, everything from ultra-sharp and complicated to level or even boring positions, all depending on your temperment.

4 g3 Ba6

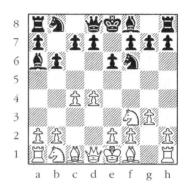

Nowadays this is the preferred continuation, even if it is an old idea by Nimzowitsch himself. The main alternative is of course the more obvious 4...Bb7, which tends to lead to more balanced positions, e.g., 5 Bg2 Be7 6 0-0 0-0 7 Nc3 Ne4! (if Black wants a more complicated position then 7...d5 or 7...Na6 are alternatives to consider) 8 Qc2 (8 Bd2 Bf6 is also popular) 8...Nxc3 9 Qxc3 f5 with perhaps slightly better chances for White. Finally, Black can also play 4...Bb4+, taking the game to a Bogo-Indian type of position.

5 b3

This is one of several continuations for White. Also to be considered are 5 Qc2, 5 Qa4 and 5 Nbd2, all with interesting play to follow.

5...Bb4+

Black can also play 5...d5 or 5...Bb7, but the text move aims to exploit the fact that White cannot develop the knight to its natural square on c3 at the moment.

6 Bd2 Be7

This looks like Black has lost a tempo by playing ...Bb4+ and then retreating to e7, but keep in mind that the white bishop on d2 is not on its ideal square either.

7 Bg2 c6 8 Bc3 d5

With this move, Black finally starts challenging the white center.

9 Ne5 Nfd7 10 Nxd7 Nxd7 11 Nd2 0-0 12 0-0 Rc8 13 e4 c5 and the battle is in full swing, with more or less even chances.

The Bogo-Indian Defense

This opening is sometimes called the Bogoljubow Indian after the two-time world championship challenger to Alekhine.

1 d4 Nf6 2 c4 e6 3 Nf3 Bb4+

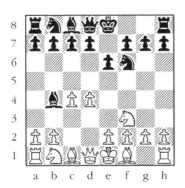

Black's main idea is to exchange his dark-squared bishop for its white counterpart. White may choose to avoid this approach, trying to show that Black's development is somewhat awkward.

4 Bd2

Usually White obliges by playing this move, but a sharper alternative exists in 4 Nbd2, for instance 4...0-0 5 a3 Be7 6 e4 d5 7 Qc2 dxe4 8 Nxe4, with complicated play.

4...Qe7

This is Black's most popular move, though by no means the only one; other perfectly reasonable moves include 4...c5, 4...a5, 4...Be7 and 4...Bxd2. All of these moves are still being played on a regular basis at all levels of competition, though White is considered to have a slight edge in most of these lines. The idea behind the text move is not immediately obvious, but soon will be.

5 g3 Nc6 6 Bg2 Bxd2+ 7 Nbxd2

Ideally, White would have liked to play 7 Qxd2 followed by Nc3 with a pleasant position and the better chances. However, here we see the point behind Black's 4th move – on 7 Qxd2?!, Black plays 7...Ne4, and then 8 Qc2 Qb4+! 9 Nc3 Nxc3 10 Qxc3 Qxc3+ 11 bxc3, and Black has the slightly better chances because of White's weakened pawn structure.

7...d6 8 0-0 a5 9 e4 e5 10 d5 Nb8

This may look a little odd: why does Black develop the knight to c6 and then retreat it to b8 rather than perhaps playing it to d8? In this case it is because from b8 it can move to both a6 and d7, after which it can go to c5 or continue to the kingside.

11 Ne1 h5 12 h4 Bg4 13 f3 Bd7 with chances for both players.

The King's Indian Defense

The King's Indian is a perennial favorite at all levels of play, though it has been in and out of fashion many times. At top levels, it was incredibly popular in the 1950s and 1960s, then disappeared somewhat after that until Kasparov started playing it in the late 1980s. After suffering some defeats against Kramnik, Kasparov gave up on it and its popularity once again faded. Nowadays Teimur Radjabov in particular happily takes on the black pieces in the King's Indian and has scored much better than could have been expected against his super-grandmaster colleagues.

1 d4 Nf6 2 c4 g6 3 Nc3 Bg7

This is the starting position of the King's Indian Defense, though if White doesn't play e2-e4, Black can still transpose to the Grünfeld Indian with

...d7-d5. Now the main continuations are: **(a) 4 e4 d6 5 f3** (Sämisch Variation); **(b) 4 e4 d6 5 f4** (Four Pawns' Attack); **(c) 4 e4 d6 5 Be2 0-0 6 Bg5** (Averbakh Variation); **(d) 4 e4 d6 5 Nf3 0-0 6 Be2** (Classical Variation); and **(e) 4 Nf3 d6 5 g3** (Fianchetto Variation). White has several other reasonably popular lines, but we will limit ourselves to the above.

The Sämisch Variation

One of the sharpest ways for White to meet the King's Indian is the Sämisch, which has drawn both attacking and positional players in amongst its adherents.

4 e4 d6 5 f3 0-0

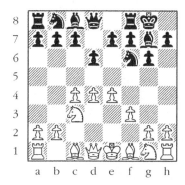

White wants to build a strong center and develop his pieces behind the central pawns, and then once development is complete, attack on whichever wing suits the position.

6 Be3

White can also opt for 6 Bg5, which tends to transpose to the Kapengut Variation in the Modern Benoni, when Black plays the customary 6...c5, e.g., 7 d5 e6 8 Qd2 exd5 9 cxd5. A third option is 6 Nge2, though this usually only leads to a transposition into the lines after 6 Be3.

6...e5

Black has many alternatives at this particular juncture, for example 6...c6, 6...b6, 6...a6, 6...Nc6 and 6...c5!?. In this last line, it looks like White can win a pawn with 7 dxc5 dxc5 8 Qxd8 Rxd8 9 Bxc5, but Black obtains sufficient counterplay after 9...Nc6 10 Nd5 (or 10 Ba3 a5 11 Rd1 Be6 12 Nd5 Bxd5 13 cxd5 Nb4) 10...Nd7! 11 Bxe7 Nxe7 12 Nxe7+ Kf8 13 Nd5 Bxb2 14 Rd1 Nc5 with compensation for the pawn. Therefore White often prefers 7 d5, which transposes to Benoni-like positions after 7...e6 or 7 Nge2, which may in turn transpose to a Sicilian Accelerated Dragon after 7...cxd4 8 Nxd4 Nc6.

7 d5

The closing of the center is the most common choice for White, though 7 Nge2 has also been played frequently.

7...Nh5

Also possible is 7...c6.

8 Qd2 f5

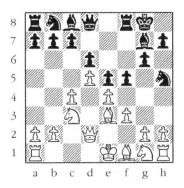

The creative mind of Russian grandmaster David Bronstein came up the fantastic, but not 100% correct queen sacrifice 8...Qh4+ 9 g3 Nxg3 10 Qf2 Nxf1 11 Qxh4 Nxe3 12 Ke2 Nxc4. Black gets decent compensation for the queen, but White maintains the better overall chances.

9 0-0-0 a6

Despite having started action on the kingside, it doesn't make sense for Black to open a full-scale battle on that wing with his own king in the line of fire. Therefore Black has to seek counterplay on the queenside as well.

10 Kb1 Nd7 11 Bd3 Nc5 12 Bc2 b5!?

Black sacrifices a pawn to open files and diagonals for his pieces.

13 cxb5 axb5 14 Nxb5 Ba6 15 Nc3 Qb8 and Black has compensation for the pawn.

Four Pawns Attack

An attractive plan for White is to attempt to gain complete control over the game with the space grabbing Four Pawns' Attack.

4 e4 d6 5 f4

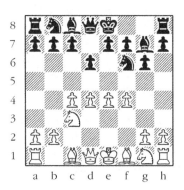

This looks impressive, but looks can be deceiving. Black can obtain an adequate game in several ways.

5...0-0 6 Nf3 Na6

The other main continuation is 6...c5; now 7 d5 e6 8 Be2 exd5 9 cxd5 lead to a line we will discuss below under the Modern Benoni. However, there are some alternatives for both sides. For example, White can also recapture on d5 with the e-pawn, 9 exd5, though this is considered quite harmless after several moves including 9...Re8 and 9...Nh5 (intending 10...Bxc3+ 11 bxc3 f5). Other options for White are 7 dxc5 and 8 dxe6. Black can also consider the Benko-style 7...b5. The text move became popular in the 1980s and proved a solid alternative to the sharp 6...c5.

7 Be2 e5 8 fxe5 dxe5 9 d5

9 Nxe5 c5 10 Be3 Nb4 is pleasant for Black.

9...Nc5 10 Bg5 h6 11 Bxf6 Qxf6 12 b4 Na6 13 a3 c5 with a complicated struggle ahead.

The Averbakh Variation

In many lines in the King's Indian, Black seeks to gain counterplay with ...e7-e5. In the Averbakh Variation White aims to limit this possibility.

4 e4 d6 5 Be2 0-0 6 Bg5

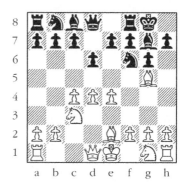

If Black now plays 6...e5?, he will lose material after 7 dxe5 dxe5 8 Qxd8 Rxd8 9 Nd5. If Black insists on playing ...e7-e5, the way to do it is 6...Na6 7 Qd2 e5 8 d5 c6 9 f3 cxd5 10 cxd5 Bd7 with a sharp position.

6...c5

In addition to the previous possibilities, Black can also play 6...Na6, 6...Nbd7 and 6...h6.

7 d5 e6 8 Qd2

8 dxe6 Bxe6 is fine for Black.

8...exd5 9 exd5 Re8 10 Nf3 Bg4 11 0-0 Nbd7 and Black should not have much to worry about.

Classical Variation

The main battle ground for many years has been the Classical Variation, where Black usually ends up attacking on the kingside and White on the queenside. This of course leads to sharp and fascinating play.

4 e4 d6 5 Nf3 0-0 6 Be2 e5

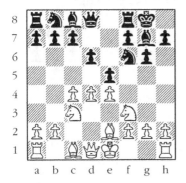

Black can also choose 6...Bg4 and 6...c5, though both of these lines are considered slightly better for White. Finally Black can try both 6...Nbd7 and 6...Na6, but these usually transpose to lines covered below.

7 0-0

White has several important alternatives at this juncture: **(a) 7 d5** (The Petrosian Variation) 7...a5 8 Bg5 h6 9 Bh4 Na6 10 Nd2 Qe8 11 0-0 Nh7 with chances for both sides; **(b) 7 dxe5** (The Exchange Variation) 7...dxe5 8 Qxd8 Rxd8 9 Bg5 Re8 10 Nd5 Nxd5 11 cxd5 c6 12 Bc4 cxd5 13 Bxd5 Nd7 with equality; and **(c) 7 Be3** Ng4 8 Bg5 f6 9 Bh4 Nc6 10 d5 Ne7 11 Nd2 Nh6 with a complicated struggle ahead.

7...Nc6

Again on this move, there are several alternatives. The most important of these are: **(a) 7...exd4** 8 Nxd4 Re8 9 f3 c6 10 Kh1 Nbd7 11 Bg5 h6 12 Bh4 Nc5 13

Rc1 a5 with a typical King's Indian position where both sides have chances; **(b) 7...Na6** 8 Re1 (8 Be3 Ng4 9 Bg5 Qe8 is also possible) 8...Qe8 9 Bf1 Bg4 10 d5 Nb4 11 Be2 (Black threatened 11...Bxf3 12 Qxf3 Nc2) 11...a5 12 Be3 Bd7 13 Nd2 Na6 14 Rb1 h5 with a double-edged position; and **(c) 7...Nbd7** 8 Re1 (or 8 Qc2) 8...c6 9 Bf1 a5 10 h3 (10 Rb1 Re8 12 d5 Bd7 leads to a different type of position that is also very common in this variation) 10...exd4 11 Nxd4 Re8 12 Bf4 Nc5 13 Qc2 Nh5 14 Be3 a4 with fairly even chances.

8 d5

White can also consider 8 Be3 in this position, after which Black usually replies either 8...exd4 or 8...Ng4.

8...Ne7

This is a crucial position that has been reached in many games.

9 Ne1

A testament to the popularity of the line can be found in how many different continuations White has tried at this juncture: **(a) 9 b4** is the so-called Bayonet Attack, which nowadays is

White's most popular option: 9...Nh5 (this is preferred by Radjabov, but 9...a5 10 Ba3 axb4 11 Bxb4 b6 12 a4 is also playable) 10 Re1 f5 (or 10...a5) 11 Ng5 Nf6 12 Bf3 c6 with a sharp position with chances for both sides; **(b) 9 Nd2** a5 (or 9...c5 10 Rb1 b6 11 b4 Ne8 12 bxc5 bxc513 Nb3 f5 leads to an unclear position) 10 a3 Nd7 (10...Bd7 is also playable) 11 Rb1 f5 12 b4 Kh8 13 Qc2 Ng8 14 f3 Ngf6 with double-edged play. White also plays 9 Bd2, 9 Bg5 and 9 a4, but less frequently.

9...Nd7

With this move Black guards against White's plan of c4-c5, but blocks the path of the bishop on c8. The sharper alternative is 9...Ne8, which is also fully playable.

10 Nd3

The other main line is 10 Be3, and here the play usually continues: 10...f5 11 f3 f4 12 Bf2 g5 13 Rc1 Ng6 14 c5!? Nxc5 15 b4 Na6 16 Nd3 Rf7 17 Nb5, and White has compensation for the pawn because of Black's poorly coordinated pieces.

10...f5 11 Bd2 Nf6 12 f3 f4 13 c5 g5

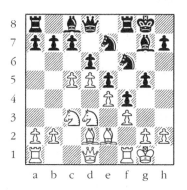

The battle lines are being drawn.

14 cxd6 cxd6 15 Rc1 a6 16 Nf2 Rf7 17 a4 Ng6 18 b4 b6 and the typical pattern of White attacking on the queenside and Black on the kingside is evident. A complicated struggle can be expected.

The Fianchetto Variation

One of the most solid ways for White to meet the King's Indian is the Fianchetto Variation. White aims to develop his pieces to good squares before starting the battle with Black for the control over the center.

4 Nf3 d6 5 g3 0-0 6 Bg2 Nbd7

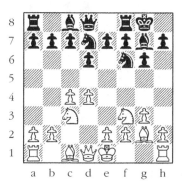

Black's main alternative is the sharp Panno Variation **6...Nc6**, which starts complications immediately: 7 0-0 a6 (Black can also play 7...Bf5, 7...Rb8 and 7...e5) 8 d5 (also 8 Bg5 and 8 h3 are worth consideration) 8...Na5 9 Nd2 c5 10 Qc2 Rb8 11 b3 b5 12 Bb2 Bh6 (12...h5!?) 13 f4 bxc4 14 bxc4 Ng4 15 Nd1 Rxb2 16 Qxb2 Bg7 17 Qc1 e5! 18 dxe6 Bxe6 with an unclear position, but Black has full compensation for the exchange thanks to his strong bishops.

Alternatively, Black can play **6...c5** 7 0-0 Nc6, which, after 8 d5 Na5 9 Nd2, can lead to the Panno Variation with 9...a6 or to independent play after 9...e5.

7 0-0 e5 8 e4 c6 9 h3 exd4

Black has several other options here, e.g., 9...Re8, 9...Qa5 and 9...Qb6, all leading to approximately even chances.

10 Nxd4 Re8 11 Rb1 a5 12 Re1 Nc5 13 b3 Nh5 14 Be3 Qe7 15 Qd2 and White has a space advantage, which offers him the slightly easier game, but not necessarily a guaranteed advantage.

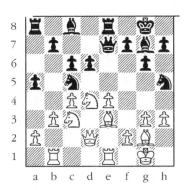

The Grünfeld Indian Defense

The Grünfeld is a provocative opening in the sense that Black hands White a broad, well-supported pawn center with easy development and a space advantage, yet Black does this willingly and with good results. Its popularity has been up and down over the years, but the fact is that it has been a successful weapon for Black for three world champions – Botvinnik, Fischer and Kasparov – in three different eras.

1 d4 Nf6 2 c4 g6 3 Nc3 d5

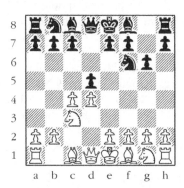

White has four main responses to Black's opening: **(a) 4 cxd5** (Exchange Variation); **(b) 4 Nf3** (Three Knights); **(c) 4 Bf4**; and **(d) 4 g3** (Fianchetto Variation).

The Exchange Variation

The most logical and in many ways the most critical response to the Grünfeld is the Exchange Variation. White builds a broad center, which Black aims to break down with careful play.

4 cxd5 Nxd5 5 e4 Nxc3 6 bxc3 Bg7

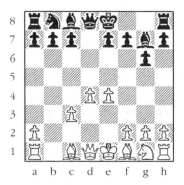

This is the starting position of the Exchange Variation, a line which looks awfully good for White unless you are familiar with the intricacies of the variation and this particular pawn structure. The theory of the lines in this variation often runs 20 or more moves deep, which may serve as a deterrent for many to take up this opening as Black, but there are many alternatives that are less steeped in theory but should allow prospective Black players to take up this opening.

While Black seems to start the game fighting from behind in this variation, he is planning to attack White's center with ...c7-c5 and ...Nb8-c6, attacking the white d4-pawn. White's objective obviously is to hold on to the center Black has so graciously handed to him.

Exchange Variation, Modern Variation

In the 1980s, White developed a new plan that gained enormous popularity, and even today it remains one of White's most popular lines in the Exchange Variation and indeed against the Grümfeld as a whole.

7 Nf3 c5 8 Rb1

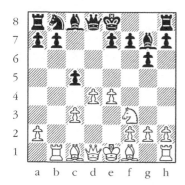

White's last move doesn't immediately strike you as particularly logical. However, the idea is to tie Black's bishop to the defense of the b7-pawn and thus prevent it from going to g4

where it would help undermine the protection of the white pawn center.

8...0-0 9 Be2 cxd4

Black occasionally plays 9...Nc6, forcing White to play 10 d5 Ne5 (10...Bxc3+ 11 Bd2 Bxd2+ 12 Qxd2 is also possible, but it is considered quite dangerous for Black) 11 Nxe5 Bxe5 12 Qd2. White will often follow up with f2-f4 and even c3-c4 with an even broader center; Black's counterplay on the dark squares is usually sufficient to balance the chances.

10 cxd4 Qa5+ 11 Bd2 Qxa2

This pawn hunt looks risky and quite hazardous for Black, but theory has established that Black should be fine. However, the variations are very long, exceedingly complicated and not always particularly logical. Therefore players on either side of the board should not enter this particular variation unless very well-prepared. I would discourage you, dear reader, to spend your time more productively than memorizing the minutiae of this variation.

Exchange Variation, Main Line

One of the most popular ways for White to play the Exchange Variation is called the Main Line. It is a very logical way for White to play and every move serves to protect the white center.

7 Bc4 c5 8 Ne2 0-0 9 0-0 Nc6 10 Be3

Thus far both sides have attacked and defended the center in the prescribed fashion, and it looks like White has won

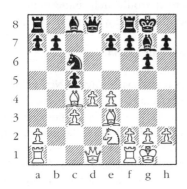

the first battle by holding on to the center.

10...Bg4

At first glance, this move makes no sense at all, because White can just play f2-f3 and break the pin. Yet this innocent pawn move in fact also results in the weakening of the dark squares around White's king and the b6-g1 diagonal.

Black also has a less theoretical alternative in 10...Qc7, intending ...Rd8, putting even more pressure on the center.

11 f3 Na5!

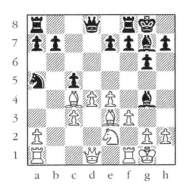

12 Bd3

In 1987, Karpov in his world championship match against Kasparov in Seville repeatedly – and with some success – played 12 Bxf7+ Rxf7 13 fxg4 Rxf1+ 14 Kxf1. Despite winning a pawn, this variation is considered harmless because Black has ample compensation for the pawn.

12...cxd4 13 cxd4 Be6 14 d5!?

The old main line runs 14 Rc1 Bxa2 15 Qa4 Be6 16 d5 Bd7 17 Qb4 with chances for both sides. Black has an extra pawn, but White has more space and a strong center as compensation. With the text move, White sacrifices the exchange to gain control over the dark squares which, in the absence of Black's dark-squared bishop, become quite weak.

14...Bxa1 15 Qxa1 f6 16 Bh6 Re8 17 Kh1 Bd7 18 e5 with a sharp game and chances for both sides. This too is a line that neither side should venture into without having first analyzed it carefully.

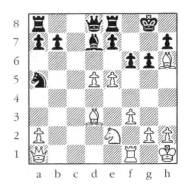

Three Knights

Another popular continuation is the development of the kingside knight, yet this, as we will soon see, is not necessarily a recipe for quiet play.

4 Nf3 Bg7 5 Qb3

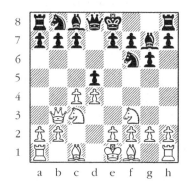

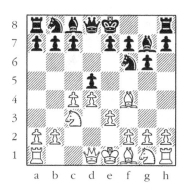

5...c5

As we have seen, there isn't much in the Grünfeld that seems to follow the normal rules of engagement. This particular line has been the battleground for world champions and other grandmasters for decades.

Another popular continuation is 5 Bf4, which can be met with 5...c5 6 dxc5 Qa5 7 cxd5 Nxd5 8 Qxd5 Bxc3+ 9 Bd2, with a complicated game and chances for both sides.

5...dxc4 6 Qxc4 0-0 7 e4 a6

This is just one of many possible continuations for Black in this position. Other possible and fully adequate moves are 7...Bg4, 7...Na6, 7...Nc6, 7...c6, and 7...b6.

8 Be2 b5 9 Qb3 c5 10 dxc5 Nbd7 11 e5 Nxc5 12 Qb4 Nfd7 with mutual chances.

4 Bf4 Variation

4 Bf4 Bg7 5 e3 (D)

Here 5 Nf3 will transpose to the previous line.

5...0-0 is also of interest. White can win a pawn with 6 cxd5 Nxd5 7 Nxd5 Qxd5 8 Bxc7, but Black is thought to have full compensation for the pawn thanks to his active pieces and easy development.

6 dxc5 Qa5 7 Rc1 Ne4 8 cxd5 Nxc3 9 Qd2 Qxa2 10 Rxc3 with unbalanced complications and chances for both players.

The Fianchetto Variation

This line is often arrived at many different ways, e.g., 1 d4 Nf6 2 c4 g6 3 g3 Bg7 4 Bg2 d5 or 3 Nf3 Bg7 4 g3 d5. White usually holds off on playing his knight to c3 until a little later.

1 d4 Nf6 2 c4 g6 3 g3 Bg7 4 Nf3 d5 (D)

5 cxd5

Former world champion Anatoly Karpov often played 5 Bg2 0-0 6 0-0 c6 (6...dxc4 is also fine for Black) 7 cxd5 cxd5 8 Ne5 with perhaps a trace of an edge for White. This type of position demands a thorough understanding

and Karpov frequently managed to squeeze out wins in this line.

5...Nxd5 6 Bg2 0-0 7 0-0 Nb6 8 Nc3 Nc6 with approximately even chances.

Old Indian Defense

The last and least common of the Indian Defenses is the Old Indian, which is considered passive, without offering Black much in the way of active counterplay. But for solid players in no rush to equalize, it can be a perfectly good weapon, particularly if you are facing an aggressive player with a great deal of theoretical knowledge; chances are that the player with the white pieces may get impatient and push too hard.

1 d4 Nf6 2 c4 d6 (D)

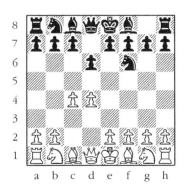

Black wants to play ...e7-e5, either straightaway or prepared by ...Nbd7.

3 Nc3

If White plays 3 Nf3, Black has the additional options of 3...Bf5 and 3...Bg4, and therefore White usually develops the knight on b1 first.

3...e5

Black isn't overly concerned about the loss of the right to castle after 4 dxe5 dxe5 5 Qxd8+ Kxd8, because White's pawn structure is actually slightly weakened by c2-c4; after 6 Nf3 Nfd7! (6...Nbd7 7 Rg1!, intending g2-g4, is actually better for White) 7 Bd2 c6 8 0-0-0 f6 with a balanced game.

4 Nf3 Nbd7 5 e4

White can also consider 5 g3 and 5 Bg5.

5...Be7 6 Be2 c6 7 0-0 0-0 8 Re1

This is just one of many possible continuations for White who can also consider 8 b3, 8 Rb1, 8 Qc2 and 8 Be3. All of these offer White good chances of a small plus.

8...a6 9 Rb1 Re8 10 b4 exd4 11 Nxd4 Bf8 12 Bf1 c5 and White is slightly better.

Modern Benoni

In my old opening books, it is explained that Benoni means "the son of sorrow," which may well be the case. There are, as we shall see, several versions of the Benoni, some see the dark-squared bishop develop to e7, others to g7. The most popular of the Benoni systems is the Modern Benoni.

1 d4 Nf6 2 c4 c5 3 d5 e6 4 Nc3

Another option is 4 g3, which allows 4...exd5 5 cxd5 b5 6 Bg2 d6 with a complicated game.

4...exd5 5 cxd5 d6

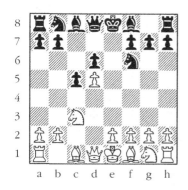

The so-called "Snake" Benoni arises after 5...Bd6 6 Nf3 0-0 7 g3 Bc7 8 Bg2 d6 9 0-0, and White has the better chances.

After the text move, we have reached the starting position of the Modern Benoni. Black intends to follow up with ...g7-g6 and ...Bg7. Now the main continuations are: (a) **6 e4 g6 7 f3** (Kapengut Variation); (b) **6 e4 g6 7 f4**

(Pawn Storm Variation); (c) **6 e4 g6 7 Nf3 Bg7 8 h3** (Modern Variation); (d) **6 e4 g6 7 Nf3 Bg7 8 Be2** (Classical Variation); (e) and **6 Nf3 g6 7 g3** (Fianchetto Variation).

The Kapengut Variation

The name of Soviet international master Albert Kapengut may not ring a bell with all chess players, but for those interested in the Modern Benoni, it will soon become a familiar one once you start studying the theory, because he is a major contributor to the development of most of the lines in the Modern Benoni. He is also known as the coach for several top players including Gelfand.

6 e4 g6 7 f3

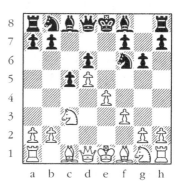

The lines in this section can often arise via transposition from the King's Indian Sämisch (see above), when Black chooses the lines with ...c7-c5, and White answers d4-d5.

7...Bg7 8 Bg5

White can also play 8 Bd3, 8 Nge2 or 8 Be3, but none of these lines is particularly problematic for Black.

8...0-0 9 Qd2 a6

The theoretical main line is 9...h6!?, but it demands a lot of theoretical knowledge. For instance, on 10 Bxh6, Black has 10...Nxe4! 11 Nxe4 Qh4+ 12 g3 Qxh6 13 Qxh6 Bxh6 14 Nxd6 Nd7, with complications and 10 Be3 a6 11 a4 h5 12 Nge2 Nbd7 13 Nc1 Re8 14 Nd3 Ne5 15 Bf2 Nh7 16 Be2 f5 with very sharp play, are just a couple of strands in the massive web of variations that make up this line.

10 a4 Re8 11 Nge2 Nbd7 12 Ng3 h5 13 Be2 Qa5 with chances for both sides.

The Pawn Storm Variation

One of the most critical approaches Black faces is the Pawn Storm Variation; it can be difficult to play for Black.

6 e4 g6 7 f4 Bg7

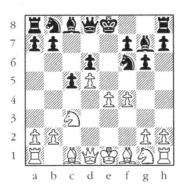

If Black is afraid of the complicated lines are covered below, Black can also consider 7...Qe7, which avoids a lot of the theory and is reasonably playable.

8 Bb5+

This is the so-called Taimanov Variation, which has deterred many players from playing the Modern Benoni with the standard move order (2...c5 3 d5 e6), only opting for the Modern Benoni with 2...e6 3 Nf3 c5.

White, of course, can also play 8 Nf3 0-0 9 Be2, after which Black can play the solid **9...Bg4** 10 0-0 Nbd7 11 h3 Bxf3 12 Bxf3 Re8 13 Re1 a6 14 a4 Rb8, with chances for both sides, or enter the maddeningly sharp lines after **9...Re8** 10 e5 (White can also avoid this line with 10 Nd2 Nbd7 11 0-0 c4 12 a4 Nc5, with adequate chances for Black) 10...dxe5 11 fxe5 Ng4 12 Bg5 Qb6 13 0-0 Nxe5 14 d6 Qxb2 15 Nd5 Bf5, with an unclear position.

8...Nfd7

Black can also play 8...Nbd7, but this is an invitation for trouble after 9 e5 dxe5 10 fxe5 Nh5 11 e6 Qh4 12 g3 Nxg3 13 hxg3 Qxh1 14 Be3, with complications that are supposed to be better for White.

9 a4 0-0

9...Qh4+ and 9...a6 can also be tried in this position.

10 Nf3 Na6 11 0-0 Nc7 12 Bc4 Nb6 13 Ba2 Bg4 14 a5 Nd7 with chances for both players.

The Modern Variation

Like many "modern" variations, this line was well-known before it became popular in the 1980s. In the beginning of its new-found popularity, it caused a lot of headaches for black players, but Black now has several ways to fight for equality.

6 e4 g6 7 Nf3

Actually I have to mention that White often plays 6 Nf3 Bg7 7 h3 and only then 8 e4, because after the text move, Black can play 7...Bg4 with a likely transposition to the Classical Variation after 8 e4 Bg7 9 Be2 0-0.

7...Bg7 8 h3 0-0 9 Bd3 a6

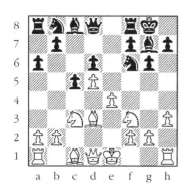

Black also has another extremely sharp alternative available in 9...b5!?, e.g., 10 Bxb5 Nxe4 11 Nxe4 Qa5+ 12 Nfd2 Qxb5 13 Nxd6 Qa6 14 N2c4 Rd8 15 Bf4 Bf8 16 Qe2 Bb7 17 Nxb7 Qxb7 and Black has

excellent compensation for the pawn; or 10 Nxb5 Re8 11 Nd2 Nxd5 12 Nc4 Re6 13 0-0 Nb4 14 Be2 Ba6 15 Nc3 Nd7, and Black is doing fine.

10 a4 Re8 11 0-0 Nbd7 12 Re1 Nh5 13 Bg5 Bf6 14 Be3 Ne5 15 Be2 Nxf3+ 16 Bxf3 Ng7 and the chances are approximately balanced.

Classical Variation

While the Classical Variation is typical of Modern Benoni play for both sides, it is also difficult to play and it takes a lot of understanding from both players to play this variation well.

6 e4

I should point out that White often plays 6 Nf3, and then after 6...g6, rather than playing 7 e4, which allows 7...Bg4, he plays 7 Nd2, and then after 7...Bg7 8 e4 0-0 9 Be2 Re8 10 0-0 we have transposed to a position in the Classical main line.

6...g6 7 Nf3 Bg7 8 Be2 0-0 9 0-0

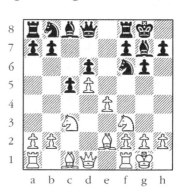

This is the real starting point of the Classical Variation.

9...Re8

Black has several alternatives here, of which the following lines are the most interesting ones: 9...Na6 10 Nd2 (10 Bf4 is probably better) 10...Nc7 11 a4 b6 12 Nc4 Ba6; 9...Bg4 10 h3 Bxf3 11 Bxf3 Re8 12 Bf4 a6 13 Re1 Bf8; and 9...a6 10 a4 Bg4 11 Bf4 Bxf3 12 Bxf3 Qe7 13 Re1 Nbd7 all leave the chances more or less balanced. However, there is an enormous amount of theory that must be learned in these lines.

10 Nd2 Na6

An important alternative is 10...Nbd7 11 a4 Ne5 12 Qc2 g5!? 13 Ra3 g4 14 Nc4 Nh5 with a sharp and unclear position.

11 f3 Nc7 12 a4 b6 13 Nc4 Ba6

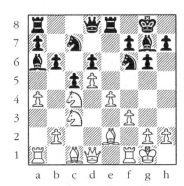

White would like to break in the center with e4-e5 when it suits him and therefore Black needs to prepare to prevent this. By exchanging the light-squared bishop for the knight, Black usually can put a temporary end to White's ambitions in the center; at the moment, the bishop pair is of secondary importance.

14 Kh1 Rb8 15 Bg5 Qd7 16 Re1 Bxc4 17 Bxc4 a6 18 Bf1 h6 19 Bh4 Nh5 20 Qd2 g5 21 Bf2 f5 and Black has opened the battle on the kingside where his

pieces are more active than the white counterparts. The chances are fairly balanced.

Fianchetto Variation

If White wants to avoid the often sharp battle that can ensue in the lines previously covered, he can consider the solid Fianchetto Variation, which doesn't offer the same tactical fireworks, but will allow the better player a chance to outplay the opponent.

6 Nf3 g6 7 g3 Bg7 8 Bg2 0-0 9 0-0

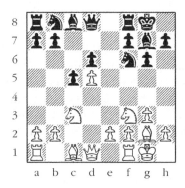

Here Black has to make an initial choice about which direction he wants to take the game. In addition to our main line, he can also consider 9...Na6, 9...Re8 and 9...Nbd7.

9...a6 10 a4 Nbd7 11 Nd2

Another interesting possibility is 11 Bf4, but Black should be fine in this line too.

11...Re8 12 h3 Rb8 13 Nc4 Ne5 14 Na3

This move looks strange: why would White allow Black to take the e5-square, while he himself retreats his knight to the ugly a3-square? On a3, the knight,

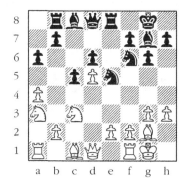

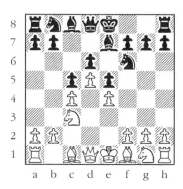

along with its colleague on c3 and the pawn on a4, helps to prevent Black from playing ...b7-b5; White would like to extract the knight on e5 with e2-e4 followed by f2-f4, though this is easier said than done.

14...Nh5 15 e4 Bd7 with an unclear position and chances for both players.

Czech Benoni

The Czech Benoni, like the Old Indian, is a solid and somewhat passive opening that should be played by patient players who don't seek immediate, active counterplay, but who can wait for the opponent to overreach.

1 d4 Nf6 2 c4 c5 3 d5 e5 4 Nc3 d6 5 e4 Be7 (D)

Black intends to castle and then slowly build up on the kingside with ...Ne8, ...Nd7,...g7-g6, ..Ng7 and then at some point ...f7-f5. White can claim an edge according to the theoretical works, but in practice, it is rather more difficult. **(D)**

6 g3

Another setup is 6 Nf3 0-0 7 h3 Ne8 8 Bd3 Nd7 9 g4!? a6 10 a4 g6 11 Bh6 Ng7

12 Qd2 Nf6 followed by ...Kh8 and ...Ng8, and though White has more space and the somewhat better chances, Black has a solid position with long-term counterplay.

6...0-0 7 Bg2 Ne8 8 Nge2 Nd7 9 0-0 a6 10 a4 g6

We see Black employ the same plan time and again in this opening, which makes it an easy opening for Black to learn.

11 Bh6 Ng7 12 Qd2 Nf6 13 h3 Kh8 followed by ...Ng8 (or ...Nd7) and ...f7-f5 with some counterplay eventually.

Schmid Benoni

1 d4 c5 2 d5 Nf6 3 Nc3

Before proceeding any further, I should also mention that 3 Nf3 will likely transpose to the main line, but it can also lead to independent play if Black goes in for the sharp 3...b5, and now 4 Bg5 Qb6 5 Bxf6 gxf6 leads to a complicated game, where White is supposed to be better, but proving it may not be so easy.

3...g6 4 Nf3 Bg7 5 e4 d6

191

Occasionally Black plays 5...0-0, but 6 e5 Ne8 7 h4 d6 8 e6!? fxe6 9 h5 is very dangerous for Black, and 6...Ng4 7 Ng5 h5 8 f4 doesn't look promising for Black either.

6 Be2

White can also consider 6 Bb5+, but Black should be okay after 6...Nbd7.

6...0-0 7 0-0 Na6 8 Bf4 Nc7 9 a4 b6 10 Re1 a6 11 h3 Bb7 12 Bc4 Qd7 with a dynamically balanced position.

Old Benoni

This line resembles the Czech Benoni, but leaves White with more options and thus is easier to play for White.

1 d4 c5 2 d5 e5 3 e4 d6

In contrast to the Czech Benoni, White has yet to play c2-c4, which gives him the option of Bb5+.

4 Nc3 Be7

Black can also play 4...a6 5 a4 Be7 6 Be2 Bg5 – a standard maneuver in this

opening – 7 Bxg5 Qxg5 8 Nf3 Qd8 9 Nd2 Nd7 10 a5, and White is slightly better.

5 Bb5+ Kf8

Both 5...Nd7, blocking the c8-bishop, and 5...Bd7, exchanging the light-squared bishop are in White's favor.

6 f4 exf4 7 Bxf4 Bg5 8 Qd2 and White has the upper hand.

Benko Gambit

In Europe, this opening is often called the Volga Gambit, named after the Russian river because some players from that region helped develop and popularize it. In English-speaking countries, it is named after the former world championship candidate Pal Benkö.

1 d4 Nf6 2 c4 c5 3 d5 b5 (D)

Nowadays this opening isn't seen very frequently at the very top level, but is otherwise played enthusiastically by players at all other levels. Black sacrifices a pawn to gain counterplay along the a- and b-files with support on the long diagonal from g7 to a1.

White now has several options, the most important ones being: **(a) 4 Nf3**; 4 cxb5 a6 5 Nc3 (Zaitsev Variation); **(b) 4 cxb5 a6 5 e3** (Modern Variation); **(c) 4 cxb5 a6 5 b6**; and **(d) 4 cxb5 a6 5 bxa6** (Benko Gambit Accepted).

4 Nf3 Variation

Just because White doesn't accept the pawn doesn't mean that he has peaceful intentions.

4 Nf3

4 a4 is another way of declining the pawn; Black is considered to be fine after both 4...bxc4 and 4...b4. Other ideas include 4 Qc2 and 4 Nd2 with similar intentions.

4...g6

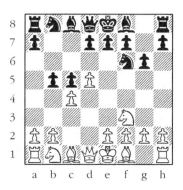

In my opinion, this is Black's best option, but many other moves have been tried, e.g., 4...b4, 4...Bb7, 4...bxc4 as well as 4...e6, which transposes to the Blumenfeld Gambit, covered below.

5 cxb5

White can also consider 5 a4, after which both 5...b4 and 5...bxc4 are adequate for Black, or 5 Qc2 a6 with a sharp game.

5...a6 6 Nc3

This is just one of several sharp lines that include 6 Qc2 and 6 e4.

6...axb5 7 d6!? Qa5+ 8 e3 exd6 9 Bxb5 Ne4 10 Bd2 Nxc3 11 Bxc3 Qxb5 12 Bxh8 Ba6 and thanks to the white king being stuck in the center, Black has compensation for the exchange.

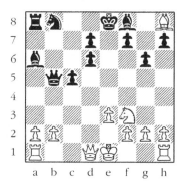

The Zaitsev Variation

A popular sharp option for White is the variation named after one of Karpov long-time seconds, Igor Zaitsev.

4 cxb5 a6 5 Nc3

 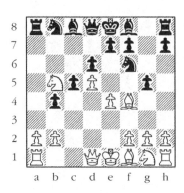

White gives back the pawn in the hope that he can gain a lead in development. White can try something similar with 5 f3, e.g., 5...axb5 6 e4 Qa5+ 7 Bd2 b4 8 Na3 d6 9 Nc4 Qc7, with approximately even chances. In addition, Black can keep it a gambit with 5...e6 and 5...g6.

5...axb5 6 e4 b4 7 Nb5

Despite its apparently vulnerable location, the knight is usually quite safe on b5 from where it helps White to generate an attack.

7...d6

Black cannot take the e4-pawn: 7...Nxe4?? 8 Qe2 Nf6 9 Nd6 mate. Who said the knight was out of play on b5?

8 Bf4

White can also consider 8 Bc4 and 8 Nf3.

8...g5!? (D)

Other options include 8...Nbd7, 8...g6 and even 8...Nxe4, but the text move has been determined to be the best and safest for Black.

9 Bxg5 Nxe4 10 Bf4 Bg7

The alternative is 10...Qa5, which also leads to an unclear position.

11 Qe2 Nf6 12 Nxd6+ Kf8 13 Nxc8 Qxc8 14 d6 exd6 15 Bxd6+ Kg8 with a complicated and unclear position. White has won a pawn and Black's king is awkwardly placed on g8, but Black has a lead in development, and it is not at all that easy to determine who is better. However, note that the continuation given in the *Encyclopedia of Chess Openings* – 16 Nf3 Qf5 – is flawed because White can win with 17 g4!. If you are not sure why, try to analyze the position.

The Modern Variation

In the 1980s, this variation gained a lot of support, but it has since been determined that Black gets full compensation in several ways.

4 cxb5 a6 5 e3

If Black takes on b5, White will take with the bishop and follow up with Nc3, a2-a4, Nf3 (or Nge2), 0-0 and finally e3-e4, with a clamp on Black's position.

However, Black doesn't have to be that accommodating.

5...g6

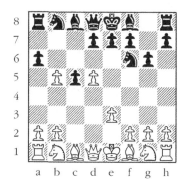

Or 5...axb5 6 Bxb5 Qa5+ 7 Nc3 Bb7 8 Bd2 Qb6 9 Qb3 e6 10 e4 Nxe4 11 Nxe4 Bxd5 12 Qd3 Qb7 13 f3 c4, and Black wins back the piece after 12 Bxc4 Bxc4 13 Qxc4 d5 with a complicated position. This is just one of the many variations in which the players need first-hand knowledge if they are to play this, so be prepared to do some studying if you want to play 5 e3 as White. The text move keeps the game in more Benko-like positions.

6 Nc3 Bg7 7 Nf3 0-0 8 a4 Bb7 9 Ra3 axb5 10 Bxb5 e6 11 dxe6 fxe6 and both players have their share of the chances; White has an extra pawn, but Black is better developed and his pieces are better coordinated.

The 5 b6 Variation

The Latvian grandmaster Alexei Shirov introduced some new ideas in the late 1980s in this otherwise largely ignored line against the Benko Gambit. But it was soon determined, that the variation had other benefits to offer White other than just the violent approach endorsed by Shirov.

4 cxb5 a6 5 b6

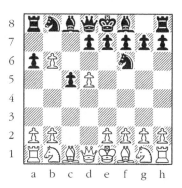

White argues that with the black pawn on a6, Black's position on the queenside is a bit clumsy and White therefore has the better chances because Black will not have a sufficient answer to White's play in the center.

5...Qxb6

Black has several alternatives including 5...e6 6 Nc3 exd5 (another idea is 6...Bb7, with which I experimented back when 5 b6 was considered a problem for Black) 7 Nxd5 Nxd5 8 Qxd5 Nc6 9 Nf3 Rb8 10 e4 Be7 11 Bc4 0-0 with even chances.

6 Nc3 d6 7 e4 g6 8 a4

White often plays 8 Nf3, which can also be quite tricky for Black to meet.

8...Bg7 9 a5 Qb4!?

If Black plays passively, e.g., 9...Qc7, then White will follow up with 10 f4 and 11 Nf3 with a strong initiative in the center.

10 Ra4 Qb7 11 Bc4 Bd7 12 Ra3 0-0 13 Nf3 Bb5 and Black has a pleasant game.

The Benko Gambit Accepted

The critical response against the Benko Gambit is undoubtedly to accept the pawn sacrifice.

4 cxb5 a6 5 bxa6 g6

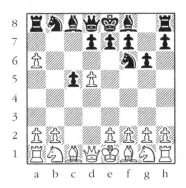

Black can also take the pawn on a6 immediately, but by playing ...g7-g6 first, Black limits White's options.

6 Nc3 Bxa6 7 Nf3

White's main alternative, 7 e4 Bxf1 8 Kxf1 g6 9 g3 (other choices here are the sharp 8 g4 and 8 h3, after which the king travels to h2 instead of g2) 9...Bg7 10 Kg2 0-0 11 Nf3 Nbd7 12 h3 Qa5 13 Re1 Rfb8, and Black's pressure on the a- and b-files compensate for the sacrificed pawn.

7...d6 8 g3 Bg7 9 Bg2 Nbd7 10 0-0 0-0
Black here often plays 10...Nb6 first, which eliminates some options for

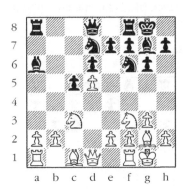

White, but adds others. The chances are approximately even.

11 Qc2 Qa5 12 Rd1 Rfb8 and Black has the typical kind of compensation he receives in the Benko Gambit.

Blumenfeld Gambit

There are many gambits that have a somewhat dubious reputation, and the Blumenfeld Gambit belongs in that group, but perhaps this is unjustified. In recent years, the Romanian grandmaster Nisipeanu has taken up the opening against top level competition with decent results, so maybe the winds are shifting.

1 d4 Nf6 2 c4 e6 3 Nf3 c5 4 d5 b5!?

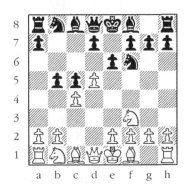

This sharp position can also be reached via the Benko Gambit move order 1 d4

Nf6 2 c4 c5 3 d5 b5 4 Nf3 e6. Black hopes to build a broad center to compensate for the pawn. However, the main recipe for White is usually to decline the pawn sacrifice.

5 Bg5

White can of course accept Black's gambit with 5 dxe6 fxe6 6 cxb5, but Black has a decent initiative after 6...d5 7 e3 Bd6 8 Be2 0-0 9 0-0 Nbd7 10 Nbd2 Bb7 11 b3 Qe7 12 Qc2 Rac8 thanks to his broad center and well-placed pieces. However, we have to remember that White has an extra pawn in return for Black's attractive position.

5...h6

Many things have been tried for Black, including 5...exd5, 5...b4 and 5...Qa5+, and some of them definitely should be given attention, if this main line is not to Black's liking.

6 Bxf6 Qxf6 7 Nc3

7 Qc2 exd5 8 cxd5 Na6 9 Nc3 Rb8 is another possibility.

7...b4 8 Nb5 Kd8

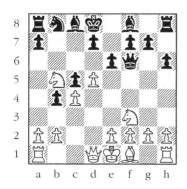

8...Na6 is also a possibility.

9 e4 g5!? 10 Bd3 Bb7 11 0-0 g4 12 e5 Qg7 13 Nd2 Qxe5 14 Re1

And White has a dangerous initiative for the pawn. This is hardly what Black was hoping for when he played 5...b5: being a pawn up, but struggling to get pieces into play with the king stuck on d8.

Budapest Gambit

While the Budapest Gambit can lead to Black's sacrificing a pawn, Black usually wins the pawn back rapidly.

1 d4 Nf6 2 c4 e5

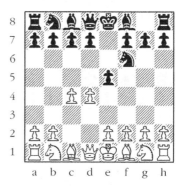

In principal this is a sharp opening, but the main lines tend to lead to a small plus for White, though well-prepared black players should not have too much to fear.

3 dxe5 Ng4

Black has a fun and sharp alternative in the Fajarowicz Gambit, which arises after 3...Ne4. In this line Black usually doesn't get his pawn back, but hopes that his slight lead in development will compensate for the sacrificed pawn. One line runs 4 a3 d6 5 Qc2 (White has to be careful, for instance 5 exd6 Bxd6 6 g3?? runs into 6...Nxf2! 7 Kxf2 Bxg3+, and White loses the queen) 5...d5 (Black would love to play 5...Bf5, but it doesn't work here because of 6 Nc3! Ng3 7 e4 Nxh1 8 exf5 dxe5 9 Be3 Nc6 10 Rd1!, and White is much better) 6 cxd5 Qxd5 7 Nf3 Nc6 8 Nc3 Nxc3 9 Qxc3 Bg4 10 Bf4 with a better game for White, though Black is not entirely without counterplay.

4 Nf3

Other options include the sharp 4 e4 Nxe5 5 f4 Nec6 6 Be3 Bb4+ 7 Nd2 Qe7 and 4 Bf4 Nc6 5 Nf3 Bb4+ 6 Nbd2 Qe7 7 e3 Ngxe5 8 Nxe5 Nxe5 9 Be2 b6, in both cases with complicated play and chances to both sides.

4...Bc5

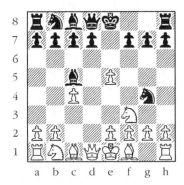

Accuracy is necessary, for instance 4...Nc6?! is met by 5 Bg5 Be7 6 Bxe7 Qxe7 7 Nc3 0-0 8 Nd5 Qd8 9 e3 with the better game for White.

5 e3 Nc6 6 Nc3 Ngxe5 7 Nxe5 Nxe5 8 Be2 0-0 9 0-0 Re8 10 b3 a5 11 Bb2 Ra6 and White chances are considered slightly preferable, though Black has excellent counterchances.

Dutch Defense

Some openings go in and out of favor for no real reason, and that has certainly been the case with the Dutch Defense, which re-emerged after a long period of obscurity and was very popular in the late 1980s and early 1990s, only to disappear again. By its very nature it is a sharp opening, but there are also many solid lines.

1 d4 f5

Black weakens, apparently without any reason, the king's pawn shield by advancing the f-pawn on the very first move. This weakness has caused a lot of people to attempt to take advantage of this by means of all sorts of gambits and sharp lines. However, all these lines have one thing in common: they don't work very well! Usually, Black obtains at least equal chances if well prepared. So I recommend that if you consider taking up the Dutch, study the small side lines first and carefully since you are likely to run into them quite frequently.

> *Flank play should only take place in conjunction with healthy development, with a particular goal in mind and with a reasonably stable center.*

The coverage divides as follows: **(a) 2 c4 Nf6 3 g3** (Main Lines); and **(b) Various** Anti-Dutch Setups.

The Main Lines

The scope and extent of these lines is quite amazing. From the solid Stonewall to the sharp Leningrad.

2 c4 Nf6 3 g3

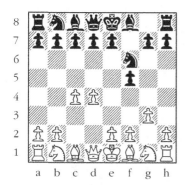

White can also play the immediate 3 Nf3, but it limits White's options considerably, and should be postponed. Now Black can go in several directions: **(a) 3...g6** (Leningrad Variation); **(b) 3...e6 4 Bg2 d5** (Stonewall Variation); and **(c) 3...e6 4 Bg2 Be7** (Classical Dutch).

The Leningrad Variation

Black's sharpest option is undoubtedly the Leningrad Dutch.

3...g6 4 Bg2 Bg7 5 Nf3

This is the normal move, but White can also choose a setup with 5 Nc3, followed by 6 d5 and 7 Nh3.

5...0-0 6 0-0 d6 7 Nc3

Again we will follow the main line, but

White frequently plays either 7 b3 or 7 d5, in both cases with chances for both sides.

7...Qe8

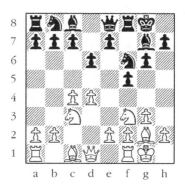

This is currently one of the most popular moves in this position, but other moves have also been played frequently here, e.g., 7...c6, 7...Na6, and 7...Nc6.

8 d5

There are several other perfectly playable alternatives at this juncture, for example, 8 Nd5, 8 Re1 and 8 b3, but Black has excellent chances of equalizing against all of them.

8...Na6 9 Rb1 c5 10 dxc6 bxc6 11 b4 Bd7 with a complicated game and chances for both sides.

The Stonewall Variation

This variation first came to prominence when Soviet world champion Mikhail Botvinnik began employing it regularly.

3...e6 4 Bg2 d5

Black can also play 4...Be7 before ...d7-d5, but it limits his options and adds some for White.

5 Nf3

White can also consider 5 Nh3.

5...c6 6 0-0 Be7

The so-called Modern Stonewall Variation sees Black playing the more aggressive 6...Bd6, immediately fighting for the control over the e5-square. One variation runs 7 b3 Qe7 (to prevent White from playing Ba3 and exchanging the dark-squared bishops) 8 Bb2 0-0 9 Ne5 Bd7 10 Qc1 Be8 11 Ba3 Nbd7 12 Nd3, and White has perhaps the slightly better chances.

7 b3 0-0 8 Qc2 Ne4 9 Bb2 Nd7 10 Nbd2 Qe8 11 Ne1

Why Ne1? Ideally, White wants to place his knights on d3 and f3 (or e5) to control the weakened e5-square and

thus restrain Black's movements. The knight retreat also creates the possibility of f2-f3, kicking Black's knight from the e4-square.

11...Qh5 12 f3 Ng5 12 Nd3 Nh3+ 13 Kh1 Bd6 14 f4 and White has the slightly better chances.

The Classical Dutch

This actually covers many variations, some quite common, others relatively rare.

3...e6 4 Bg2 Be7

Another line is 4...Bb4+.

5 Nf3 0-0 6 0-0 d6

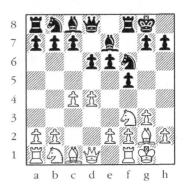

Alekhine on occasion favored 6...Ne4, but White obtains better chances after both 7 Nbd2 and 7 b3, though not all the lines are entirely clear.

7 Nc3 Qe8

In this line Black can also consider 7...c6.

8 b3 a5 9 Bb2 Na6 10 e3 c6 11 Qe2 Nc7 and both sides have their chances, though White is generally considered to be slightly better in this position.

Various Anti-Dutch Set-ups

White has tried many different plans against the Dutch and to examine them individually in detail would require a separate book. So what follows is a brief review of each of them:

(a) 2 e4 (The Staunton Gambit) 2...fxe4 3 Nc3 Nf6 4 Bg5 (4 f3 d5 5 Bg5 Bf5 is better for Black) 4...Nc6 (4...d5? 5 Bxf6 exf6 6 Qh5+) 5 d5 Ne5 6 Qd4 Nf7 7 Bxf6 exf6 8 Nxe4 Be7 9 0-0-0 0-0, and although White has won back the pawn, Black is at least equal.

(b) 2 Bg5 g6 (note that White doesn't lose the bishop after 2...h6 3 Bh4 g5, because of 4 e3, but 4...Nf6 5 Bg3 d6 is about equal) 3 Nd2 Bg7 4 e3 d6 with equal chances.

(c) 2 Nc3 d5 3 Bg5 (3 e4 has to be met by 3...dxe4, and transposes into a version of the Blackmar-Diemer Gambit, that is playable for White: 4 Bf4 Nf6 5 f3 exf3 6 Nxf3 e6 with chances for both sides) 3...g6 (or 3...Nf6 4 Bxf6 exf6 with more or less equal play) 4 h4 Bg7 5 e3 c6 6 Bd3 Be6 7 Nf3 Nd7 8 h5 Ngf6, and Black has equalized.

(d) 2 g4 (2 h3 followed by g2-g4 is another version of the Wing Gambit) 2...fxg4 3 e4 (3 h3 d5! 4 hxg4 Bxg4 5 Bg2 Nf6 is better for Black) 4...d5 4 e5 c5 5 dxc5 Nc6 6 Bf4 Be6 7 h3 g5 8 Bxg5 Bg7 with sharp complications.

(e) 2 c4 Nf6 3 Nc3 e6 (3...g6 4 Bg5 Bg7 5 Qd2 c5 6 d5 d6 is also possible with unclear play) 4 Nf3 Bb4 5 Bg5 0-0 6 Rc1 d6 with chances for both players.

Knight's Tango

One of Black's most provocative openings is the Knight's Tango, which isn't as bad as it may look at first glance.

1 d4 Nf6 2 c4 Nc6!?

This move dares White to push the pawns forward, but White doesn't have to oblige.

3 Nc3

White's alternatives are also of interest: 3 Nf3 e6 4 Nc3 Bb4 5 Qc2 leads to a variation of the Nimzo-Indian that is considered slightly better for White, but which is fully playable for Black or 3 d5 Ne5 4 Qd4 Ng6, intending ...e7-e5 or ...e7-e6, depending on White's next move; in either case, Black is doing fine.

3...e5 4 d5 Ne7 5 e4

If White plays 5 h4 to discourage Black from playing ...Ng6, Black instead plays 5...Neg8! followed by development of the dark-squared bishop to b4 or c5, then ...d7-d6 and ...Ne7.

5...Ng6 6 Bd3

6 Be3 Bb4 7 f3 Bxc3+ 8 bxc3 d6 is fine for Black.

6...Bc5 7 h3 d6 8 Nge2 a6 with perhaps slightly better chances for White, but Black's position is fully playable.

King's Fianchetto

In this short section, there are two move orders worth noting.

1 d4 d6

The other move is the immediate 1...g6, which often transposes to other openings, e.g., 2 c4 Bg7 3 Nf3 (3 Nc3 c5 4 d5 Bxc3+ 5 bxc3 f5 is a fun line, that isn't particular easy to play for either side) 3...c5 4 e4, and now 4...cxd4 (also 4...Qb6 and 4...Qa5 are possible) 5 Nxd4 Nc6 is a Sicilian Accelerated Dragon, Maroczy Bind.

2 c4

2 Nf3 may transpose, but Black can also play 2...Bg4, which leads to an unbalanced game after both 3 e4 Nf6 4 Nc3 e6 and 3 c4 Bxf3 (or 3...Nd7 4 Qb3 Rb8) 4 exf3 g6 5 Nc3 Bg7. These lines are considered better for White, but are difficult to play.

2...g6 3 Nc3 Bg7 4 e4

After 4 Nf3 Bg4 5 e3, Black can play 5...c5 with more or less equal chances.

4...e5

Black has other choices available at this juncture: 4...Nc6 5 d5 Nd4 6 Be3 c5 7 Nge2 Qb6 with a complicated position or 4...Nd7 5 Nf3 e5 6 Be2 Ne7 7 0-0 0-0 8 Be3 h6 with a position somewhat similar to the King's Indian.

5 Nf3 exd4 6 Nxd4 Nc6 7 Be3 Nge7 8 h4

8 Be2 0-0 9 0-0 f5 is considered fully acceptable for Black.

8...f5 9 h5 fxe4 10 hxg6 hxg6 11 Rxh8 Bxh8 12 Nxe4 Bf5 with an unclear position, considered slightly better for White, but which demands very accurate play.

Keres-Mikenas Defense

This opening is a sort of an accelerated Bogo-Indian, where both sides have some extra options to sharpen the game.

1 d4 e6 2 c4 Bb4+ *(D)*

Black can also play 2...b6 which leads to the English Defense.

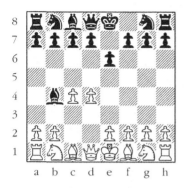

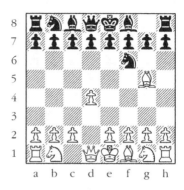

3 Bd2 a5

Or 3...Qe7 4 e4 Nc6 5 Nf3 Nf6 6 Bd3 Bxd2+ 7 Nbxd2 d6 8 0-0, and White has the slightly better chances. Black can also transpose to a line in the Dutch with 3...Bxd2+ 4 Qxd2 f5 5 g3 Nf6.

4 Nc3 d6 5 e4 e5 6 a3 Bxc3 7 Bxc3 Nf6 8 f3 exd4 9 Qxd4 and White's position is preferable.

Trompowsky Attack

For a long period of time, this opening was relegated to relative obscurity, but in recent years it has developed a large following; the theory has developed greatly in part because of several excellent books on the topic.

1 d4 Nf6 2 Bg5 (D)

White threatens to exchange on f6 and give Black a doubled f-pawns. This in itself is no disaster for Black, but it takes the game out the normal types of positions Black is seeking in the Semi-Closed Games.

2...Ne4

Other continuations include **2...d5** 3 Bxf6 exf6 (3...gxf6 is also playable) 4 e3; **2...e6** 3 e4 h6 4 Bxf6 Qxf6 5 Nc3 Bb4 6 Qd2 c5 or **2...c5** 3 Bxf6 (3 d5 Qb6 4 Nc3 Qxb2 5 Bd2 Qb6 6 e4 with compensation for the pawn is also possible) 3...gxf6 4 d5 Qb6 5 Qc1 f5 6 g3 Bg7 7 c3 d6 8 Nd2 0-0, in all cases with interesting play and chances for both sides.

3 Bf4

3 Bh4 d5 4 f3 Nd6 5 Nc3 Nf5 6 Bf2 c5 is another strange line of this exciting opening.

3...c5 4 f3 Qa5+ 5 c3 Nf6 6 Nd2 cxd4 7 Nb3 Qb6 8 cxd4 d5 9 Rc1 Nc6 and Black has succeeded in equalizing.

Torre Attack

1 d4 Nf6 2 Nf3 e6

2...g6 doesn't prohibit White from playing the Torre either, for instance 3 Bg5 Bg7 4 Nbd2 0-0 (or 4...c5!? to sharpen the game) 5 c3 (5 e3 d6 6 Bd3 Nbd7 7 0-0 h6 8 Bh4 e5 is fine for Black) 5...d6 6 e4 Nbd7 7 Bc4 h6 8 Bh4 e5 with more or less even chances.

3 Bg5

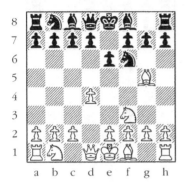

This is a well-respected way for White to avoid the theoretical main lines after 3 c4 and has been regularly played at all levels, including in some world championship matches.

3...c5

An interesting alternative is 3...h6 4 Bxf6 Qxf6 5 e4 d6 6 Nc3 Nd7 7 Qd2 a6 with sharp play.

4 e3 Be7

The immediate 4...b6?! runs into 5 d5! exd5 6 Bxf6 Qxf6 7 Nc3 with the better chances for White.

5 Nbd2 b6 6 Bd3 Bb7 7 c3 cxd4 8 exd4 Nc6 9 0-0 0-0

Black should usually be careful castling kingside, waiting to first see where White castles.

10 Qe2 Nd5 11 Bxe7 Ncxe7 and Black has equalized.

London System

The London can be considered an even more solid version of the Torre Attack. It is hardly ever played at grandmaster level, but has numerous fans at lower levels because it is an easy opening to play as White.

1 d4 Nf6 2 Nf3 e6

The London can also be played against 2...g6: 3 Bf4 Bg7 4 e3 d6 5 h3 0-0 6 Be2 c5 7 c3 b6 8 0-0 Bb7 9 Nbd2 Nbd7 10 a4 a6 with fairly even chances.

3 Bf4 c5 4 e3 b6 5 Bd3 Bb7 6 h3 Be7 7 c3 0-0 8 0-0 d5 9 Nbd2 Qc8 10 Re1 Ba6 with an even game.

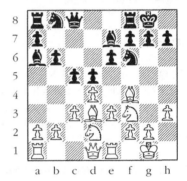

Fianchetto System

This careful setup can often transpose to the Catalan, the King's Indian, the Queen's Indian, the Pirc or even the English Opening, depending on Black's replies, so both sides have to be careful in order not to transpose into an inferior line of these openings.

1 d4 Nf6 2 Nf3 e6

Or 2...g6 3 g3 Bg7 4 Bg2 0-0 5 0-0 d6 6 b3 (6 Re1, 6 Nc3 and 6 a4 are other possibilities) 6...e5!? 7 dxe5 Nfd7 8 Bb2 Nc6 9 e4 dxe5 with a balanced game.

3 g3 b5!? (D)

Black can also play 3...c5 4 Bg2 Nc6 5 0-0 cxd4 6 Nxd4 Qb6 7 Nxc6 dxc6 8 Nd2 e5 9 Nc4 Qc7, with equality.

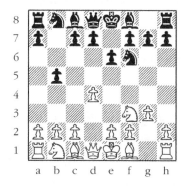

4 Bg2 Bb7 5 0-0 c5 6 c3 Na6 7 Bg5 Be7 8 Nbd2 0-0 with more or less even chances.

Lesser Variations

Englund Gambit

1 d4 e5?!

This gambit is entirely unsound, but has a nasty trap that has worked for me several times in blitz games when I was much younger.

2 dxe5 Nc6 3 Nf3 Qe7 4 Bf4 Qb4+ 5 Bd2 Qxb2 6 Nc3!

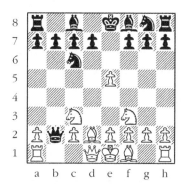

The trap occurs if White here plays 6 Bc3?, which is strongly met by 6...Bb4, and now 7 Qd2? Bxc3 8 Qxc3 Qc1 mate

ends the game rather abruptly. But after the text move, Black's position is quite awful. He has only just managed to level the material imbalance, but has done so at the cost of three queen moves and picking up the "poisoned" b2-pawn. He is now far behind in development and will have to spend time getting the queen back to safety as well as pieces into play.

Polish Defense

1 d4 b5 2 e4 Bb7

Of course, if Black played 2...a6, then we would enter the line 1 e4 a6 2 d4 b5, covered in chapter 6. But the line here is slightly better.

3 f3 a6 4 Be3 e6 5 Nd2 d5 6 Bd3 Nf6 7 e5 Nfd7 8 f4 c5 9 c3

This position very much resembles one that could have arisen from the Classical French, 1 e4 e6 2 d4 d5 3 Nc3 Nf6 4 e5 Nfd7 and the play that arises is also quite similar in style. White is marginally better, but since White played 1 d4 on the first move, he may not be all that familiar with the specific plans that are commonplace with this pawn structure. Therefore the chances are more or less equal, with perhaps a slight preference for White.

Accelerated Knights Tango

1 d4 Nc6

The play that we will see in this line will often be able to transpose to the Knights Tango covered above, after 1 d4 Nf6 2 c4 Nc6, but there are a number of clearly defined differences.

2 c4

A fun alternative is 2 d5 Ne5 3 e4 e6 4 f4 Ng6 5 dxe6 fxe6 6 Nf3 Bc5 7 Nc3 Nh6 with a messy position where White perhaps has the slightly better of it, but not by much.

2...e5 3 d5 Bb4+

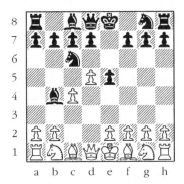

Both with 2...Nf6 and 3...Nce7 4 e4 Ng6 5 Nf3 Nf6, play could transpose to the "normal" Knights Tango. The text move takes the game in a slightly different direction.

4 Nd2 Nce7 5 a3 Bxd2+ 6 Bxd2 d6 7 e4 f5!? with a sharp position in which both sides have chances.

Queen's Fianchetto

1 d4 b6 2 c4 Bb7

2...e6 would be a direct transposition to the English Defense.

3 Nc3

3 d5 e6 is also possible, again transposing to the English Defense.

3...Nf6 4 Nf3 d5

4...e6 transposes to a Queen's Indian.

5 cxd5 Nxd5 6 a3 Nd7

6...e6 would again lead to a Queen's Indian, this time the Petrosian Variation.

7 Qc2 e6

Transposing into a more standard Queen's Indian Defense, with chances for both sides.

Do not think you can match the repertoires of top grandmasters; their repertoires are far to detailed and will contain several very theory-laden lines that you will have no capacity to learn properly and even less chance of understanding.

Chapter 9

Flank Openings

The openings in this chapter are an odd blend of flexible and popular openings such as the English and the Reti and the weird and rare such as the Orangutan and Grob. Though they are called "Flank Openings," their aim is to get some pieces into play before occupying the center. You may notice the "reverse" nature of some of these openings. For instance 1 d4 f5 is the Dutch, whereas 1 f4 d5 is the Bird; 1 d4 Nf6 2 c4 e6 3 Nf3 b6 is the Queen's Indian, and 1 b3 d5 2 Bb2 c5 3 e3 is the Nimzo-Larsen Attack, etc.

English Opening

1 c4

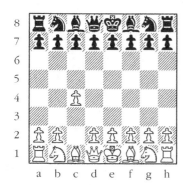

The naming of 1 c4 as the English Opening stems back to the 19th-century British master Howard Staunton's use of this move. It is a very flexible opening that can lead to numerous transpositions to other openings. It is mostly a dynamic, positional opening, but it can also turn very sharp. Among its adherents are all sorts of players from mostly positional players like Smyslov

and Kramnik to dynamic tactical players like Kasparov, who in the late 1980s injected several new ideas into the opening. As previously noted, this is my favorite opening and it is the first opening I ever studied. I have since written two books exclusively devoted to the theory on this opening.

There is a large body of theory, and we will cover it in the following sections: **(a) 1...e5** (King's English); **(b) 1...c5** (Symmetrical English); **(c) 1...Nf6** (Anti-Indians); **(d) 1...b6** (English Defense); and **(e)** Other English Variations.

The King's English

You wouldn't be completely wrong if you describe this opening as the Sicilian Reversed. Indeed some of the sub-variations use this description, but this opening is a lot more than that.

1 c4 e5

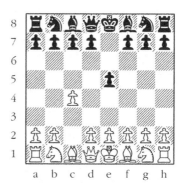

This appears to be the most logical answer to the English opening, giving Black easy access to the development of his kingside. Personally I think that this is the easier move for White to play against, because it gives White a greater opportunity to dictate the direction of the game. Indeed when I first started playing the English, I felt that after 1...e5, I was already reasonably sure that I was on the way to winning the game. What the mind can do to you...

2 Nc3

Normally White chooses this move, the natural follow-up to his first move, because it continues development and takes control over the e4- and d5-squares. However, because Black has had a fair amount of success with the sharp 2...Bb4, many players have started to use a different move order and play 2 g3 to prevent this possibility for Black. This line usually transposes to other variations with g2-g3, but the main exception is when Black counters it with 2...Nf6 3 Bg2 c6, which resembles an Alapin Sicilian with the colors reversed, but in the English Opening, the setup is named after the Estonian world championship candidate Paul Keres. After 4 d4 (4 Nf3 e4 5 Nd4 d5 is also possible) 4...exd4 (4...Bb4+ 5 Bd2 Bxd2+ Qxd2 d6 6 Nc3 0-0 is also feasible, if easier to play for White) 5 Qxd4 d5 6 Nf3 Be7 7 cxd5 cxd5 9 Qa4 0-0 (9...Qb6 can also be considered) 10 Be3 Ne4 11 Rd1 and White is better.

After 2 Nc3, the main options for Black are: **(a) 2...d6; (b) 2...Nf6;** and **(c) 2...Nc6.** And of course we have previously noted 2...Bb4, which intends to disrupt White's game with an exchange on c3, if White allows it. Therefore White's best is 3 Nd5, and then after 3...Be7

(both 3...Ba5 and 3...Bc5 are met with 4 b4 with the better game for White) 4 d4 d6 5 e4 Nf6 6 Nxe7 Qxe7 7 f3, and now Black can play either 7...exd4 8 Qxd4 Nc6 or 7...Nh5 followed shortly by ...f7-f5. In both cases I think White is better, but this type of position is very different from solid, maneuvering types of positions that White usually hopes for in the English Opening.

2...d6 Variations

After the flexible 2...d6, the game may take three distinctively different directions, all depending on White's third move.

2...d6 3 Nf3

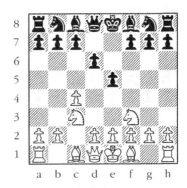

White's alternatives are the central response with 3 d4, after which Black usually gets an adequate game with 3...exd4 4 Qxd4 Nc6 (4...Nf6 is also playable) 5 Qd2 Nf6 6 b3 (6 g3 Be6 7 e4 a5 is fine for Black) 6...g6 (or 6...Be6 7 e4 a5 8 Bd3 g6 also leads to approximately even chances) 7 Bb2 Bg7 8 g3 0-0 9 Nh3 (note that 9 Bg2 Re8 10 Nh3 can be met with the surprising 10...d5 with very sharp play) 9...Re8 10 Nf4 Ne5 11 Bg2 with a position that is slightly easier for White to play.

The second alternative to the main line is 3 g3, which leads to a position that resembles the Closed Sicilian Reversed, which we will cover in the section on 2...Nc6. For instance 3...g6 (3...f5 4 Bg2 Nf6 is also playable though 5 e3 Be7 6 Nge2 followed by 0-0, d2-d3, f2-f4 and b2-b4 is better for White) 4 Bg2 Bg7 5 d3 f5 6 e3 Nf6 7 Nge2 a5 8 0-0 0-0 with a sharp battle ahead.

3...f5 4 d4

Here 4 g3 would transpose to 3 g3. Instead, with the text move, White attacks the black center hoping that the weaknesses in Black's position will compensate for the time White invests in probing them.

4...e4 5 Ng5 c6

5...Be7 6 Nh3 c6 is also possible, and then of course 5...h6 6 Nh3 g5 looks tempting, but White has the surprising 7 Ng1 followed by h2-h4, with the better chances.

6 g3 Be7 7 Nh3 Nf6 8 Bg2 0-0 9 0-0 Na6 10 d5

White has to be careful not to let Black play ...d6-d5 and consolidate the center.

10...Nc7 11 f3 with a complicated battle ahead, the chances are more or less balanced.

2...Nf6 Variations

Very often, Black develops both knights early in the English. Those lines will be covered in the next section; below we will only look at lines in which Black does not play ...Nc6 on one of the next few moves.

2...Nf6 3 g3 g6

This line takes the game closer to King's Indian setups for Black. Black's two main alternatives are 3...Bb4 4 Bg2 0-0 5 e4 (or 5 Nf3 Re8 6 0-0 e4 7 Ne1 Bxc3 8 dxc3 d6 with chances for both sides) 5...Bxc3 6 bxc3 c6 7 Ne2 d5 8 cxd5 cxd5 9 exd5 Nxd5 10 0-0 Nc6 with a balanced game, and the Keres Variation, 3...c6 4 Nf3 e4 5 Nd4 d5 6 cxd5 Qb6 7 Nb3 cxd5 8 Bg2 Bf5 9 d3 Bb4 10 0-0, with a better game for White.

4 Bg2 Bg7 5 Nf3 d6 6 0-0 0-0 7 d3

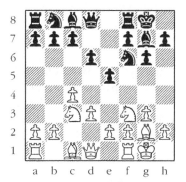

This position is often reached when Black seeks a King's Indian Defense, but White doesn't want to oblige. The move order is therefore frequently: 1 c4 (or 1 Nf3 first and only c2-c4 later) 1...Nf6 2 Nf3 g6 3 g3 Bg7 4 Bg2 d6 5 0-0 0-0 6 Nc3 e5 7 d3. If White had played d2-d4 anywhere in the above sequence, the game would have transposed to the Fianchetto Variation of the King's Indian.

The position that arises after 7 d3 was the subject of some scrutiny in several chapters of the second edition of *A Strategic Opening Repertoire* which I co-authored with John Donaldson.

7...Nc6

This is the more common move, but Black can also play moves like 7...Re8, 7...Nh5, 7...Nbd7, 7...c6 and even 7...h6, all in line with a typical King's Indian for Black. You could argue that with the text move, we have transposed to the King's English Four Knights which belongs in the next section, but the position we have reached here very rarely comes from a traditional Four Knights move order.

8 Rb1 a5 9 a3 h6

Black often plays this move to prevent White from playing Bg5, pinning the knight and gaining more control over the d5-square.

10 b4 axb4 11 axb4 Be6 12 b5 Ne7 13 Bb2 with a sharp battle ahead, in which the play is clearly defined: White tries to break through on the queenside and Black hopes to get a kingside attack rolling.

2...Nc6 Variations

For the sake of simplicity, we will cover the remaining lines in this section, even if the positions reached in this section just as often come from Black playing 2...Nf6, before ...Nc6 is played. For example, in the Four Knights, it usually does not matter which knight is developed first.

2...Nc6 3 Nf3 *(D)*

White commonly plays **3 g3** here as well. It can easily transpose to other lines, but many times it does not: **3...g6 4 Bg2 Bg7**, and here White has several specialties like **5 Rb1**, **5 e3** (my childhood favorite) and **5 Nf3** (here or

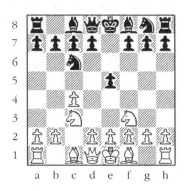

on the next move) which can transpose to the main line covered in the previous section. The main move, however, is **5 d3**, and then after **5...d6**, White has several interesting moves available: **6 e3**, e.g., 6...f5 7 Nge2 Nf6 8 0-0 0-0 9 Rb1 a5 10 a3 Ne7 11 b4 axb4 12 axb4 with chances for both sides; **6 Rb1**, aiming for an immediate queenside attack before bothering with kingside development, e.g., 6...a5 7 a3 Nf6 8 b4 axb4 9 axb4 0-0 10 b5 Nd4 11 e3 Ne6 12 Nge2 Re8 and the chances are about balanced; and **6 e4**, which can be difficult to play against as Black; the main line runs 6...f5 7 Nge2 Nf6 8 0-0 0-0 9 Nd5 Be6 10 Bg5 Qd7 11 Rc1 Nh5 12 exf5 Bxf5 13 Qd2 with a better game for White. Finally, **6 Nf3** transposes to the main line in the previous section. These lines all fall within the category of the Closed Sicilian Reversed.

3...Nf6

The starting position in the King's English Four Knights. Black can also try 3...g6 and 3...Bb4, but these are less common. A sharper alternative can be found in 3...f5, and now 4 d4 e4 5 Ng5 Nf6 6 e3 h6 7 Nh3 g5 8 f3 exf3 9 Qxf3 leads to a double-edged position.

4 g3

White has an amazing variety of choices available at this juncture, and all of them have found a following, even at grandmaster level. Some of these lines are positional and slow, others are quite sharp and complicated:

(a) 4 a3 d6 5 e3 g6 6 d3 Bg7 7 Be2 0-0 and 4 d3 Bb4 5 Bd2 0-0 6 e3 Re8 7 Be2 are positional lines, where neither side tends to get hurt early on.

(b) The illogical-looking **4 e4** Bb4 (or 4...Bc5 5 Nxe5 Nxe5 6 d4 Bb4 7 dxe5 Nxe4 8 Qd4 Nxc3 9 bxc3 Be7 with an unclear position) 5 d3 d6 6 g3 0-0 7 Bg2 a6 8 0-0 is an interesting and somewhat off-beat line.

(c) The sharp **4 d4** also leads to unusual pawn structures after 4...exd4 5 Nxd4 Bb4 6 Bg5 h6 7 Bh4 Bxc3+ 8 bxc3 Ne5 9 f4 Ng6 with a complicated struggle ahead.

(d) Of the "minor" alternatives to the text move, **4 e3** is the most common: 4...Bb4 (4...Be7 is the more solid alternative) 5 Qc2 0-0 (Black can also play 5...Bxc3 6 Qxc3 Qe7 7 a3 d5 8 cxd5 Nxd5 with an even game) 6 Nd5 Re8 7 Qf5 (hello, what was that?) 7...d6 8 Nxf6 Qxf6 (Black can also take the with pawn, but that is very complicated) 9 Qxf6 gxf6 10 a3 Bc5 11 b4 Bb6 12 Bb2, and White may have a tiny edge, but nothing that should overly concern Black.

Note that it may be tempting for Black to play an early ...d7-d5 against 4 d3, 4 a3 and 4 e3, but this is usually something White is hoping for Black to play, and why play straight into White's hands?

4...Bb4

Again Black has several worthy alternatives to choose from: **4...Bc5** 5 Bg2 d6 6 0-0 0-0 7 d3 h6 8 a3 a6 9 e3 Bb6 10 b3 Bf5 with chances for both sides; **4...Nd4** is an idea of Kortschnoi's that has become popular relatively recently: 5 Bg2 Nxf3+ 6 Bxf3 Bb4 7 Qb3 Bc5 8 0-0 0-0 9 d3 h6 10 e3 a6 11 Rd1, and White has the somewhat better chances; and **4...d5**, the Reversed Dragon Variation, is one of Black's main alternative to the text move and is also popular. After 5 cxd5 Nxd5 6 Bg2 Nb6 7 0-0 Be7 8 d3 (White can also play 8 Rb1 0-0 9 b4 or 8 a3 0-0 9 b4 Be6 10 Rb1 f6 11 d3 in both cases with plenty of play for both sides) 8...0-0 9 a3 Be6 10 b4 f6 11 Bb2 a5 12 b5 Nd5 13 Nd2 with a sharp position and chances for both players.

5 Bg2

White also often plays 5 Nd5, e.g., 5...Bc5 6 Bg2 d6 7 0-0 0-0 with a somewhat different type of position.

5...0-0 6 0-0 e4

On 6...Re8, White usually plays 7 Nd5, e.g., 7...Bc5 8 d3 Nxd5 9 cxd5 Nd4 10 Nd2 d6 11 e3, and White has a more comfortable game.

7 Ng5

Or 7 Ne1 Bxc3 8 dxc3 h6 9 Nc2 Re8 10 Ne3 d6, and Black is doing okay. The text move forces Black's next two moves.

7...Bxc3 8 bxc3 Re8 9 f3 exf3

In their 1987 World Championship match, Karpov surprised Kasparov with the sharp pawn sacrifice 9...e3, which is best not accepted, but after 10 d3 d5 11 Qb3 Na5 12 Qa3 c6 13 cxd5 cxd5 14 f4, White has slightly better chances.

10 Nxf3 d5 11 cxd5 Qxd5 12 Nd4 Qh5 13 Nxc6 bxc6 with an unclear position and approximately even chances.

The Symmetrical English

One of the common misconceptions about the Symmetrical English is that it is a boring opening. The opening is as varied as many of the sharp lines in the Sicilian.

1 c4 c5 (D)

The coverage will be broken up into the following sections: **(a) 2 Nf3 Nf6 3 d4** (Anti-Benoni); **(b) 2 Nf3 Nf6 3 g3 b6** (Hedgehog); **(c) Asymmetrical Lines;**

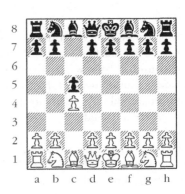

and **(d) 2 Nc3 Nc6 3 g3** (Pure Symmetrical).

The Anti-Benoni

This name appears to be confusing; you would think that by playing 1 c4 and 2 Nf3, White has avoided all of the Benonis. The label comes from the fact that we can reach these lines after 1 d4 Nf6 2 c4 c5, and now 3 Nf3 avoids the Benoni, and we have the same position as with our move order.

2 Nf3 Nf6 3 d4 cxd4 4 Nxd4 e6

Black can play 4...Nc6 and then follow up with 5...e6, which will transpose to the main line. However, there are some independent alternatives. For instance,

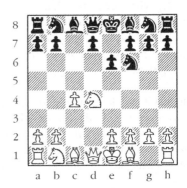

the sharp 4...e5, the so-called Kasparov Gambit, sacrifices a pawn for fast and easy development: 5 Nb5 d5 6 cxd5 Bc5 (6...Nxd5?? loses a piece to 7 Qxd5 Qxd5 8 Nc7+) 7 N5c3 0-0 8 e3 e4 9 Be2 Qe7 10 a3 Rd8, and Black has compensation for the pawn; he is likely to pick up the d-pawn sooner or later.

4...b6 is also commonly seen, e.g., 5 Nc3 Bb7 6 f3 e6 7 e4 d6 8 Be2 a6 9 Be3 Be7 10 0-0 0-0 11 Qd2 Nbd7 where Black has chosen a so-called Hedgehog (see below for further explanation) against a Maroczy Bind setup from White. The chances are approximately equal.

5 Nc3

Often White plays 5 g3 immediately, against which Black has tried just about any available move. The best moves for Black are probably 5...Bb4+ 6 Bd2 Qb6, 5...Nc6, 5...Qb6 and 5...Qc7 and in all cases, Black has excellent chances of equalizing.

5...Nc6

Here both 5...a6 and 5...Bb4 are equally good options, but carry a lesser theoretical burden.

6 g3

White has a complicated-looking alternative in 6 Ndb5, but it usually quickly fizzles out to an even endgame after 6...d5 7 Bf4 e5 8 cxd5 exf4 9 dxc6 bxc6 Qxd8+ Kxd8 11 Rd1+ Bd7 12 Nd6 Bxd6 13 Rxd6 Rb8, and most of the excitement is behind the players.

6...Qb6 7 Nb3 Ne5

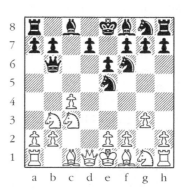

This provocative move forces White to play e2-e4, a move which he would rather have saved for later. The fact that Black spends a move to provoke it and then loses a tempo when White chases the queen away later, speaks to the significance of luring the e-pawn forward.

8 e4 Bb4 9 Qe2 d6 10 f4 Nc6 11 Be3 Bxc3+ 12 bxc3 Qc7 13 Bg2 0-0

Amazingly, this is more or less the starting position when playing this variation. White can now sacrifice a pawn with 14 0-0 b6 15 Nd4 Nxd4 16 cxd4 Ba6 with a complicated game or play it safer with 14 c5 dxc5 15 Bxc5 Rd8 with another sharp position. Needless to say, you really need to know this variation well before you include it in your repertoire, and unless you have studied the theory carefully, you should avoid this line with either color.

The Hedgehog

One of the most popular defensive setups for Black in the Symmetrical English is the so-called Hedgehog. The variation, much like its real-life counterpart, is an odd creature, that gives the appearance of being shy, unassuming and very careful, but when you provoke it, its nastier side may emerge, and you will likely hurt yourself on its spikes.

2 Nf3 Nf6 3 g3 b6 4 Bg2 Bb7 5 0-0 e6 (D)

The Hedgehog has a cousin in the so-called double fianchetto, which is also seen quite frequently, e.g., 6 Nc3 (also 6 b3 Bg7 7 Bb2 0-0 8 Nc3 Na6 9 d4 d5 is possible) 6...Bg7 7 d4 cxd4 8 Qxd4 (like in the Hedgehog, it is Black's interest

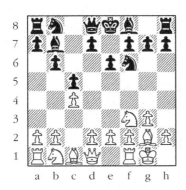

to exchange the light-squared bishops, and therefore White usually avoids 8 Nxd4 Bxg2 9 Kxg2 0-0 with equal chances) 8...Nc6 9 Qf4 0-0 10 Rd1 Rc8 with an interesting struggle ahead. White has more space, but Black's position is solid and loaded with dynamic counterplay.

6 Nc3 Be7 7 d4

White has two main alternatives at this juncture. 7 b3 is considered fairly harmless and offers Black a relatively easy game, whereas 7 Re1 is much

sharper: 7...d6 8 e4 a6 9 d4 cxd4 10 Nxd4 (now this move is possible thanks to Re1 and e2-e4) 10...Qc7 11 Be3 Nbd7 (the c-pawn looks tasty, but after 11...Qxc4 12 Rc1, the threat of Nd5 or Ncb5 will cause Black serious problems) 12 Rc1 0-0 13 f4 Rfe8 14 g4 Nc5 with an unclear position and chances for both sides. White has more space, but he has to be careful because Black's pieces are ready to jump into action after a well-timed ...e6-e5 or ...d6-d5.

7...cxd4 8 Qxd4 d6 (D)

This is the starting position of the main line Hedgehog. White has several good

options to choose from, 9 b3 and 9 Bg5 for instance, in addition to our chosen main line...

9 Rd1 a6 10 b3 Nbd7 11 e4 Qc7 12 Ba3 Nc5 13 e5 dxe5 14 Qxe5 Rc8 and White has at best a tiny advantage. The Hedgehog setup for Black is very solid and can arise from any number of different openings – the Kan and Paulsen Sicilians, the Queen's Indian, and several different lines in the English. White does best to play carefully, but actively, Black on the other hand should maintain a flexible position and usually wait for White to weaken himself, though sometimes a little provocation is needed for this to happen. Needless to say, the Hedgehog has an enormous amount of theory attached to it. Entire books have been devoted to the study of this opening, and in fact a recent one covered the subject in depth in 575 pages! Do not play this line unless you have studied it very carefully.

The Asymmetrical Variations

This appears to be a contradiction of terms – how can the Symmetrical English be asymmetrical? Well, in the Symmetrical English it is a way to describe those lines that do not fall in under the label *Pure Symmetrical*, which we will cover below. In my opinion, some of the most interesting lines of the Symmetrical English are those we will look at in this section.

2 Nc3 Nf6 3 Nf3

White can also play 3 g3 after which 3...d5 4 cxd5 Nxd5 5 Bg2 Nc7 leads to a variation of the Rubinstein Variation, which we will look a little closer at below.

3...d5 (D)

Black has several interesting alternatives, e.g., 3...e6, which after 4 g3 d5 5 cxd5, can either lead to a Tarrasch Queen's Gambit after 5...exd5 6 d4 or a Semi-Tarrasch after 5...Nxd5 6 d4. The latter doesn't allow an isolated d-pawn, but is in many other ways more difficult to play for Black. Also 3...b6, trying for a Hedgehog is possible, but aside from 4 g3, which will take us to the lines covered above, White can also

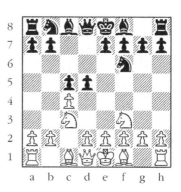

choose 4 e4 d6 5 d4 cxd4 6 Nxd4 followed by Bd3 and Qe2.

4 cxd5 Nxd5 5 g3

If White is the type of player to be satisfied with a small edge from the opening, then 5 d4 is a good choice, e.g., 5...cxd4 (5...Nxc3 6 bxc3 Bg7 is similar to a Grünfeld Indian) 6 Qxd4 Nxc3 7 Qxc3 Nc6 8 e4 e6 (now Black threatens ...Bb4, pinning the queen) 9 Bb5 Bb7 10 0-0, and White is a tiny bit more comfortable. For the more adventurous, White can play Nimzowitsch's 5 e4, which can be a lot of fun if both players are up for it: 5...Nb4 (5...Nxc3 6 dxc3 - 6 bxc3 g6 7 d4 Bg7 is a Grünfeld – 6...Qxd1+ 7 Kxd1 looks boring, but is difficult for Black to play) 6 Bc4 (6 Bb5+ N8c6 7 d4 cxd4 8 a3 dxc3 9 Qxd8+ Kxd8 10 axb4 cxb2 11 Bxb2 12 0-0 f6 leaves White with adequate compensation for the pawn, but not much more than that) 6...Nd3+ 7 Ke2! Nf4+ 8 Kf1 Ne6. **(D)**

White has lost the right to castle, but Black has spent six moves to put a knight on e6 and has not developed any other pieces! White now usually sacrifices a pawn with 9 b4, hoping to get even further ahead in development: 9...cxb4 10 Ne2 Nc7 11 d4 e6 12 h4 and

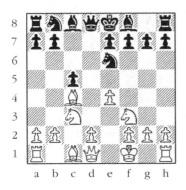

White has excellent compensation for the pawn.

5...Nc6 6 Bg2 Nc7 7 0-0 e5

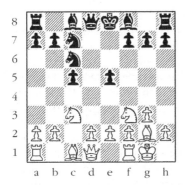

The so-called Rubinstein Variation, which essentially is a Accelerated Dragon, Maroczy Bind, with the colors reversed, and many of the same ideas apply for both players.

8 d3 Be7 9 Nd2 Bd7

Black does not allow White to exchange his light-squared bishop on c6 as the pawns will be difficult to guard long-term.

10 Nc4 f6 with approximately even chances.

The Pure Symmetrical

When people think of the Symmetrical English as dull, the lines in this section is what they have in mind. However, as with many other openings where the lines are finely balanced, the player with the better understanding has an excellent chance for winning the game.

2 Nc3 Nc6 3 g3 g6 4 Bg2 Bg7 5 Nf3 (D)

I can already hear the yawns. White has several alternatives, e.g., 5 e4, which does not carry the same punch as when

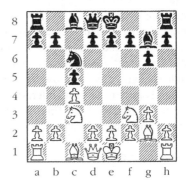

Black has a pawn on e5 instead of c5, but nevertheless still is quite interesting: 5...Nf6 6 Nge2 0-0 7 0-0 d6 8 d3 Ne89 Be3 Nd4 with even chances or 5 e3 e5 (5...e6 6 Nge2 Nge7 7 0-0 0-0 is truly boring, no excuses here) 6 Nge2 Nge7 7 0-0 0-0 8 a3 d6 9 Rb1 a5, again with chances for both sides or 5 a3 a6 6 Rb1 Rb8 7 b4 cxb4 9 axb4 b5 10 cxb5 axb5 and despite the obvious symmetry, there is plenty to play for although the position is quite difficult to play well.

5...Nf6

The so-called Wedberg Variation arises after 5...e5, and now 6 0-0 Nge7 7 a3 0-0

216

8 d3 d6 9 Rb1 a5 10 Ne1 Be6 11 Nc2 d5 12 cxd5 Nxd5 13 Ne3 Nde7 with a complicated struggle ahead. 5...e6 and 5..d6 are also fully playable.

6 0-0 0-0 7 d4

Nothing exciting is created after 7 d3 or 7 b3.

7...cxd4 8 Nxd4 Nxd4

Black can also play 8...Ng4, though the position that arises after 9 e3 d6 10 b3 Nxd4 11 exd4 Nh6 is easier for White to play.

9 Qxd4 d6 10 Qd3 a6 11 Bd2 Rb8 12 Rac1 b5 with chances for both sides, and the position is by no means boring.

The Anti-Indians

The label for the variations in this section stems from Black wanting to play one of the Indian openings, such as the Nimzo-Indian, the Queen's Indian or the Grünfeld Indian, but White does not oblige, avoiding d2-d4, yet Black goes ahead with his plan anyway.

1 c4 Nf6 2 Nc3

And now: **(a) 2...d5** 3 cxd5 Nxd5 (Anti-Grünfeld); **(b) 2...e6** 3 Nf3 Bb4 (Anti-Nimzo); and **(c) 2...e6 3 e4** (Flohr-Mikenas Attack).

The Anti-Grünfeld

There are a couple of different versions of this variation.

2...d5

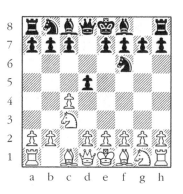

Frequently Black plays 2...g6 first, which usually transposes, but can have independent relevance after 3 Nf3 d5 4 Qa4+ which is very popular at the moment at top levels: 4...Bd7 5 Qb3 dxc4 6 Qxc4, and it seems a little odd that White has invested so many queen moves on forcing the black bishop to d7, but the truth is that the bishop does not stand well on this square and Black would also rather have his knight on f6 relocated to the queenside.

3 cxd5 Nxd5 4 Nf3

Or 4 g3 g6 5 Bg2 Nxc3 (5...Nb6 is also possible but leads to a better game for White) 6 bxc3 Bg7 7 Rb1 Nd7 8 Nf3 0-0 with chances for both players.

4...g6 5 Qa4+

If White is satisfied with a draw then 5 e4 is a decent choice, e.g., 5...Nxc3 6 dxc3 (6 bxc3 is a regular Grünfeld) 6...Qxd1+ 7 Kxd1 Nd7 8 Bf4 c6 9 Kc2 f6 10 Nd2 e5 with equality. *(D)*

5...Bd7 6 Qh4 Nxc3

Here 6...Bc6 7 Qd4 f6 8 e3 leads to a somewhat better game for White.

7 bxc3 Nc6 8 e4 e5 9 Bg5 Be7 and Black is fine.

The Anti-Nimzo

This is an opening you hardly ever see used by anyone except very strong players.

2...e6 3 Nf3 Bb4

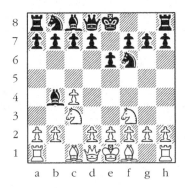

3...b6 is met by 4 e4 Bb7 5 Bd3 (or 5 Qe2) 5...d6 6 Bc2 c5 7 d4 cxd4 8 Nxd4 a6 9 b3 Be7 with another version of a Hedgehog; in this case White has the better chances.

4 Qc2

White has several alternatives available at this juncture, e.g., 4 Qb3 and 4 g3, which are commonly seen and are fairly

solid, whereas 4 g4!? is sharp and fun: 4...h6 5 Rg1 d6 6 h4 with an unclear position.

4...0-0 5 a3 Bxc3 6 Qxc3 b6

Black can also consider 6...d6 and 6...Nc6.

7 b4 Bb7 8 Bb2 d6 9 e3

9 g3 is also an accepted continuation for White.

9...Nbd7 10 Be2 Qe7 11 0-0 c5 12 d3 and while the chances are considered approximately even, White's position is far easier to play and the results in this variation are heavily in White's favor.

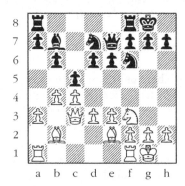

The Flohr-Mikenas Attack

In addition to allowing Black to enter the Anti-Nimzo, White has a sharp alternative with which he immediately provokes a crisis in the center.

2...e6 3 e4 (D)

Because of the direct threat of e4-e5, Black has to react immediately. After facing this as Black in one of the first games with this variation, Nimzowitsch used this move on several occasions.

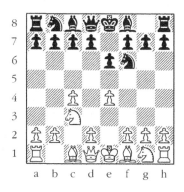

3...d5

An even sharper option is available with 3...c5, allowing White to play e4-e5: 4 e5 Ng8 5 Nf3 (or 5 d4 cxd4 6 Qxd4 Nc6 7 Qe4 d6 with good chances to equalize) 5...Nc6 6 d4 cxd4 7 Nxd4 Ne5 8 Ndb5 a6 9 Nd6+ Bxd6 10 Qxd6 f6 11 Be3 Ne7 12 Bb6 Nf5 13 Qc5, and White has excellent compensation for the pawn thanks to his active pieces, more space and bishop pair.

4 e5 d4 5 exf6 dxc3 6 bxc3

6 fxg7 cxd2+ is quite harmless for Black.

6...Qxf6 7 d4

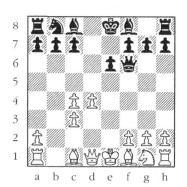

More recently, it has been established that White has a good alternative in 7 Nf3. After 7...e5, White can of course transpose back to our main line with 8 d4, but also continue down an independent path with 8 Bd3 Bd6 9 0-0 Na6 10 Bc2 Bg4 11 d4 Bxf3 12 Qxf3 Qxf3 13 gxf3 exd4 14 Re1+ Kd8 15 cxd4 with a slight initiative for White.

7...e5 8 Nf3 exd4 9 Bg5 Qe6+ 10 Be2 Be7 11 cxd4 and White has the initiative thanks to his lead in development.

The English Defense

After having lived a life in relative obscurity, the English Defense gained popularity in the 1970s when a number of the strongest English players included it in their repertoires.

1 c4 b6 2 d4

White can stay in the English Defense proper with 2 Nc3 Bb7 3 e4 e6 4 Nf3 Bb4 5 Bd3 Ne7, but this is not considered critical for Black. The only way to test Black is with the text move, which makes the game a kind of Queen's Pawn Opening.

2...e6 3 Nc3

3 e4 is also possible, but White has to

be a little careful when playing against the English Defense, because the center pawns can easily become vulnerable, and hanging on to them usually mean creating further weaknesses: 3...Bb7 4 Bd3 (4 Qc2 Qh4!? 5 Nd2 Bb4 6 Bd3 f5 is a good example of the mischief Black may create) 4...Nc6 5 Ne2 Nb4 6 Nbc3 Nxd3+ 7 Qxd3 d6 8 0-0 Nf6, and White has the more active position and has slightly better chances.

3...Bb7 4 a3

Again White can consider 4 e4, and again the complications start immediately: 4...Bb4 5 f3 (also 5 Qc2 and 5 Bd3 are possible) 5...f5 6 exf5 Nh6! 7 fxe6 (7 Bxh6 is met by 7...Qh4+, leaving Black with excellent compensation) 7...Nf5! (threatening ...Qh4+) 8 Bf4 dxe6, and Black has sufficient compensation for the pawn.

4...f5

With 4...Nf6 5 Nf3 the play transposes to the Petrosian Variation of the Queen's Indian.

5 d5

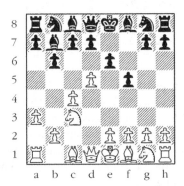

White can also play the normal 5 Nf3 and the somewhat offbeat 5 Nh3, which has scored quite well for White.

5...Nf6 6 g3 Na6 7 Bg2 Nc5 8 Nh3 Bd6 9 0-0 Be5 10 Qc2 0-0 with a dynamically complicated position where both sides have chances.

Reti Opening

Before we start discussing the Reti in this section and the King's Indian Attack in the next, we need to understand the differences between the two openings. In the Reti, White follows up with c2-c4 at some point, whereas in the King's Indian Attack, White plays his pawn to e4, sometimes as in e2-e4, but also as in e2-e3-e4. So for example, 1 Nf3 d5 2 g3 c6 3 Bg2 Nf6 4 0-0 Bf5 5 d3 e6 6 Nbd2 h6 7 b3 Be7 8 Bb2 0-0, and now White can play 9 c4 and it is a Reti or 9 Re1 followed by 10 e4 and it is a King's Indian Attack.

1 Nf3 d5

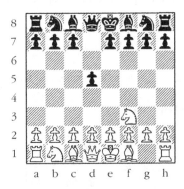

As you can probably imagine from reading the previous comment, the Reti can be terribly confusing and reached through a number of different move orders. For the sake of both the reader and author's sanity, I will stick with this move order, because Black can also play 1...Nf6 first followed by 2...d5 or 2...e6 or 2...c6.

The coverage will be split into two sections: White plays 2 c4; and White plays c2-c4 later.

White plays 2 c4

In this section we cover what I call the Reti proper.

2 c4 d4

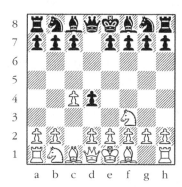

White has had a hard time proving an advantage after the simple 2...dxc4, e.g., 3 Na3 a6 4 Nxc4 b5 5 Ne3 Bb7 6 g3 Nf6 7 Bg2 e6 8 0-0 Nbd7 and the chances are fairly even. Also after the alternatives 3 e4, 3 Qa4+, 3 g3 and 3 e3, Black has equalized with relative ease. White's best may well be to transpose to a Queen's Gambit Accepted with 3 e3 followed by Bxc4 and d4.

3 g3

The most interesting alternative for White is undoubtedly 3 b4 which, after 3...c5 can lead to a Benko Gambit Reversed or Blumenfeld Gambit Reversed, depending on White's follow up. Also 3...f6 4 e3 e5 5 c5 could be fun, if quite unclear.

3...Nc6

With 3...c5, the game can become a Benko Gambit Reversed with 4 b4 or a Benoni Reversed with 4 Bg2 Nc6 5 d3 e5 6 0-0 Nf6 6 e3; both lead to approximately equal chances.

4 Bg2 e5 5 d3 Nf6 6 0-0 a5 7 Na3

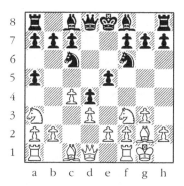

White can also break immediately in the center with 7 e3, which will normally transpose to other lines with 7...Be7 8 exd4 exd4, but here Black can also opt for 7...dxe3 8 Bxe3 Be7 with a sharp, unbalanced position.

7...Be7

7...Bc5 is also played in this position.

8 Nc2 0-0 9 b3 Re8 10 a3 h6 and the chances are about even.

White plays c2-c4 later

For the sake of simplicity, we will discuss the lines in this section with White playing c2-c4 on move 4, because it gives us the opportunity to look at things in a somewhat simpler light.

2 g3 Nf6 3 Bg2 (D)

And now we will look at two separate lines: **(a)** 3...c6 4 c4 (Slav Set-ups); and **(b)** 3...e6 4 c4 (Semi-Catalan).

The Slav Setups

The Slav (1 d4 d5 2 c4 c6) is easily one of the most popular ways to meet the Queen's Gambit today, and therefore many of the Slav players aim to reach it through English or Reti move orders as well.

3...c6 4 c4

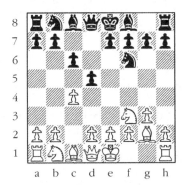

Many white players prefer to play 4 b3 first in order to avoid Black playing 4...dxc4. After 4 b3 Bf5 (or 4...Bg4 5 c4 e6 6 Bb2 Nbd7 7 0-0 Bd6 8 d3 0-0 with fairly even chances) 5 c4 e6 6 Bb2 Nbd7 7 0-0 h6 8 d3 Be7 9 Nbd2 0-0 10 a3 a5 with chances for both players.

4...Bg4

This is the so-called Capablanca Variation. Black has three alternatives worth mentioning: **(a) 4...g6** 5 b3 Bg7 6 Bb2 Nbd7 7 0-0 Bg4 8 d3 Nbd7 9 Nbd2 Re8 10 Rc1 with a slightly better game for White; **(b) 4...Bf5** (The Lasker or New York Variation) 5 0-0 (or 5 cxd5 cxd5 6 Qb3) 5... e6 6 d3 h6 7 cxd5 exd5 8 Nc3 Be7 9 Nd4 Bh7 10 e4 with the better chances for White; and **(c) 4...dxc4**, which can be a little problematic for White unless he doesn't mind sacrificing a pawn: 5 0-0 Nbd7 6 Qc2 Nb6 7 Na3 Qd5 8 Nh4 Qe6 9 e4 g6 10 b3 Bg7 11 Bb2 cxb3 12 axb3 0-0 13 d4 with good compensation for the pawn.

5 0-0 e6 6 cxd5 exd5 7 d3 Nbd7 8 Qc2

White can also play 8 Nc3 Bd6 9 Qc2 intending e2-e4.

Be7 9 e4 0-0 10 Nc3 Nc5 and chances are about even.

The Semi-Catalan

The name of this variation is not exactly official, but makes sense to me because it is quite similar to the Catalan, even though White normally does not play d2-d4.

3...e6 4 c4 Be7

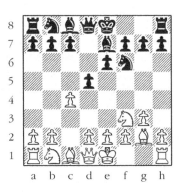

In this position Black often plays 4...dxc4, thus avoiding the Catalan proper, which would arise if Black played 4...Be7, and White then replied 5 d4. 4...dxc4 is usually met by 5 Qa4+ Nbd7 6 Qxc4 c5 7 Qb3 (7 d3 and 7 0-0 are also frequently played) 7...Rb8 8 d3 Bd6 9 a4 b6 10 Nc3 a6 with chances for both players.

5 0-0 0-0 6 b3 b6

Or 6...c5 7 Bb2 Nc6 8 e3 d4 9 exd4 cxd4 10 Re1 Ne8 11 d3 f6 12 Na3 e5 13 Nc2 and although the chances are more or less even, the white position has proven easier to play.

7 Bb2 Bb7 8 e3 c5 9 Nc3 dxc4 10 bxc4 Nc6 11 Qe2 Qc7 with a balanced game and approximately even chances.

King's Indian Attack

The King's Indian Attack can arise from a surprising number of openings: the French (1 e4 e6 2 d3 d5 3 Nd2 or 2 Qe2), the Caro-Kann (1 e4 c6 2 d3 d5 3 Nd2), the Sicilian (1 e4 c5 2 Nf3 e6 3 d3 or 2...d6 3 c3 Nf6 4 d3) and in its original form, which we will focus on here. The King's Indian Attack looks like a fairly harmless opening, but has been a favorite of attacking champions like Bobby Fischer and Leonid Stein as well as many other grandmasters.

1 Nf3 d5 2 g3 Nf6

Black can also play 2...c5, and then 3 Bg2 Nc6 (or 3...g6 4 0-0 Bg7 5 d3 Nc6 followed by Nbd2 and e4) 4 0-0 e5 5 d3 Nf6 6 Nbd2 Be7 7 e4 0-0 with approximately even chances. Compared

to a normal King's Indian Defense, White's extra tempo does not mean that much.

3 Bg2 c6

Another setup for Black involves 3...g6 4 0-0 Bg7 5 d3 0-0 6 Nbd2 c6 7 e4, which is in my opinion easier to play for White.

4 0-0 Bg4

Another popular setup is, just like in the Reti, 4...Bf5 and now White can choose to include b3 and Bb2 before playing d3, Nbd2, Qe1 and e4 or play d3, Nbd2, Qe1 and e4 directly. In either case the chances are more or less even, but shouldn't be underestimated by Black.

5 d3 Nbd7 6 Nbd2

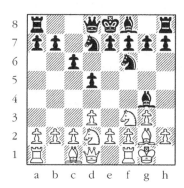

White often dispenses with the text move and plays 6 Qe1 directly, e.g., 6...e5 7 e4 dxe4 8 dxe4 Bc5 9 Nbd2 0-0 10 h3 Bh5 11 Nc4 with an easier game for White.

6...e5

Or 6...e6 7 h3 Bxf3 8 Nxf3 Be7 8 Qe1 0-0 9 e4 dxe4 10 dxe4 e5, and Black has equalized.

7 e4 dxe4 8 dxe4 Bc5 9 Nc4 0-0 10 h3 Bh5 11 Qd3 and White has a tiny advantage.

1 Nf3 Specialties

The Reti and the King's Indian Attack are not exactly the favorite openings to play against for a lot of black players, so it is hardly surprising, that Black has tried several offbeat ideas to unsettle things a bit when facing 1 Nf3.

1 Nf3

And now we will look briefly at the following lines: **1...Nf6 2 g3 b5** (Polish Defense); and **1...f5** (Reti-Dutch).

The Polish Defense

This opening comes in several variations; we will look at two of the more common ones after 1 Nf3.

1...Nf6 2 g3 b5 *(D)*

In recent years, Black has frequently employed a different line: 2...a6 3 Bg2 b5 4 b3 Bb7 5 c4 e6, which often is reached via 2 c4 e6 3 g3 a6 4 Bg2 b5 5 b3 Bb7. White appears to obtain the

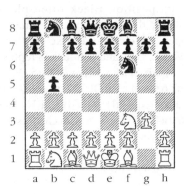

somewhat better chances after 6 0-0 c5 7 Nc3 Qb6 8 e3 Be7 9 Qe2.

3 Bg2 Bb7 4 0-0

White can also consider 4 Na3 followed by c2-c4.

4...e6 5 d3 d6

5...d5 is another option.

6 e4 Be7 7 Nbd2 0-0 8 Ne1 Nfd7 and Black is doing fine.

The Reti-Dutch

When Black steers for the Dutch after 1 Nf3, he opens himself to a couple of very sharp ideas from White.

1...f5 2 d3

This move is an improved version of the Lisitsyn Gambit, which some will argue doesn't need improvement! This gambit runs 2 e4 with the idea 2...fxe4 3 Ng5 Nf6 4 d3 exd3 5 Bxd3 which already now threatens 6 Nxh7 and 7 Bg6 mate! In this particular line Black does best either play 4...e5 5 dxe4 Bb4+ 6 c3 Bc5 or 3...d5 4 d3 Qd6, in either case the positions are complicated and unclear. Probably Black's best option is 3...Nc6 4 d3 e5 5 Bxe3 e5 with more or less equal chances.

2...d6

Obviously 2...Nf6 3 e4 fxe4 4 dxe4 Nxe4? 5 Bd3 Nf6 6 Ng5 leads to the previous line.

3 e4 e5 4 Nc3 Nc6

4...Nf6 looks more logical, but 5 exf5 Bxf5 6 d4 e4 7 Nh4 has been found to be better for White.

5 exf5 Bxf5 6 d4 Nxd4 7 Nxd4 exd4 8 Qxd4 c6 and Black has solved his opening problems successfully.

Bird's Opening

White's sharpest opening in this chapter is undoubtedly the Bird, which has never had a great following at any level. Nevertheless, for players who know what they are doing, it offers White excellent attacking chances and good opportunities to shake things up, while forcing both players to think for themselves right from the beginning of the game.

1 f4

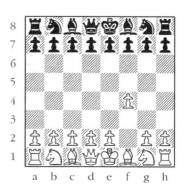

1...d5

This is like a Dutch with colors reversed. A popular alternative for Black is the sharp From's Gambit, which aims to exploit the fact that White has weakened his kingside structure and made the king somewhat vulnerable. After 1...e5!? 2 fxe5 (note that 2 e4 is a King's Gambit by transposition) 2...d6 3 exd6 Bxd6 4 Nf3 g5, and here both 5 g3 g4 6 Nh4 Ne7 7 d4 Ng6 8 Nxg6 hxg6 9 Qd3 Nc6 and 5 d4 g4 6 Ne5 Bxe5 7 dxe5 Qxd1+ 8 Kxd1 Nc6 9 Nc3 Bc6 lead to positions with chances for both players.

Another option is 1...Nf6, after which White can try Larsen's 2 Nf3 g6 3 b4 Bg7 4 Bb2 0-0 5 e3 d6 with an approximately balanced game.

2 Nf3 Nf6

2...Bg4 has also been recommended, but White gets to play 3 e3 Nc6 4 h3 Bxf3 5 Qxf3, and now 5...e5 will be met with 6 g4, with a sharp position.

3 e3

Or 3 g3 g6 4 Bg2 Bg7 5 0-0 0-0 6 d3 c5 7 c3 Nc6 and both sides have their chances.

3...g6 4 Be2

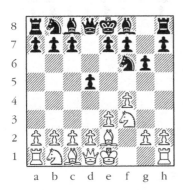

4 b3 is also interesting, for instance 4...Bg7 5 Bb2 0-0 6 Be2 c5 7 0-0 Nc6 8 Ne5 Bd7 and the chances are about even.

4...Bg7 5 0-0 0-0 6 d3 c5 7 Qe1 Nc6 8 Qh4 b6 9 Nbd2 Ba6 and the play resembles a sharp Classical Dutch with the colors reversed and a double-edged position.

Barcza Opening

There are very few lines that retain independent significance when White opens with 1 g3, but those that do are often called the Barcza Opening. Aside from the inventor, Gideon Barcza, and his countryman Istvan Bilek, it was also employed occasionally by Larsen early in his career.

1 g3 e5 2 Bg2 d5 3 d3 (D)

Larsen tried 3 Nf3 once and won a beautiful game against Geller, but Black gets the better chances after 3...e4 (Geller played 3...Nc6) 4 Nd4 c5 5 Nb3 c4 6 Nd4 Bc5, and the fact that White has an extra tempo over a similar line

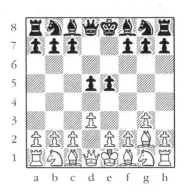

the Alekhine Defense actually worsens his position.

3...Nf6 4 Nf3 Bd6 5 0-0 0-0 and we have reached a Pirc Defense Reversed, where Black has no problems maintaining the balance.

Grob Attack

Of the more unusual openings in this chapter, this opening is probably the most dubious one.

1 g4

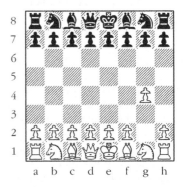

White weakens the kingside for no real compensation; it cannot be recommended for anything other than blitz games.

1...e5

White players tend to hope for continuations like 1...d5 2 Bg2 Bxg4 3 c4 after which 3...c6 4 cxd5 cxd5 5 Qb3 with queenside pressure. However, Black can get a pleasant game with 3...dxc4!? 4 Bxb7 Nd7, and Black gets amble compensation for the exchange. Of course, the solid 2...c6 is also playable, avoiding the sharp lines altogether.

2 Bg2 d5 3 h3 c6
Also 3...Nc6 4 c4 dxc4 is possible for Black, though it may lead to wild positions.

4 d4 e4 5 c4 Bd6 6 Nc3 Ne7 7 Bg5 f6 8 Bd2 0-0

Black is already very comfortable, and White's early kingside pawn thrust has done nothing, but weakened the dark squares.

Nimzo-Larsen Attack

There are a few nuances I should point out from the outset regarding this opening. Nimzowitsch, the inventor of so many opening lines, usually played this opening with 1 Nf3 followed by 2 b3 or 2 e3 and then 3 b3; my compatriot Bent Larsen took it a step further and played 1 b3, thus allowing Black some extra options, most importantly 1...e5. Thanks to the efforts of Larsen, this opening saw a fair amount of action at top levels in the late 1960s and early 1970s, but has been seen much less frequently.

1 b3

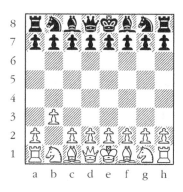

The move order with 1 Nf3 prevents Black from playing 1...e5, but adds other options for Black: 1...d5 2 b3 Bg4 (2...c5 3 e3 Nf6 4 Bb2 followed by Bb5 was Nimzowitsch's idea, just like in the Nimzo-Indian) 3 Bb2 (3 e3 e5 is fine for Black) 3...Bxf3 4 gxf3 e6 5 e3 Nf6 with chances for both players.

1...e5

Many other moves, including 1...d5, 1...c5, and 1...Nf6, are possible.

2 Bb2 Nc6 3 e3

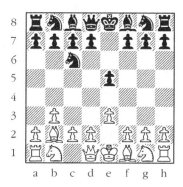

Or 3 c4 Nf6 4 e3 d5 5 cxd5 Nxd5 6 a3 Bd6 with a position that is a Sicilian with colors reversed.

3...d5

Or 3...Nf6 4 Bb5 d6 (or even 4...Bd6!? with chances for both players) 5 Ne2 a6 6 Bxc6 bxc6 7 0-0 Be7 8 d3 0-0 with approximate equality.

4 Bb5 Bd6 5 c4

White has the ultra-sharp 5 f4 available as well, for instance, 5...Qh4+ 6 g3 Qe7 7 Nf3 f6 8 Qe2 exf4 9 gxf4 with a double-edged position.

5...dxc4 6 bxc4 Bd7 7 Nf3 Qe7 and the chances are more or less even.

Orangutan/Sokolsky Opening

White's opening is either named after an orangutan in New York's Central Park Zoo or the Soviet master Alexei Sokolsky. I am personally familiar with the opening because my father played it regularly and it was featured in the first tournament game between us, which ended in a draw after a short, but intense battle. With best play from Black, White shouldn't expect to be able to gain an advantage, but it is perfectly playable.

1 b4 e5

A safer and more solid setup for Black is 1...d5, e.g., 2 Bb2 Nf6 3 Nf3 e6 4 b5 c5 5 e3 Be2 b6 6 Be2 Bb7 followed by ...Bd6, ...Nbd7, ...0-0 and ...Qe7, with a pleasant game for Black.

2 Bb2 Bxb4 *(D)*

2...f6 is also possible, though both 3 b5 and the sharp 3 e4 Bxb4 4 Bc4 followed by f2-f4 are interesting options for White.

3 Bxe5 Nf6 4 c4 0-0 5 e3 Nc6

Or 5...d5 6 cxd5 Nxd5 followed by either ...Nc6 or ...c7-c5, and then ...Nc6, and in either case Black has a comfortable game.

6 Bb2 d5 7 cxd5 Nxd5 8 Nf3 Bg4 9 Be2 Re8 10 0-0 with chances for both sides. White has to be careful not to let Black develop an initiative on the kingside, whereas Black has to watch White's central pawns.

The Dunst

This is an opening that has more names than it merits: Der Linksspringer (German for "the knight on the left"), the Van Geet, the Queen's Knight Attack, and the Dunst.

There are a number of independent lines in this opening, but it contains numerous transpositions to other openings; one of the more tricky aspects of playing this opening for Black is to stay clear of possible unfavorable transpositions.

1 Nc3 d5 *(D)*

Clearly this is far from Black's only move in this position. 1...e6 or 1...c6, can

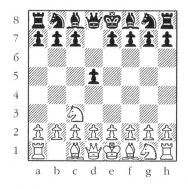

transpose to the French or Caro-Kann respectively if White then plays 2 e4. Another option is 1...c5, after which 2 Nf3 Nc6 (or 2...e6 and 2...d6, in either case Black is also fine) 3 d4 cxd4 4 Nxd4 g6 (4...Nf6 5 Bg5 is one of the lines White is hoping for, though it is by no means lethal for Black) 5 Be3 (5 e4 is an Accelerated Dragon) 5...Bg7 6 Nxc6 bxc6 7 Bd4 Nf6, and Black is doing fine. Finally 1...e5 is possible, after which 2 e4 leads us to the Vienna Game, but 2 Nf3 Nc6 3 d4 exd4 4 Nxd4 Nf6 5 Bg5 is not easy to play against for Black. Also after 1...e5 2 e3, Black should avoid 2...d5 because of the sharp 3 Qh5, and Black will have a very hard time hanging on to both central pawns. So if Black usually answers 1 e4 with 1...e5, the answer to 1 Nc3 should be 1...Nf6, intending to meet 2 e4 with 2...e5.

2 e4

2 d4 Nf6 3 Bg5 transposes to the Richter-Veresov, which is covered in the chapter on closed games.

2...dxe4

Of course 2...d4 is entirely possible, but these lines are often what White is seeking, e.g., 3 Nce2 c5 (or 3...e5 4 Ng3 Be6 5 Nf3 Nd7 6 c3 c5 7 cxd4 cxd4 8 Be2 with chances for both sides) 4 Ng3 Nc6 5 Bb5 e5 6 Bxc6+ bxc6 7 d3, followed by f2-f4 with the type of position White is hoping for.

3 Nxe4 Nd7

Black has a number of perfectly playable moves available here, including 3...c6, 3...e6, 3...Nf6, 3...Bf5, 3...e5 and even 3...Qd5, since 4 Nc3 transposes to the Scandinavian.

4 Bc4 e6

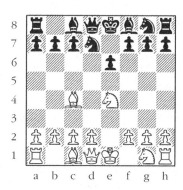

The normal-looking 4...Ngf6 allows the ultra-sharp 5 Bxf7+ Kxf7 6 Ng5+ Kg8 7 Ne6, which is reasonably playable for White.

5 d3 Ngf6 6 Nf3 Be7 7 0-0 0-0 and Black follows up with ...a7-a6 and ...b7-b5 with equal chances.

Other Flank Openings

The remaining opening are not even really worth spending much time on, but should still be mentioned:

(a) 1 a3 (Anderssen's Opening) 1...g6 (1...d5 and 1...e5 are of course also perfectly playable, but White has the advantage of actually being able to transpose to several different lines where a2-a3 is a sensible move, such as 1...e5 2 c4) and now 2 b4 Bg7 is obviously comfortable for Black, so 2 c4 Bg7 3 Nc3 d6 4 Nf3 Nf6 (or even 4...f5 with a Leningrad Dutch set-up, where a2-a3 doesn't make a particularly great impression) 5 d4 0-0, and we have a King's Indian where White has wasted a tempo.

(b) 1 c3 (Saragossa Opening) is in my opinion best met by 1...e5 (1...d5 2 d4 transpose to a number of Queen's Pawn openings, such as the Torre, London or Colle, which are all perfectly playable for White, if not exactly threatening to Black) 2 d3 (2 e4 Nf6 is pleasant for Black, and 2 d4 exd4 3 cxd4 d5 is an Queen's Gambit, Exchange Variation, where White has given Black a lot of extra options that aren't normally available when starting from a Queen's Gambit move order) 2...d5 3 Nf3 Nc6 4 g3 Be7 with a version of the King's Indian Attack that is quite harmless for Black.

(c) 1 e3 (Van't Kruij's Opening) doesn't have any real independent relevance, and will normally transpose to other openings, such as the Colle (when White plays d2-d4), the English (when c2-c4 follows), or the Nimzo-Larsen Attack (b2-b3). The only thing Black shouldn't do is underestimate the opponent's play, because the move order employed may be an attempt to transpose into a favorable line of a standard opening.

(d) 1 Nh3 (Paris Opening) 1...e5 is fine for Black, e.g., 2 g3 d5 3 Bg2 c6 4 f3 Bd6 5 Nf2 Nf6, and Black has already at least equalized.

Viktor Kortschnoi has said that implementing new openings into your repertoire keeps your game fresh and broadens your understanding of chess overall. You should heed his advice, but not do it too frequently.

If you are at a level where the material in this book is new to you, then you ought to stay well clear of the main lines and instead seek refuge in some of the numerous respectable sidelines that objectively offer chances that are just as good as anything you will come across in the main lines.

Chapter 10

Where do I go from here?

Having finished the chapters on opening theory, you are undoubtedly motivated to try all sorts of openings, and quite possibly feeling confident about your understanding and ability to handle these openings. After all, wasn't that the purpose of studying the chapters on opening theory? My answer to you is a resounding "No!" Just hit the brakes and settle down for a bit!

Before you get upset, thinking I have made you waste your time studying the previous chapters, know that I have had severe bouts of this ailment on several occasions before developing the understanding to know what I was doing wrong. As mentioned in the chapter "An Introduction to Opening Theory," the theoretical chapters only skim the surface of the vast ocean of opening theory, and while your knowledge and understanding of these opening has probably increased many-fold, you still essentially know little compared to what is recommended before starting to play an opening with confidence.

Therefore, instead of falling into the very common trap of thinking you now know enough, it is now time to go back to chapter 3 and review the process of building an opening repertoire, and this time you have the added benefit of actually having studied a little opening theory and thus knowing slightly more about what you are doing.

Once you have gone over the exercise

of building an opening repertoire again, you can start thinking about how you continue your opening studies. The first most obvious step is…

Which opening books should you buy?

New opening books are published every week, and therefore it can be very difficult to decide which books to buy and which to avoid. Before even thinking about browsing for opening books to buy, you should take a good look at yourself and ask the following questions:

– *Am I reasonably certain about my decisions regarding my future opening repertoire?*

This is an important question because a lot of chess libraries, my own included, are filled with books on openings that players thought they would be playing even though they had not made clear decisions regarding their own repertoires. It is a very quick way to spend too much money and time on openings if you have not sorted out which openings you are going to play.

– *Which openings are the cornerstones of my repertoire (both colors)?*

In many ways, this question is an direct continuation of the previous one, but it is also important by itself. Initially, do *not* spend money on books that are not crucial to your opening repertoire. It is more important that you get a grasp of the openings that you really need to understand, such as your key replies to 1 d4 and 1 e4, as well as the main answers to your opening move of choice. For the openings that are in the periphery of your main repertoire, they can be covered by lines suggested in either encyclopedic type books or in repertoire books (more about both types below).

– How much money should I to spend on opening books?

There is an almost never-ending flow of opening books appearing, and therefore it is quite easy to end up spending a disproportionately high amount of money on opening books if you buy all titles that pertain to even just the key parts of your opening repertoire. Therefore decide how much money you are going to spend on books and software overall and how much of the overall budget you will spend on opening books.

– Do I really need the book I'm about to order?

Before buying a new book on an opening, did you really read and study the other book(s) you bought on that opening? If you didn't, don't purchase another on the same opening until you have finished the previous one you bought. It is common sense, but that is often not what considered first when most people shop for books. The same principle should be used on books on any topic. For instance, there is no reason to buy another book on the endgame if you haven't read the previous one you bought; the new book is just as likely to collect dust on the shelf.

– How can I find out if a book is good before I order it?

Read the reviews before buying any chess book. You can find reviews several places, on the internet (e.g., www.chesscafe.com), in many chess magazines and a few other places. Many of the reviews you will read are either very short and therefore not particularly informative or don't tell prospective buyers for whom the book is most relevant. In my opinion, you should not buy a book unless you know it is relevant for you, which puts the burden on you to seek out reviewers that tell the readers which audience a particular book is written for, along with other pertinent details of the book, including of course which lines are covered. Few things are more frustrating than buying a book that you think covers an opening you are playing, but the lines you use in your repertoire are only covered briefly.

Furthermore, you can also seek out bookstalls at tournaments, where you can see for yourself if a book meets your needs. In addition, many of the major book chains will allow you to special order books.

– Where should I buy my chess books?

Personally, I think you should support an exclusive chess store, which is more likely to be able to give advice as to which books are good and relevant for a player of your level, but is also more likely to have a wider selection of books than the local chain bookstore. The third option is to go to one of the many on-line vendors that offer books at often much deeper discounts than what you will find other places. However, regardless of where you order your books, check out the return policies first; often there is a re-stock fee if you return books, so think first before ordering.

Software

There is a great deal of chess software available and even what seems to be basic software can be expensive, so let us quickly go over what is available and what you may need. In addition, keep in mind that once you have brought the program home and opened it, you will in most cases not be able to return the item unless it is damaged.

Database programs

Nowadays everybody seems to have a database program. It isn't strictly necessary, though it does make studying openings somewhat easier, but for the vast majority of players it really is quite unimportant.

Should you, however, feel you need to have one, there are some freeware options such as, e.g., ChessBase Light, which will do just fine for most players.

Engines / Analysis modules

While I find most software superfluous for beginners, I think that most chess engines will be able to assist players of nearly every strength. One program will normally be adequate and it doesn't even have to be the latest version. Keep in mind that the earliest versions of Fritz, Junior, Hiarcs, etc., were also used by grandmasters in their studies, and therefore should be quite capable of assisting you for your relatively simple objectives. Chess engines for lower-rated players should really only be used as "blunder checkers" and to suggest

better moves when you go over your games at home. You can also use them to practice openings you are intending to use, playing them against the program, perhaps even from a particular starting position.

Opening CD-ROMs

Most of these cater to players rated above certain levels, so before buying these, check the reviews.

Opening DVD-ROMs

DVD-ROMS usually feature video recordings by a well-known player or coach. Some are very good, some are not. Again, I strongly suggest you check the reviews before purchasing an item. But see the next section for some general issues regarding this type of product.

DVDs / VHS

There are many products available in this category, and again some are quite useful and others considerably less so. Not many of these are reviewed regularly, so you will not find much help there. However, should you feel tempted by some titles, buy one item by a particular presenter and see if you like the presenter's style and the level of player the product is aimed at; that should give you a clear idea about whether you want to buy more in the future.

One note of warning, however: many of these products seem to be assembly-line material, quickly put together without too much effort. Keep in mind that material presented in a video would rarely be thorough enough to make it to book format. Too many lines are covered very superficially or for more problematic lines, perhaps not at all.

ChessBase Magazine

As far as I'm aware, *ChessBase Magazine* is the only digital magazine published. You get a DVD-ROM every two months with a great deal of top quality material, including numerous opening specials, usually written by top talent. For an ambitious player, it is worth the investment as it contains so much study material on all phases of the game, openings, tactics, strategy, endgames, annotated games and much more. Specifically regarding the openings, I would still qualify much of it as being too advanced for novice or beginning players, but the rest of the magazine definitely caters to a wide audience of all levels.

On-line Sources

While we are looking at the digital and electronic media, we should mention the wide selection of material online. Online sources for games, such as *The Week in Chess*, have already been noted, but other websites offer regular opening updates, the most prominent being www.chesspublishing.com which offers monthly updates in twelve different categories. The updates are written by grandmasters or international masters who are all specialists on the topics about which they are writing. The price is affordable, and in my opinion, in fact, a bargain, considering the volume of material that is available to you from day one of your subscription. However, much of the material is quite advanced and it rarely caters to weaker players. Other websites offer opening analysis as part

of overall concept. However, be a little skeptical as the quality of the material may vary a lot.

Types of Books

In this section, I will quickly peruse the most common types of opening books.

Starting Out...

This series from Everyman Chess is by and large written for players at a level that would include most readers of this book, though occasionally some of their titles may be more advanced. They tend to be instructive and are a good place to start when getting acquainted with an opening for the first time.

Chess Explained...

Gambit Publications, another of the big chess publishers, releases this series, which is aimed at a slightly higher level than the "Starting Out" series. This includes players rated as low as 1500, but probably not much lower than that. They have a great emphasis on explanations and typical ideas, with lesser emphasis on theory.

Winning with... and *Repertoire Books*

Any book promising you easy wins or guaranteed advantages out of the opening should carry a warning label, because they usually don't deliver on their promise. That being said, they are not all bad, and many of these books are reasonably well-written and will in many cases put you in a position to get a decent position from the outset.

A repertoire book is a different kind of opening book. Many titles are very good and if the author does his or her job properly, the suggested repertoire is consistent, leading to positions that are explained and discussed in detail. It is worth checking reviews of these kinds of books because some repertoire books are very advanced, loaded with theory and do not offer many explanations; you should stay away from those books if you are rated below 2000.

Opening Monographs

Monographs focus on one opening or even just one line and vary tremendously in quality and style. Some are excellent and some are not that good, though in recent years, chess publishers have been more careful about the books they published, trying to ensure good value for the reader. However, this fact should not make you purchase opening books indiscriminately, because the target audience of a book may not be right for your level of play. Another thing to keep in mind is that many books focus on an opening with an emphasis on either a white or black perspective, so while a book may have received great reviews, it may not help you very much if it presents material only "from one side of the board." Another piece of advice is to be careful when it comes to books on obscure openings and gambits. They are rarely objective, and often the authors are weaker compared to those who write monographs on more mainstream openings.

Yearbooks

The main "yearbooks" at the time of this writing are *Chess Informant* and *New In Chess Yearbook*, both excellent books with a great deal of quality material. Note however that they cater to more advanced players. The former is primarily a game collection of the best games played in the previous 3-4 months period, but there are a number of other features which makes it very attractive for training purposes. There are combinations, endgames from recent games, as well as a section on endgame studies (compositions), along with a lot more interesting material. As an overall source of study material, it is very good, but everything is in "languageless annotations" (i.e., using symbols to indicate evaluations of moves) which can be difficult for the inexperienced player. *New In Chess Yearbook* has a lot more text, but the majority of the games are also presented with languageless annotations, and the focus is entirely on openings.

Hopefully this chapter has given you the guidance you need to make good decisions about how to consider which books to buy, and which to avoid. In conjunction with the advice in the previous chapters, all that remains is to wish you good luck in your opening endeavors, though I will repeat what I have previously said: Don't spend too much time on the opening compared to the other phases of the game. It is a tempting trap into which that too many players over the years fall.

On-line learning

Since the first edition of this book, there has been a huge development in the material that is available on-line both for free through social media, the playing platforms (such as Chess.com and lichess.org) and educational platforms (such as Chessable). In this section, we will take a quick look at the various sources, what to look out for and what to avoid.

Facebook

Social media can be wonderful but there are some serious caveats and this is particularly the case with Facebook. There are great Facebook groups where there is an abundance of excellent information, these tend to be run by stronger or more experienced players. Those groups are often smaller and the posts managed carefully. If you can become part of such groups, go for it. The counterpart are those groups that are big and everybody joins in. They can be fun, but the amount of bad information and recommendation that is being handed out is astounding. Usually, it is done with the best of intentions, but the advice of someone rated 700 on-line, an experienced club player, and a titled player should not have equal weight, but that is often what happens in these groups, so the best advice is to be very careful what and who you listen to.

YouTube

YouTube is not unlike Facebook in that there is plenty of material to choose from and there is both good and bad providers. However, unlike Facebook, those channels with the greatest number of subscribers are usually those that deliver the greatest value. Some of my personal favorites are John Bartholomew, Eric Rosen, GothamChess (Levy Rozman), Chess24, ChessBase India, but there are many other great channels to choose from. The biggest channel at the moment is Agadmator who is closing in on a million subscribers and he has a lot of great content as well.

Other Social Media

I'm less impressed with what can be learned from other social media channels such as Instagram, Twitter, twitch, Snapchat, Pinterest, etc. That being said, it is more sporadic in terms of quality, so for now, my advice would be to focus on YouTube and Facebook.

Playing Platforms

Nearly all of the platforms have educational materials. The quality is a bit of a mix and usually, the good stuff only becomes available once you pay a subscription fee. Nevertheless, it is worth checking out what is available, particularly in the openings you are interested in.

Learning Platforms

There are many to choose between, but the current king is Chessable. There are many courses on openings, including several by world-class authors and grandmasters. Check out the "Short & Sweet" before opting in.

Index of Names & Variations

240

Books by Carsten Hansen

Winning Quickly Series:
Catastrophes & Tactics in the Chess Opening - Volume 1: Indian Defenses
Catastrophes & Tactics in the Chess Opening - Volume 2: 1.d4 d5
Catastrophes & Tactics in the Chess Opening - Volume 3: Flank Openings
Catastrophes & Tactics in the Chess Opening - Volume 4: Dutch, Benonis & d-pawn Specialties
Catastrophes & Tactics in the Chess Opening - Volume 5: Anti-Sicilians
Catastrophes & Tactics in the Chess Opening - Volume 6: Open Sicilians
Catastrophes & Tactics in the Chess Opening - Volume 7: Minor Semi-Open Games
Catastrophes & Tactics in the Chess Opening - Volume 8: 1.e4 e5
Catastrophes & Tactics in the Chess Opening - Volume 9: French & Caro-Kann
Catastrophes & Tactics in the Chess Opening – Volume 10: Selected Brilliancies from Volumes 1-9
Entire series also available in Large Print Format

Chess Miniatures Series:
Winning Quickly at Chess: Miniatures in the Sicilian Najdorf
Winning Quickly at Chess: Miniatures in the Queen's Indian Defense: 4 g3
Winning Quickly at Chess: Miniatures in the Ruy Lopez: Main Lines
Upcoming Volumes:
Winning Quickly at Chess: Miniatures in the King's Indian Defense: Fianchetto Systems
Winning Quickly at Chess: Miniatures in the Slav Defense: Main Lines
Winning Quickly at Chess: Miniatures in the Scotch Game

Specialized Chess Tactics Series:
Specialized Chess Opening Tactics: Budapest & Fajarowicz Gambits
Upcoming Volumes:
Specialized Chess Opening Tactics: Caro-Kann - Main Lines
Specialized Chess Opening Tactics: Caro-Kann - The Panov, Advance & Specialties
Specialized Chess Opening Tactics: Benko & Blumenfeld Gambits
Specialized Chess Opening Tactics: The Sicilian Dragon – Classical Lines
Specialized Chess Opening Tactics: The Sicilian Dragon – Yugoslav Attack

Daily Chess Training Series:
Chess Tactics – Volume 1 (404 puzzles from 2nd half of 2018)
Chess Tactics – Volume 2 (404 puzzles from 1st half of 2019)
Chess Tactics – Volume 3 (404 puzzles from 2nd half of 2019)
Chess Tactics for Improvers – Volume 1 (808 puzzles from 2019)
Upcoming Volumes:
Chess Tactics – Volume 4 (404 puzzles from 1st half of 2020)
Chess Tactics for Improvers – Volume 2 (808 puzzles from 2019-20)

For updates and free material, please visit www.winningquicklyatchess.com

Other books by Carsten Hansen:

The Sicilian Accelerated Dragon: Improve Your Results with New Ideas in This Dynamic Opening (with Peter Heine Nielsen, Batsford 1998)

The Gambit Guide to the English Opening: 1...e5 (Gambit Publications 1999)

The Symmetrical English (Gambit Publications 2001)

The Nimzo-Indian: 4 e3 (Gambit Publications 2002)

Improve Your Positional Chess (Gambit Publications 2004) - also available as e-book (Gambit Publications 2016) and in a Spanish-language edition *Mejore su ajedrez posicional* (Editorial La Casa Del Ajedrez 2008)

A Strategic Opening Repertoire (with John Donaldson, Russell Enterprises 2008) - also available as an e-book (Russell Enterprises 2015)

Back to Basics: Openings (Russell Enterprises 2008) - also available as an e-book (Russell Enterprises 2016)

The Sicilian Dragon: Move by Move (Everyman Chess 2016) - also available as an e-book (Everyman Chess 2016)

The Closed Sicilian: Move by Move (Everyman Chess 2017) – also available as an e-book (Everyman Chess 2017)

The Chameleon Variation – Confronting the Sicilian on Your Own Terms (Russell Enterprises 2017) – also available as an e-book (Russell Enterprises 2017)

The Full English Opening – Mastering the Fundamentals (New in Chess 2018) – also available as an e-book (New In Chess 2018)

The Sicilian Accelerated Dragon – 20th Anniversary Edition (with Peter Heine Nielsen - CarstenChess 2018) – Expanded version of the 1998 edition with approximately 15%new material)

Marvelous Modern Miniatures – 2020 games in 20 or less (Russell Enterprises 2020) - also available as an e-book (Russell Enterprises 2020)

Upcoming books:

The Modernized Accelerated Dragon (Thinkers Publishing 2021)

Made in the USA
Monee, IL
28 April 2023

32586839R00138